Antitrust Guidelines
for the Business Executive

Antitrust Guidelines for the Business Executive

Richard M. Calkins

Dow Jones-Irwin   Homewood, Illinois 60430

© Dow Jones-Irwin, Inc. 1981

ISBN 0-87094-231-X

Library of Congress Catalog Card No. 81-65229
Printed in the United States of America

1 2 3 4 5 6 7 8 9 0 K 8 7 6 5 4 3 2 1

To: Anita, Chrissy, Tad, and Kathie Calkins

Contents

Chapter Three
Violations of Section 1 of the Sherman Act   57

Table of Cases

Preface

This book is not intended to make the business executive a "Do It Yourself Lawyer," but rather to assist him in identifying the danger signals that are found throughout the antitrust laws and in seeking the assistance of counsel.

Unlike most legal texts, this book presents the antitrust laws through the cases themselves rather than as a straight legal discussion. By analyzing the facts of the many cases that make up the laws, the reader is studying the business acts of other businessmen and the reasons those acts led to trouble and even a jail sentence. In this way the reader can better relate his own activities to that of other businessmen who have suffered the consequences of the antitrust laws, and thereby avoid the same pitfalls through ignorance or misunderstanding of the law.

The renewed vigor in recent years of antitrust enforcement by federal and state authorities has burdened the businessman with a new realization that he can and will go to jail for conduct that ten years ago would have enjoyed no more than a passing glance. The antitrust laws today demand a greater sophistication on the part of the business executive. This book is intended to initiate an educational process that will lead to that sophistication.

When one has completed this book he no doubt will note that every American corporation worthy of note has been sued under the anti-trust laws. Indeed, a corporation in this country that has not felt the sting of those laws has not yet "arrived" on the business scene. Thus, involvement with the Sherman Act or Clayton Act, for example, does carry with it a certain symbol of status—which for many is perhaps better forgotten.

I wish to thank David A. Schlanger, a student at John Marshall Law School, and Christine Marshall of Drake University Law School, for their invaluable and dedicated assistance in preparing this book.

Antitrust Guidelines
for the Business Executive

Chapter One

Historical Perspective of the Antitrust Laws

The historical background of the antitrust laws is of little moment to the businessman indicted under the Sherman Act and facing a potential $100,000 fine and three years in a federal penitentiary. Yet an examination of the historical forces that brought the Sherman Act, the Clayton Act, the Robinson-Patman Act, and the Federal Trade Commission Act into being might help explain the severity with which the antitrust laws are enforced today. Unquestionably, the antitrust laws, even their historical background, deserve the businessman's close scrutiny, for they are "here to stay." They are, as one president of the United States stated, "as much a part of the American way of life as the due process clause of the Constitution."[1]

The very simplicity of the wording of the Sherman Act, Section 1—"Every contract, combination in the form of trust or otherwise, or conspiracy, in restraint of trade or commerce among the several States, or with foreign nations, is hereby declared to be illegal"—is its web of entrapment to the unwary businessman. No longer is it sufficient to rely on the advice of general counsel unless he is specially

1. Letter from President Franklin D. Roosevelt to Secretary of State Cordell Hull (Sept. 6, 1944).

trained in the antitrust laws, for these laws are evolving at a pace that only the trained expert can digest. No longer can the business-man find comfort in the fact that an attorney is present at industry meetings to foreclose illegal discussions, for in one case the attorney was indicted along with members of the trade association he was retained to monitor. And no longer will a company memorandum that each employee must read and sign attesting that he has not fixed prices, or a company movie on the antitrust laws, shield the business executive from indictment because of the illegal conduct of subordinates. Today, the businessman, as in every other aspect of business life, must demonstrate a new sophistication in his awareness of the antitrust laws, unheard of ten years ago. This new sophistication requires careful consideration of the historical forces that brought the antitrust laws into the mainstream of American business life.

1. Earliest origins of antimonopoly laws

Society's aversion to monopolies, price fixing, and the allocation of business among competitors finds an early expression predating the common law of England. In AD 483, the Emperor Zeno issued to the Practorian Prefect of Constantinople an edict, which provided:

> We command that no one may presume to exercise a monopoly of any kind of clothing, or of fish, or of any other thing serving for food, or for any other use, whatever its nature may be, either of his own authority or under a rescript of an emperor already procured, or that may hereafter be procured, or under an Imperial decree, or under a rescript signed by our Magesty; nor may any persons combine or agree in unlawful meetings, that different kinds of merchandise may not be sold at a less price than they may have agreed upon among themselves. Workmen and contractors for buildings, and all who practice other professions, and contractors for baths are entirely prohibited from agreeing together that no one may complete a work contracted for by another, or that a person may prevent one who has contracted for a work from finishing it; full liberty is given to anyone to finish a work begun and abandoned by another, without apprehension of loss, and to denounce all acts of this kind without fear and without costs. And if any one shall presume to practice a monopoly, let his property be forfeited and himself condemned to perpetual exile. And in regard to the principals of other professions, if they shall venture in the future to fix a price upon their merchandise, and to bind themselves by agreements not to sell at a lower price, let them be condemned to pay 40

pounds of gold. Your court shall be condemned to pay 50 pounds of gold if it shall happen, through avarice, negligence or any other misconduct, the provisions of this salutary constitution for the prohibition of monopolies and agreements among the different bodies of merchants, shall not be carried into effect.[2]

2. Common law of England

The federal antitrust laws find their origin in the common law of England as well as in the common law of the various states of the United States. As Senator John Sherman, after whom the Sherman Act was named, stated:

> This bill, as I would have it, had for its single object to invoke the aid of the courts of the United States to . . . supplement the enforcement of the established rules of the common and statute laws by the courts of the several states in dealing with combinations that affect injuriously the industrial liberty of the citizens of those States.
>
> It does not announce a new principle of law, but applies old and well-recognized principles of the common law to the complicated jurisdiction of our State and Federal Government.[3]

The concept that monopolies violated the common law was first perceived by Sir Edward Coke, who argued in the late 1500s that monopolies violated the civil law, the Magna Carta, and certain statutes of Edward III's reign.[4] Coke (1552–1634) was a brilliant English courtroom lawyer who rose to prominence as speaker of Parliament in 1593 and in 1594 was selected over Sir Francis Bacon as Queen Elizabeth's attorney general. In 1606 he became chief justice under King James I, at which time he insisted that even the king was subject to the law.

Coke's thesis—radical for that Elizabethan age—was predicated on a case decided two centuries earlier. One John Pecche obtained an exclusive patent in 1373 through the king's son, John of Gaunt, to sell sweet wines at retail in London.[5] At the time, the king's son was virtual ruler of England due to the king's age and the illness of

2. Code IV, 59. Translation of A. H. Marsh, Q. C., reprinted in 23 *Am. Law Rev.* 261 (1889).

3. 21 *Cong. Rec.* 2456, 2457 (1890) (speech of Sen. Sherman).

4. Wagner, "Coke and the Rise of Economic Liberalism," *Econ. Hist. Rev.,* VI.; 30 (1935).

5. Coke, Institutes, III, 181; *Cf.* Holdsworth, *History,* IV, 344 n. 6 (1937).

the immediate heir. John Pecche, a merchant, alderman, and once mayor of London, purchased the patent for a fee of 10 shillings on each pipe of wine sold, which was to be paid to the king. After three years, however, the political climate changed and John of Gaunt began losing favor. Parliament met in 1376 and, in an effort to discredit John of Gaunt, attacked his associates for artificially raising prices of "all the merchandise that came into England," for taking bribes and misappropriating funds, and for obstructing justice. Pecche was charged with having fraudulently obtained and excessively exploited his patent and for having failed to pay the king the required fees. He was subsequently sentenced "to be imprisoned, to make fine and ransom to the King, and also to give satisfaction to the parties complaining of his extortionate prices."[6] Pecche spent only a short time in prison and was then given a pardon excusing him from paying any further penalties or outstanding license fees.[7] Although his patent was not revoked, its value was lost when Parliament repealed the former prohibition, thereby permitting anyone to sell sweet wine at retail.[8]

In 1599, Sir Edward Coke's opportunity to apply his thesis came in the first recorded antitrust case of *Davenant* v. *Hurdis,* also known as *The Merchant Tailors' Case.*[9] The case arose out of a 1571 bylaw, entitled "An Ordinance for Nourishing and Relieving the Poor Members of the Merchant Tailors Company,"[10] passed by the London tailors' guild. This ordinance required every guild member who sent cloth to be finished by outside labor to have at least half the work done by fellow members of the guild. Davenant challenged the bylaw by sending out twenty cloths to be finished, but refusing to give an equal number to members of his guild. He was assessed a fine of ten shillings per cloth, as provided in the bylaw, and he refused to pay. When Davenant's goods—equal in value to the fine—were seized, Coke filed a lawsuit on behalf of Davenant.

Coke argued that the bylaw was unreasonable and contrary to law

6. *Rot. Parl.,* 50 *Edw. III,* No. 33 (1376).
7. *C.P.R.,* 51 *Edw. III,* 448, 457 (April 10, 1376).
8. *Rot. Parl.* 50 *Edw. III,* No. 14 (1376).
9. Moore 576, 72 Eng. Rep. 769 (K.B. 1599).
10. The preamble of the ordinance stated that "Forasmuch as it is the duty of every Christian society to help and relieve every willing labouring brother in the Commonwealth, and especially such as are incorporated, grafted, and knit together in brotherly society ..." Clode, *Merchant Taylors,* I, (1918).

because, while it absolutely required merchants to give their business to clothworkers belonging to the guild, it did not require the latter to provide quick service, good workmanship, or reasonable prices in exchange. As a result the merchants might be "utterly impoverished and forced to deceive their customers."[11] Coke argued that the bylaw was illegal because if the guild could keep half of the cloth dressing for its members, it could gradually appropriate the balance. He concluded that such a bylaw, which might create such monopoly powers, was against the public good and void. The court agreed, holding that "a rule of such nature as to bring all trade or traffic into the hands of one company, or one person, and to exclude all others, is illegal."[12] With that solitary pronouncement was launched a vague concept that monopolies were bad and contrary to the public good. For the next 300 years, the further development of this concept traveled a rather torturous path.

The next case of significance, and perhaps the most important in the common law concerning monopolies, was *Darcy* v. *Allein,* or *The Case of Monopolies,* decided in 1603.[13] Whereas *Davenant* v. *Hurdis* had established that a corporate bylaw was invalid if it created a monopoly, *Darcy* v. *Allein* went further and established the principle that even a royal grant by patent was invalid if it created a monopoly. In that case Queen Elizabeth granted Darcy, her groom, a patent for a monopoly on the manufacture and importing of playing cards. Shortly thereafter, in 1601, Allein, a London haberdasher, made and sold some playing cards and was subsequently sued by Darcy for infringement of his patent. The court held the patent void as a "dangerous" and "unprecedented" innovation and in order not to offend the Queen, adopted the fiction that "[t]he Queen was deceived in her grant; for the Queen, as by the preamble appears, intended it to be for the real public."[14] The court further held that the grant prejudiced the public good by raising prices and lowering the quality of the cards. More importantly, by depriving various workmen of their livelihood the patent was void because it violated the right of others to carry on the trade.[15]

11. Moore at 580–81, 72 Eng. Rep. at 771–72.
12. Moore at 591, 72 Eng. Rep. at 778.
13. 11 Co.Rep. 84b, 77 Eng. Rep. 1260 (K.B. 1602).
14. *Id.* at 87a, 77 Eng. Rep. at 1264.
15. Gordon, *Monopolies by Patent,* 226.

The next case of importance, the *Ipswich Tailors*'[16] case, was decided in 1614. The Tailors' Guild of Ipswich had a bylaw precluding all persons from practicing their trade in a town unless they first either served an apprenticeship under the guild or had been given its approval. One Sheninge violated the bylaw, and suit was commenced against him. The court held this bylaw invalid because "at common law, no man could be prohibited from working in any lawful trade. . . ."[17]

The Statute of Monopolies, passed in 1624, stifled further development of antimonopoly laws for nearly a century.[18] It was not until *Mitchell* v. *Reynolds*[19] in 1711 that the next important pronouncements were made.[20] This case involved an agreement among merchants not to compete. In this case the defendant assigned to the plaintiff a five-year lease of a bakery in a certain London parish, with the condition that defendant would pay damages of 50 pounds to plaintiff if he worked as a baker within the parish during the term of the lease. Defendant intentionally violated this covenant, arguing that having served his apprenticeship as a baker and being a member of the guild, no private person could lawfully foreclose him from working at his trade.

Plaintiff sued and won; however, the importance of the case is found in the language of Lord Macclesfield. He stated that all restraints of trade were either involuntary or voluntary and that this case fell within the latter category. He then distinguished between general restraints, which foreclosed a person from exercising his

16. 11 Co.Rep. 53a, 77 Eng. Rep. 1218 (K.B. 1614).

17. *Id.* at 53b, 77 Eng.Rep. at 1219.

18. Progress toward freer enterprise established by the Davenant and Darcy cases was undermined by the Statute of Monopolies of 1624. Although declaring all monopolies and grants illegal, it exempted the monopolies or grants given by cities, towns, corporations, trading companies, and guilds from its proscriptions.

19. 1 P. Williams 181, 24 Eng. Rep. 347 (K.B. 1711).

20. Some mention should be made of the common law crimes of forestalling, engrossing, and regrating, which were denounced on the ground that they concentrated the supply of commodities in the hands of a few persons, invariably resulting in higher prices. The forestaller purchased grain in the sheaf before it was winnowed or fish before the boats reached shore, thereby "intercepting the goods on their way to the market so that a higher price could be commanded." An engrosser was a person who, having bought goods at wholesale, sold them again at wholesale. And regrating simply meant retailing: buying in bulk and selling in small lots. See Thorelli, *The Federal Antitrust Policy* 15–17; Letwin, *Law and Economic Policy in America* 32–39. As the necessities of life became more abundant and the means of distribution more complex, these laws were abolished in 1772. However, judgment laws, punishing the same offenses, survived until 1844 when Parliament passed a law prohibiting the entertainment of further suits for those practices. 7 and 8 Vict., C 24.

trade anywhere in the kingdom, and particular restraints, which were limited to a particular place. The former, he held, were void and illegal as being only oppressive and of no benefit to either party.[21] As to particular restraints, he noted that there were two types: those without consideration, "all of which are void by what sort of contract soever created"; and those with consideration, such as the contract in question. As to the latter, they were enforceable. The Macclesfield rule thus established that a contract in restraint of trade would be valid only if the restraint was "particular" and the contract "appears to be made upon a good and adequate consideration, so as to make it a proper and useful contract."[22]

In *Nordenfeldt* v. *Maxim Nordenfeldt Gun and Ammunition Co.*,[23] decided in 1894, Thorsten Nordenfeldt, pursuant to a contract, agreed not to engage in the ammunition and armaments business for twenty-five years except on behalf of the Nordenfeldt company. Nordenfeldt breached the agreement, and the company sought an injunction against him. Nordenfeldt successfully argued in the lower court that the restraint was general and therefore void. The court of appeals reversed the lower court,[24] and the House of Lords, to which Nordenfeldt appealed, held that the restraint was valid because it was reasonable. Lord Macnaghten, in his opinion, enunciated a clear statement on "reasonableness":

> The public have an interest in every person's carrying on his trade freely: so has the individual. All interference with individual liberty of action in trading, and all restraints of trade of themselves, if there is nothing more, are contrary to public policy, and therefore void. That is the general rule. But there are exceptions: restraints of trade and interference with individual liberty of action may be justified by special circumstances of a particular case. It is a sufficient justification, and indeed it is the only justification, if the restriction is reasonable—reasonable, that is, in reference to the interests of the parties concerned and reasonable in reference to the interests of the public to the party in whose favour it is imposed, while at the same time it is no way injurious to the public.[25]

21. *Id.* at 182, 24 Eng. Rep. at 348.
22. *Id.* at 185–186, 24 Eng. Rep. at 348–49.
23. [1894] App. Cas. 535.
24. [1892] 1 Ch. 630.
25. [1894] App. Cas. 535, 565.

The essence of the opinion was that freedom of parties to contract and the need for "maintaining the rules of fair dealing between man and man"[26] were more important than some elusive effect which their agreement might have on the freedom of trade.[27]

Perhaps the leading common law decision on combinations in restraint of trade, decided in 1892, was *Mogul Steamship Co.* v. *McGregor.*[28] This case, perhaps more than any other, so eviscerated the common law as an antimonopoly deterrant as to make it ineffectual in any area without statutory impetus. The defendants in this case were a number of shipping lines that formed an association to regulate, by joint decision, the number of ships each would send to Hankow or Shanghai during the tea export season, the cargoes each ship would carry, and the freight rates they would charge. They further agreed to give rebates only to shippers dealing exclusively with members of the association and to prohibit their agents in China from acting on behalf of competing lines. The Mogul Company, at first a member of the association and then excluded, brought suit against the defendants when the Chinese port serviced by Mogul saw a sharp increase in defendants' ships. The defendants underbid Mogul's rates, threatened to dismiss service agents handling Mogul's account, and circulated notices that they would not give rebates to anyone shipping by Mogul. Mogul's complaint for damages, alleging a conspiracy to injure it, was dismissed by the trial court. The dismissal was affirmed by the court of appeals and affirmed by the House of Lords.[29]

All justices agreed that the agreement was unlawful in the sense that it would not be enforced between the parties thereto, but it was

26. *Id.* at 552.

27. It is interesting that many of the antimonopoly statutes enacted by Parliament were directed toward labor rather than business. For example, the Combination Act of 1799 prohibited combinations of workmen only. This was superseded by the Combination Act of 1800, which prohibited masters as well as workmen from combining. 38 Geo. III, c. 81 (1799); c. 106 (1800). It is clear that these laws were prosecuted more severely against combinations of laborers than against those of masters. *See* George, "The Combination Laws," *Econ. His. Rev.,* VI, 172 (1935). In 1824 Parliament passed an act which gave workmen, as well as masters, immunity from all statutory and common law prohibitions against restraints of trade. 5 Geo. IV, c. 95 (1824). Later excesses caused the next session of Parliament, however, to reverse the terms of the prior act and restore the power of the common law over combinations. 6 Geo. V, 129 (1825).

28. [1892] App. Cas. 25. This decision paralleled a major development in the United States; passage of the Sherman Act in 1890.

29. 21 Q.B.D. 544 (1888). 23 Q.B.D. 598 (1889). [1892] App. Cas. 25.

not illegal in the sense of being "contrary to law."[30] Under the common law a conspiracy was illegal or contrary to law only if it sought an unlawful end or used unlawful means, neither of which existed here, according to the Lord Chancellor, since the combination had neither acted with any "malicious intention to injure rival traders," nor used any unlawful means, such as violence, intimidation, molestation, or inducement, to breach contracts.[31]

On the question of whether such a combination was contrary to public policy, Lord Bramwell stated that the public policy of free trade positively authorized such combinations: "It does seem strange that to enforce freedom of trade, of action, the law should punish those who make a perfectly honest agreement with a belief that it is fairly required for their protection." Lord Bramwell further noted that employers should receive treatment equal to that of their workmen: "I have always said that a combination of workmen, an agreement among them to cease work except for higher wages, and a strike in consequence, was lawful at common law; perhaps not enforceable inter se, but not indictable. The Legislature has now so declared."[32]

By 1890 the facility of English common law to deter monopolies, restraints of trade, and combinations in restraint of trade was all but a dead letter. The common law limiting monopoly power had been abrogated by the Statute of Monopolies, and the common law deterring contracts and combinations in restraint of trade was so diluted as to be of no consequence.

In the United States, however, there emerged in the mid-1800s a line of decisions promulgated by state courts that affirmatively deterred monopolistic practices. These decisions, which formed a part of the common law, greatly influenced the molding of the Sherman Act in 1890 and therefore need to be considered.

3. Common law development in American state courts

The English courts' failure to effectively deter monopolies and restraints of trade did not leave Congress without a framework in which to draft the Sherman Act. State courts, relying on earlier

30. [1892] App. Cas. 25, 39.
31. [1892] App. Cas. 25, 36–37.
32. [1892] App. Cas. 25, 47.

English decisions curtailing monopolies and restraints of trade, began formulating their own laws to combat such conduct, particularly when perpetrated by combinations governed by "gentleman agreements" and tightly associated "pools" of business interests.

In the case of *Craft* v. *McConoughy*,[33] decided in 1875, five grain dealers in Rochelle, Illinois, combined to fix prices and divide profits. After one of the members of the combination died, his son filed a lawsuit for an accounting and distribution of profits. In refusing to enforce the agreement, thereby leaving the parties as they were, the court emphasized the fact that the dealers had a virtual monopoly: all warehouses in the city and all lots suitable for warehouse construction were controlled by the combination. Also, the court noted the combination had carried out its program in secrecy, thereby misleading the public to believe that the participants had acted unilaterally and independently in conducting their business. The court stated:

> While these parties were in business, in competition with each other, they had the undoubted right to establish their own rates for grain stores and commissions for shipment and sale. They could pay as high or low a price for grain as they saw proper, and as they could make contracts with the producer. So long as competition was free, the interest of the public was safe. The laws of trade, in connection with the rigor of competition, was all the guaranty the public required, but the secret combination created by the contract destroyed all competition and created a monopoly against which the public interest had no protection.[34]

In *India Bagging Associations* v. *B. Kock & Co.*,[35] decided in 1859, eight India bagging concerns formed an association. Each agreed not to sell any bagging for a period of three months except with the consent of the majority of members. Breach of the agreement was grounds for a fine of $10 for every bale sold. Suit was brought against one member for selling 740 bales without authorization. The court found the agreement to be in restraint of trade, contrary to the public order, and therefore unenforceable. The ultimate effect of the agree-

33. 79 Ill. 346 (1875).
34. *Id*. at 350.
35. 14 La. Ann. 168 (1859).

ment, the court declared, was to enhance the price of an article of prime necessity to cotton planters.

A third case, *Emery* v. *Ohio Candle Co.,*[36] decided in 1890, the year the Sherman Act was passed, involved a combination of manufacturers comprising 95 percent of the star candle industry in a large part of the United States. Members of the combination had been required to pay into the treasury of the association 2½ cents per pound on every pound of candles sold. At regular intervals, each member received a share of the pool's profits, in proportion to the amount of business done. A member of the association withdrew and sued for his share of the profits. The court refused to grant relief, declaring that "the objects of the association were contrary to public policy, and in no way to be aided by the courts." The court further noted that plaintiff was not an innocent victim, but rather had brought a suit to recover a portion of his "ill gotten goods" while an active member of the association.[37]

A number of early decisions, however, reached contrary results. In *Skrainka* v. *Scharringhausen,*[38] an 1880 decision, twenty-five stone quarry owners in the St. Louis area entered an agreement establishing among themselves "a fair proportionate sales of the produce of all quarries at uniform prices and living rates." An exclusive sales agent was appointed to apportion sales among the quarries and sell the stone at the agreed-upon prices. Defendant was sued for violating the agreement and for recovery of the penalty incurred. The court rejected defendant's argument that the agreement was in restraint of trade and held that where the restraint was partial and the restrictions reasonable, the restraint was not such that it would interfere with the interests of the general public. The court, in holding for plaintiff, noted that the contract was limited as to both time and place and was amongst the quarrymen of only one district of the city.

In *Dolph* v. *Troy Laundry Machinery Co.,*[39] decided in 1886, the two leading manufacturers of washing machines in the United States entered a five-year agreement to raise prices and to divide profits. Dolph had the option of manufacturing all the machines sold by both

36. 47 Ohio St. 320 (1890).
37. *Id.* at 322.
38. 8 Mo. App. 522 (1880).
39. 28 Fed. 553 (C.C.N.D.N.Y. 1886).

parties, and Troy agreed to purchase at least fifty machines annually from Dolph. Dolph sued when Troy terminated the contract prior to its expiration. The court held the contract valid, reasoning that "[t]he scheme of the parties did not contemplate suppressing the manufacture or sale of machines by others. Those who might be unwilling to pay the prices asked by the parties could find plenty of mechanics to make such machines," and this fact was enough to "effectually counteract any serious mischief likely to arise from the attempt of the parties to get exorbitant prices for their machines."[40] The court noted the distinction between internal restraints, which merely restrained the parties, and external restraints directed at actual or potential competitors. The court concluded:

> It is not obnoxious to good morals, or to the rights of the public, that two rival traders agree to consolidate their concerns, and that one shall discontinue business and become a partner with the other, for a specified term. It may happen . . . that the public may have to pay more for the commodities in which the parties deal; but the public are not obliged to buy of them. Certainly, the public have no right to complaint so long as the transaction falls short of a conspiracy between the parties to control prices by creating a monopoly.[41]

4. The rise of business trusts

Perhaps the single, most significant factor giving impetus to the Sherman Act's passage was the emergence of the uniquely American institution called the *trust*. First coming to prominence in the 1880s with the creation of the Standard Oil Company Trust, trust building entered an era of great expansion by the end of that decade. There emerged the American Cotton Oil Trust, the National Linseed Oil Trust, the Sugar Trust, the Whiskey Trust, the Cordage Trust, and the National Lead Trust, to name a few. It was not simply the size of these trusts that inflamed public resentment against them, but their ruthless methods of competition, which dragged business morality to the lowest point in the history of the country. Clair Wilcox

40. *Id.* at 555.
41. *Id.* at 555–56.

describes this climate with reference to the National Cash Register Co.:

> The National Cash Register Co., organized in 1882, set out deliberately to destroy its competitors. It hired employees away from them. It bribed their employees and the employees of common carriers and telephone and telegraph companies to spy on them and disclose their business secrets. It spread false rumors concerning their solvency. It instructed its agents to misrepresent the quality of their goods, interfere with their sales, and damage the mechanism of their machines in establishments where they were in use. It publicly displayed their cash registers under labels which read, "Junk." It made, and sold at cost, inferior machines called "Knockers," which it represented to be just as good as theirs. It threatened to bring suit against them and their customers for alleged infringement of patent rights. It induced their customers to cancel their orders by publishing lists of defunct competitors and by exhibiting in a "graveyard" at its factory samples of machines which they had formerly made.[42]

Henry Demarest Lloyd's article, "The Story of a Great Monopoly," which heavily castigated the Standard Oil Company Trust, received such prominence that the *Atlantic Monthly* reprinted the article six times.

It was the second Standard Oil Trust agreement, concluded in 1882, that became the model for subsequent trusts. It was entered into by all the stockholders and members of fourteen corporations and limited partnerships, by groups of stockholders and members of twenty-six other corporations and limited partnerships, and by some forty individuals, most of whom were associated with John D. Rockefeller. A board of nine trustees was established to control the physical properties of the industry. In turn, each party to the agreement gave up control of its respective properties as well as its shares of stock and voting power in exchange for trust certificates issued by the trustees. The certificates had a par value of $100 each. Each party was given a number of certificates corresponding to the value of its property or stock turned over.

The nine trustees of the Standard Oil Trust held staggered terms

---

42. Wilcox, "Competition and Monopoly in American Industry," *U.S. Temporary National Economic Committee Monograph* No. 21 (1940), 68.

of three years with one third elected each year by the certificate hold-
ers. The trust was to run for twenty-one years after the death of the
last survivor of the original trustees. The trustees were given power
to admit new corporations, partnerships, or individuals into the
arrangement as well as buy and sell bonds and stocks of outside corporations doing business in related fields. In effect, the oil industry in
the United States became concentrated in the hands of the nine
trustees.

In 1884 the American Cotton Oil Trust was organized by seventy
or eighty mills engaged in the production of cottonseed oil. Two years
later the trust controlled "88 percent of the entire crushing capacity
of the United States."[43] In 1887 the Sugar Trust was formed and
controlled seventeen or eighteen refineries out of twenty-one. Capitalization reached the enormous figure, for that time, of $50,000,000.
The Whiskey Trust, formed the same year, was made up of eighty-
one companies manufacturing 85 to 90 percent of the total output of
alcohol and spirits. Between 1887 and 1889 the National Lead Trust
was organized, consisting of thirty-one companies, including three
large smelters, one of the best refineries, and three linseed oil mills.
The trust controlled over 95 percent of the nation's output of lead.

Railroads had a great impact, not only in industrial development
after the Civil War, but in fostering antitrust legislation. Nothing
epitomized their unique role more than the extraordinary grants of
aid that they received from local and federal governments in the form
of land, credits, and cash. It is estimated that railroads received
242,000 square miles of land before 1912;[44] by comparison, continental France covers 204,000 square miles. The most famous instance of
federal aid was that given to the Central Pacific and Union Pacific
to build the first transcontinental railroad. The federal government
gave a cash subsidy of $16,000 per mile in level country, $32,000 in
hill country, and $48,000 in the mountains, plus 12,800 acres in
determinate sections of public lands for every mile of track laid. It is
estimated that the total aid given was $700 million.[45]

Railroads lost their favored position through outright corruption
and unscrupulous practices, and by the 1870s they had become the

---

43. "American Cotton Oil Trust," 43 Com. & Fin. Chron. (Sept. 11, 1886), 302.
44. Ripley, *Railroads: Rates and Regulation* 36 (1912).
45. *Id.* at 35f.

whipping dog of the nation. It was not uncommon for railroads to hire legislators as counsel at large salaries and grant free passes to public figures. The Erie Railroad bribed numerous New York assemblymen with $15,000 each to legalize a stock issue. The governor of New York received $20,000. Vanderbilt, who was trying to defeat the measure in order to buy out the Erie Railroad, purchased one legislator for $75,000, only to be outbid by Jay Gould, who paid $100,000.[46] In one year the Erie spent $700,000 for corruption and legal expenses while carrying the amount on the books as the "India Rubber Account."

Men like Jay Gould, Daniel Drew, and Vanderbilt manipulated their railroad stock, not for the good of their corporations, but rather to enhance their personal fortunes. At the same time, competition between railroads became intense, resulting, at first, in lower rates in competitive areas. A pricing pattern emerged, however, whereby rates at competitive points were quite low, while charges in areas where a railroad had a monopoly were unreasonably high. A rate "war" between trunk lines serving New York to Chicago in the early 1880s resulted in a charge of $1.00 for immigrants traveling from New York to Chicago.

The presence of competitive water transportation on the Great Lakes was of indispensable value to the Middle West as a check upon the railways. However, whenever they could avoid this source of competition, the trunk lines shamelessly gouged farmers and other shippers. Each year the railroads hiked their freight rates, by one to two thirds in November when ice closed the ports, and in April of each year they reverted to an honest, competitive level when navigation was again possible.[47] Meanwhile, at noncompetitive points, carriers "were able to charge monopoly prices, being limited only by what the traffic would bear, or, perhaps more accurately, by what the traffic would not bear."[48]

It was this discrimination in prices between localities that led to the first real attack on railroads in the 1870s by the granges and other farm organizations. A second practice that came under heavy attack was the railroads' practice of charging discriminatory prices to two

46. Shannon, *The Economic History of the People of the United States* 492 (1934).
47. Ripley, *Railroads: Rates and Regulations* 23.
48. *Ibid.*

customers shipping similar goods in similar quantities. Powerful and unscrupulous shippers like the Standard Oil Trust were able to exact substantial rebates or refunds over their competitors. Such discriminatory pricing was recognized in the 1880s as a source of grave danger to the very existence of competitive enterprise in other industries. The Cullum Committee, reporting to the Senate in 1886, stated that it was a common complaint that

> the effect of the prevailing policy of railroad management is, by an elaborate system of secret special rates, rebates, drawbacks, and concessions, to foster monopoly, to enrich favored shippers and to prevent the competition in many lines of trade in which the item of transportation is an important factor.[49]

The disastrous results of unscrupulous competition in the railroad industry ultimately led to concerted arrangements called pools that were intended to cushion existing rivalries. Although these agreements lessened cutthroat competition, they did nothing to do away with the system of discrimination. The pool arrangements became another grievance against railroads, which resulted in the public outcry for antitrust legislative reform.

5. Political pressure on Congress to stop the trusts and railroads

The initial impetus for antitrust legislation came from the Grangers or Patrons of Husbandry. First intended to serve the social and educational needs of rural America, the granger movement became embroiled in political and economic activities. By 1871 their watchwords were "Cooperation," which meant farmers' cooperatives and "Down with monopolies," which primarily sought regulation of railroads.[50] Through its manifesto, declarations, petitions, and statements, the movement attacked railroads and monopolies as "detrimental to the public prosperity, corrupting their management, and dangerous to republican institutions." At the Illinois Farmers Convention in 1873 a resolution was passed stating that "the railways of the world, except in those countries where they have been held under

49. Cullom Committee Report, Senate Select Committee on Interstate Commerce, S. Rep. No. 46, 49th Cong, 1st Sess. (1886), 181.
50. Buck, *The Granger Movement* 52–53, 58 (1913).

the strict regulations and supervision of the government, have proved themselves arbitrary, extortionate and as opposed to free institutions and free commerce between states as were the feudal barons of the middle ages."[51]

A broader attack was launched in the 1880s by various other sectors of the American public. One crusader condemned as monopolistic not only railroads, banks, and public utility companies, but also "speculative dealings in grains, restrictive licensing of business and professions, laws limiting the ballot to males, and those 'nurseries of caste'—West Point and Annapolis."[52] One Chicago judge, speaking at an Illinois Bar Association meeting in 1882, described the accumulation of capital into the "great moneyed institutions—private corporations—that are commonly stigmatized as monopolies" as one of America's greatest problems. As examples he listed railroad corporations, the giant wheat farms, and the "monster business establishments, owned by private individuals, of which the Standard Oil Company is the best known type."[53] General Ben Butler, the presidential candidate of the Greenback and Anti-monopoly parties in 1884, attacked the railroads, which charged excessive rates, the sewing machine monopoly, which abused the power derived from its patent, and the Standard Oil Company.[54]

By the mid-1880s, the political parties were following the lead of the granger movement, condemning trusts and monopolies. The Greenback and Anti-Monopoly parties carried on a campaign against "land, railroad, money and other gigantic monopolies."[55] The Union Labor Party, formed by a coalition of Greenbackers, Knights of Labor, and farmer organizations, included in its platform of 1888 the declaration, "The paramount issues to be solved in the interests of humanity are the abolition of usury, monopoly, and trusts, and we denounce the Democratic and Republican Parties for creating and perpetuating these monstrous evils."[56] Antimonopoly planks also

51. Periam, *The Groundswell* 286 (1874).

52. Letwin, *Law and Economic Policy in America* 68 (1965).

53. Jameson, *The Grounds and Limits of Rightful Interference by Law With Accumulation and Use of Capital* 1–7 (1882).

54. Butler, Speech of August 30, 1884, appended to his pamphlet, *Address to His Constituents*, August 12, 1884.

55. McKee, *National Conventions and Platforms*, 215, 192, 224 (1901).

56. *Id.* at 251.

appeared in the 1888 platforms of the Prohibition Party and United Labor Party.[57] The two major parties sought to disassociate themselves from the trusts. The Democratic Party, in 1880 and 1884, spoke out against trusts and monopolies, and President Cleveland, in his annual message to Congress at the end of 1887, said it was "notorious" that the "combinations quite prevalent at this time, and frequently called trusts," strangled competition. He suggested that Congress take affirmative action by reducing the custom duties protecting them.[58]

The Republican Party took a stronger position against trusts and monopolies. It had no politically sound alternative, for it was considered the party of the rich, the "Party of Monopolists."[59] This label stuck after the Republican presidential candidate was given a banquet by a group of businessmen—including Gould, Vanderbilt, and Astor—which the New York World titled, "The Royal Feast of Belshazzar Blain and the Money Kings."[60] In an effort to overcome such labels, the Republicans, at their 1888 convention, condemned "all combinations of capital, organized in trusts or otherwise, to control arbitrarily the conditions of trade among our citizens," and recommended "such legislation as will prevent the execution of all schemes to oppress the people by undue charges on their supplies, or by unjust rates for the transportation of their products to market."[61] The election of Benjamin Harrison and a Republican Congress placed in their hands responsibility for enacting appropriate legislation.

6. Congress' response to the needs of the nation

Senator Sherman, the most prominent and esteemed Republican in Congress, in 1888 introduced the first antitrust bill.[62] After committee consideration, his bill was debated in January 1889. It was

---

57. *Id.* at 247, 252.

58. Richardson, *A Compilation of the Messages and Papers of Presidents,* VIII, 588 (1900).

59. Butler, *Address to His Constituents* 8 (Pamphlet of August 12, 1884).

60. *N.Y. World,* Oct. 30, 1884, et al.

61. McKee, *National Conventions and Platforms* 241.

62. Senator Sherman had served as a representative for eight years and a senator for twenty-five years. He had been secretary of the Treasury under President Hayes and a presidential nominee in 1880 and 1888.

severely attacked by Senator James George of Mississippi, formerly a Confederate general and chief justice of the state supreme court, on the grounds that the bill would be ineffective and was unconstitutional. Although against trusts, Senator George felt that the bill would penalize southern farmers who had organized a boycott against the Jute-Bag Trust as well as all farmers who had combined to raise the prices of their products. As drafted, the bill would also have penalized laborers who unionized in order to raise their wages and even temperance societies whose members compacted not to use spirits. Some opponents argued that the bill was utterly worthless: because the bill's jurisdictional authority was based on the commerce clause of the U.S. Constitution, its scope was limited to goods actually in interstate or forcign transit and therefore would not punish the large combinations acting at local levels. Before any action could be taken on the bill, the 50th Congress disbanded.

At the commencement of the 51st Congress, Senator Sherman reintroduced the bill on December 4, 1889, and it was brought to the floor of the Senate for debate in February 1890. It declared unlawful and void all combinations preventing competition in foreign and interstate commerce, it authorized the persons injured to recover damages, and it subjected all parties found guilty to a fine and imprisonment. Senator George again attacked the bill as unconstitutional and worthless.[63] At this point interest in the bill waned. Two other bills, including one introduced by Senator George, were tied up by committee, as were seventeen bills that had been introduced in the House.

In March 1890 there was a sudden burst of energy that was perhaps motivated by increasing public agitation for antitrust legislation. Petitions and resolutions from state legislatures seeking appropriate legislation were read into the Congressional Record, including some forty-nine that were entered during the period December 2, 1889, to March 21, 1890.[64]

Senator Sherman opened the debate with a defense of his bill, explaining both the legal and political theory. He noted that the bill was not intended to destroy all combinations but merely those that

63. 21 Cong. Rec. 1765–72 (1890).

64. 20 Cong. Rec. 514, 1234, 1253, 1273, 1500, 1589, 2135 (1888–89), 21 Cong. Rec. (listed in Index, sub. "Trusts, Petitions").

the common law had always condemned as unlawful. It was aimed at combinations that restrained trade and stifled competition, such as those that dictated terms to railroads, raised prices to consumers, and controlled the price of labor. He attacked the monopolies that were engaged in a form of tyranny "of kingly prerogative," and observed that a nation that "would not submit to an emperor ... should not submit to an autocrat of trade."

Sherman cited case after case that had applied the common law to combinations in restraint of trade. The decision of the Michigan Supreme Court in *Richardson* v. *Buhl*[65] was of particular interest to him, and he read the full opinion into the record. The case struck at the Diamond Match Company's monopoly and labeled as a monopolist one of Sherman's chief rivals in 1888 for the Republican presidential nomination, General Russel Alger, whom Sherman blamed for his unexpected defeat.[66] Sherman noted that although trusts and monopolies could be attacked under the common law in state courts, there was no similar federal law. He again insisted that Congress was authorized by the commerce and revenue clauses of the Constitution to regulate combinations affecting interstate and foreign commerce.

During the following days of debate a number of objections were made, amendments were added, and the bill was referred to the Judiciary Committee—over Sherman's objection.[67] To the surprise of all, a redrafted bill, the work largely of George Edmunds of Vermont, chairman of the committee, was reported out in one week. Edmunds convinced all, including Senator George, that Congress had the constitutional power to pass a law "preventing and punishing contracts etc. in restraint of commerce between the states." He drafted the critical sections of the bill that made it a misdemeanor to engage in any combination in restraint of trade or to monopolize trade. Senator George himself drafted the section authorizing the attorney general to sue for injunctive relief, and Senator Hoar drafted a section giving private persons injured by such combination a right of recovery of damages.[68] Although the redraft was very similar to Sherman's original bill, he bitterly opposed it as "totally inef-

65. 77 Mich. 632 (1889).
66. Senator Sherman had publicly accused Alger of bribing convention delegates.
67. 21 Cong. Rec. 2600 et. seq., 2604, 2610, 2731 (1890).
68. The Committee Minute Book, 227–33, shows that sections 1, 2, 5, and 6 were drafted by Edmunds, section 4 by George, section 7 by Hoar, and the phrase "in form of trust or otherwise" by Evarts.

fective in dealing with combinations and trusts. All corporations can ride through it or over it without fear of punishment or direction."[69] However, he did vote for it, and as a consequence the law bears his name. The final Senate vote was 52 to 1.

After limited debate, the House passed the bill on May 1, 1880, with one amendment. During the next two months of conferences between the two chambers the House was finally prevailed upon to drop its amendment, and President Harrison signed the bill on July 1, 1890.

7. Early enforcement of the Sherman Act

As originally enacted, the Sherman Act was divided into eight sections. The first three defined the substantive violations and provided for certain penalties. Contrary to the felony provisions today, the original penalty was a misdemeanor of a fine not exceeding $5,000 and imprisonment not exceeding one year. Section 1 provided that "every contract, combination in the form of trust or otherwise, or conspiracy, in restraint of trade or commerce" between the states or with foreign nations was illegal. Section 2 provided that every person "who shall monopolize, or attempt to monopolize or conspire with any other person or persons, to monopolize any part of" interstate or foreign commerce was guilty of a misdemeanor, the punishment of which was the same as provided in Section 1.

Section 3 made the provisions of Section 1 applicable to commerce in the District of Columbia and the territories, as well as between them and the states and foreign nations. Section 4 vested the federal courts with jurisdiction to hear cases arising under the act and the attorney general with power to enforce the act through the commencement of injunction actions. Section 5 gave the court nationwide power to summon additional parties and subpoena witnesses. Section 7 permitted persons injured by any of the unlawful acts to sue and recover three times their loss as damages plus reasonable attorney's fees. Section 8 defined "person" or "persons," as used in the act, to include corporations and associations existing under the laws of the United States or any state or foreign country.

Passage of the Sherman Act was heralded by some as the end of trusts. It did not, however, live up to its expectations. Inaction

69. *New York Times,* Apr. 8, 1890, at 4, col. 4.

brought complaints that Congress had deliberately passed a mock law, too weak and badly worded to accomplish anything. An apologist and one of the principal authors of the act, Senator Edmunds, stated in 1892 that "the law is all right, the courts are all right, and the people are all right. Let the officers charged with the enforcement of the law do their full duty and trusts and combinations will go to pieces as quickly as they sprang up."[70]

The failure to enforce the Sherman Act might be laid, in part, at the doorstep of the attorney general's office. However, the attorney general was severely hampered from the start because of lack of funds and manpower. Congress did not appropriate funds to be used specifically for antitrust enforcement[71] until 1903, when it appropriated $500,000. In 1890 the attorney general's office had eighty employees, only eighteen of whom were lawyers. This staff, already burdened with enforcement of other federal criminal statutes, could not direct its attention to pursuing the trusts and others acting in violation of the Sherman Act.

A second obstacle to enforcement was the broad language of the act itself, as well as the lack of definitive judicial interpretations upon which individual district attorneys could rely. Indifference to the act set in during the administrations of Presidents Benjamin Harrison, Grover Cleveland, and William McKinley. Attorney General Richard Olney, in expressing his own disinterest, reported in 1893:

> There has been, and probably still is, a widespread impression that the aim and effect of this statute are to prohibit and prevent those aggregations of capital which are so common at the present day, and which are sometimes on so large a scale as to control practically all the branches of an extensive industry. It would not be useful, even if it were possible, to ascertain the precise purposes of the framers of the statute. It is sufficient to point out what small basis for the popular impression referred to.[72]

Additionally, until 1903 there was a lack of interest in the private sector to commence private treble damage actions.

The cases that were decided showed a glaring need for additional legislation to amend the Sherman Act or cover certain loopholes inherent in the act. The first major test of the act in the U.S.

---

70. *New York Times,* Nov. 25, 1892, at 4, col. 2.
71. Thorelli, *The Federal Antitrust Policy* 369 (1955).
72. 1893 Atty. Gen. Ann. Rep. XXVI f., *reproduced in* Thorelli, *supra* note 78, at 385.

Supreme Court was *United States* v. *E. C. Knight Co.*[73] or the *Sugar Trust* case. In this case the defendant, having 65 percent of the domestic sugar refining and sales capacity, purchased four smaller Pennsylvania sugar refining companies that together had about 33 percent of the domestic refining and sales capacity. It was alleged that the defendant monopolized the manufacture and sale of refined sugar in the United States, thereby controlling the price of sugar. The purchase contracts were alleged to constitute a combination and conspiracy in restraint of trade. The dismissal of the complaint by the trial court was affirmed by the Supreme Court on the ground that the complaint failed to allege a violation of the Sherman Act, because there was no evidence that there was any intention to restrain interstate trade or commerce.

As a result of the *Knight* decision, the business community concluded that a merger of competitors was the only medium for doing business free from the strictures of the Sherman Act.[74] As a result of this understanding of the law and the liberalizing of state merger laws, there was excessive growth in industrial trusts that far exceeded that during the period prior to the Sherman Act. Senator William H. Thompson of Kansas inserted in congressional debates a lengthy table showing that 628 trusts had formed from 9,877 independent companies and had a total capitalization of almost $25 billion. He testified that the greatest amount of trust formation took place between 1898 and 1908.[75]

The growing prosperity and strength of the trusts in the early 1900s gave them unbridled power over labor and prices. It was anomalous that the Sherman Act was used, not against these trusts, but by them to crush labor strikes and stifle the ability of workers to organize. Between the years 1890 to 1914, approximately 101 cases were filed in which federal courts issued injunctions against labor organizations,[76] even though the legislative history of the Sherman Act makes it clear that it was not intended to apply to such combinations.

The trusts, in their efforts to more effectively control competition, engaged in new and different restrictive practices. For example, the

73. 156 U.S. 1 (1895), *aff'd.,* 60 Fed. 934 (3d Cir. 1894).

74. Northern Securities v. United States, 193 U.S. 197 (1904), put this notion to rest, holding that the form of the combination did not matter in determining legality.

75. 51 Cong. Rec. 14217–21 (1914).

76. 51 Cong. Rec. 9173, 13665–66 (1914).

United Shoe Machinery Co. conditioned the lease of certain of its machinery upon the explicit condition that the supplies necessary to the functioning of those machines be purchased only from the company. It also inserted certain tying clauses in its leases for its basic bottoming machines requiring (1) that the lessee utilize these machines only in finishing the shoes, with other machines also leased from United Shoe performing the intermediate manufacturing processes, (2) that the lessee use the machines to their full capacity, and (3) that lessee pay to United Shoe a royalty for each pair of shoes on which the soles had been welded or stitched by machine, without regard as to whether United Shoe's machinery had been used in their manufacture. The lease also provided that failure of the lessee to use exclusively certain classes of machinery leased to it by United Shoe would constitute immediate grounds for termination. These provisions, in addition to United Shoe's policy of buying up competitors and new machinery patents from independent inventors, had given the company a virtual monopoly over the manufacture of shoe machinery in the United States by 1911.[77]

Such tying restrictions became a significant means of doing business in the early 1900s, and the U.S. Supreme Court's decision approving the practice in *Henry* v. *A. B. Dick Co.*[78] spurred further use. In the *A. B. Dick Co.* case the Court found that the patentee's practice of licensing its patented duplicating machines for use only with inks, stencils, and supplies of the patentee's own manufacture was legal under existing patent laws. The court noted that only Congress had the power to make the practice illegal.

In 1900 Congress reacted to the *Knight* decision by considering, among other things, a joint resolution proposing a constitutional amendment that would permit Congress, through a federal incorporation system, to regulate corporations engaged in interstate commerce.[79] The Republican controlled Congress also proposed amendments to the Sherman Act that would have increased the penalty for violations. New provisions were suggested that would have barred trust goods from interstate transportation, denied the use of the mails

77. Hearings Pursuant to 5 Res. 98 Before the Senate Comm. on Interstate Commerce, 62 Cong., 3d Sess (1913), 2258.

78. 224 U.S. 1 (1912).

79. H.R.J. Res. 138, 56th Cong., 1st Sess. (1900).

to convicted combinations, granted broader subpoena powers in both civil and criminal cases, and vested private citizens with the right to proceed against combinations on behalf of the government.[80]

Such efforts failed and were not renewed until after the U.S. Supreme Court's decision in *Standard Oil Co. of New Jersey* v. *United States*.[81] In that case the government brought an action against the Standard Oil Trust and named as defendants the Standard Oil companies of New Jersey, California, Indiana, Iowa, Kansas, Kentucky, Nebraska, New York, Ohio, and sixty-two other corporations and partnerships, as well as seven individuals. In an exhaustive opinion discussing the common law and the background of the Sherman Act, the Court concluded that the Standard Oil Trust was violative of the Sherman Act and ordered its dismemberment. The importance of the opinion, however, was the ruling that not all combinations in restraint of trade are illegal, but only those that are "unreasonable." Thus, the Court took upon itself the determination as to whether a restraint was reasonable or unreasonable, for only those of the latter category were said to be violative of the act.[82]

The decision brought an immediate response from Congress. Legislation was introduced in both houses to strengthen the Sherman Act.[83] Congress made it clear that it was concerned with what it considered to be a dilution of the Sherman Act as a result of the *Standard Oil* decision. In one report of the Senate Commerce Committee the following statement was made:

> The fair conclusion is that it is now the settled doctrine of the Supreme Court that only undue or unreasonable restraints of trade are made unlawful by the antitrust act, and that in each instance it is for the court to determine whether the established restraint of trade is due restraint or an undue restraint.

80. H.R. 10539, 56th Cong., 1st Sess. (1900).

81. 221 U.S. 1 (1911).

82. As a practical matter, all contracts in some sense restrain trade and commerce. Unless the Court conditioned a violation of the act upon a determination that the parties' conduct was "unreasonable," the broad sweep of the act's language would have done away with practically all contracts.

83. Senator Robert M. LaFollette (R.Wis.) introduced a bill on August 19, 1911 and a companion bill was introduced in the House on December 5, 1911 by Representative Irvine L. Lenroot (R.Wis.), S.3276, 62d Cong., 1st Sess. (1911); H.R. 15926, 62d Cong., 2d Sess. (1911).

• • •

The committee has full confidence in the integrity, intelligence, and patriotism of the Supreme Court of the United States, but it is unwilling to repose in that court, or any other court, the vast and undefined power which it must exercise in the administration of the statute under the rule which it has promulgated. It substitutes the court in the place of Congress, for whenever the rule is invoked the court does not administer the law, but makes the law. If it continues in force, the Federal Courts will, so far as restraint of trade is concerned, make a common law of the United States just as the English courts have made a common law for England.

The people of this country will not permit the courts to declare a policy for them with respect to this subject. If we do not promptly exercise our legislative power, the courts will suffer immeasurable injury in the loss of that respect and confidence so essential to their usefulness. It is inconceivable that in a country governed by a written constitution and statute law the courts can be permitted to test each restraint of trade by the economic standard which the individual members of the court may happen to approve. If we do not speedily prescribe insofar as we can a legislative rule by which to measure the forms of contract and combination in restraint of trade with which we are familiar or which we can anticipate, we cease to be government of law and become a government of men, and, moreover, of a very few men, and they appointed by the President.[84]

8. Passage of the Clayton Act

On January 20, 1914, President Wilson presented a special message before a joint session of Congress that stressed the need for certainty in the antitrust laws and endorsed the creation of an interstate commerce commission.[85] The Democratic platform on which President Wilson ran presented a list of specific trade practices, which the Democratic party pledged to eliminate. Three of these practices were ultimately incorporated in the Clayton Act itself.[86]

84. S. Rep. No. 1326, 62 Cong., 3d Sess. (1913).

85. 51 Cong. Rec. 1963 (1914).

86. The Democratic Party platform provided: "We favor the declaration by law of the conditions upon which corporations shall be permitted to engage in interstate trade, including, among others, the prevention of holding companies, of interlocking directorates, of stock watering, of discrimination in price, and the control by any one corporation of so large a proportion of any industry as to make it a menace to competitive conditions." Martin, *Mergers and the Clayton Act* 28 (1959).

The Clayton Act, as finally passed, was a direct response to the weakness inherent in the Sherman Act. Whereas the Sherman Act prohibitions are expressed in general terms, the Clayton Act prohibits specified trade practices. Furthermore, the Clayton Act, unlike the Sherman Act, condemns practices the effect of which *may be* substantially to lessen competition, rather than only those restraints which *in fact* unreasonably restrain trade.

Some of the pertinent provisions of the act provide as follows: As enacted, Section 2 of the Clayton made it unlawful for any person to discriminate in prices, services, or facilities where the effect of such discrimination may be substantially to lessen competition or tend to create a monopoly in any line of commerce. Section 3 makes illegal (1) tying (or tie-in) agreements, that is, agreements to sell a desired product only on the condition that the buyer purchases a second unwanted or less desirable product, (2) exclusive dealing contracts, that is, agreements that the buyer will purchase only from the seller and no other supplier, and (3) requirements contracts, that is, agreements that the buyer will purchase all his requirements of a certain product from the seller.

Section 4 of the Clayton Act provides that any person injured in his business or property by reason of anything forbidden in the antitrust laws may sue and recover treble damages and costs of suit, including reasonable attorney's fees.[87] Section 5, in pertinent part, provides that final judgments and decrees entered in suits brought by the United States may, in certain cases, be *prima facie* evidence in subsequent suits brought by private parties and that the running of the statute of limitations is suspended during the pendency of government proceedings and for one year thereafter.

Section 6 of the act provides that the antitrust laws are not to be construed to forbid the existence and operation of nonprofit labor, agricultural, or horticultural organizations. Section 7 prohibits certain acquisition of the stock or assets of other corporations. Section 8 prohibits interlocking directorates between banks, savings banks, trust companies, and certain corporations.

---

87. By subsequent amendment Section 4A was added to give the United States the right to sue for actual damages and costs of litigation when injured by an antitrust violation. Section 4B provides a four-year statute of limitations to commence a lawsuit. And Section 4C-H empowers state attorneys general to bring treble damage actions as *parens patriae* on behalf of consumers when their individual losses are too small to justify private litigation.

9. Passage of the Federal Trade Commission Act

The Federal Trade Commission Act, which was passed one month before the Clayton Act, in September 1914, was intended to supplement rather than to amend the Sherman Act. Like the Clayton Act, its enactment was in response to the relative inactivity generated by the Sherman Act in the first twenty-three years of its existence. During the Sherman Act's first ten years only eighteen actions were commenced by the government: seven under President Harrison, eight during Grover Cleveland's second term, and three during McKinley's term. The largest number of suits, eighty-nine, came during President Taft's administration. Forty-four suits were instituted in President Roosevelt's eight years and eleven during Woodrow Wilson's term. In many of these cases, after the *Standard Oil* decision, the propriety of business activity was determined by the social and economic theories of individual judges applying the rule of reason. Hence, both the business world and its detractors demanded a law that specified and defined activities that violated the Sherman Act. A commission, with the ability and power to establish reliable guidelines and therefore remove the element of uncertainty that had previously tainted judicial opinions, was also sought.

The Clayton Act was passed to satisfy the first demand; the Federal Trade Commission Act satisfied the second. A major consideration in passing the FTC Act was the widely felt need for an impartial body with a specialized knowledge of business and economic conditions. The act has the primary object of preventing potential harm by halting unfair methods of competition or unfair or deceptive practices in commerce.[88]

10. Passage of the Robinson-Patman Act

The fourth act of importance, enacted on June 19, 1936, is the Robinson-Patman Act. The statute, which amends the Clayton Act, was vigorously sponsored by wholesale grocers and supported by food brokers facing fierce competition and a fight for economic survival as the result of the growth of chain grocery stores, mail-order houses, and similar mass merchandisers. Impetus for this legislation was also

88. This provision is found in Section 5 of the Federal Trade Commission Act 15 U.S.C. §45 (1975).

fueled by the collapse, in 1935 and 1936, of the Codes of the National Recovery Administration after the U.S. Supreme Court found them unconstitutional in *Schechter Poultry Corp.* v. *United States.*[89] The Federal Trade Commission, pursuant to a 1928 Senate resolution, had been investigating chain store marketing practices for more than six years and in December 1934 transmitted its final report.[90] The report noted that chain store operators, by virtue of their massive economic power, were obtaining discriminatory price concessions, advertising allowances, discounts reflecting brokerage savings, and similar advantages. The Federal Trade Commission recommended that Section 2 of the Clayton Act be amended in order to outlaw these evils.

Three principal bills were introduced: The Patman Bill (H.R. 9442), in the House; the Robinson Bill (S.3154), in the Senate; and the Borah-Van Nuys Bill (S.4171), dealing with criminal penalties, in the Senate. In the case of all three bills there was acrimonious debate by those who praised the legislation as the salvation of small business and a strike at the "damnable chains," and by those who condemned the bills as a price-fixing device that would be a serious detriment to the consumer. All three bills, as amended, were passed and are now referred to as the Robinson-Patman Act.

Section 1 of the act amends Section 2 of the Clayton Act and provides for civil remedies through government enforcement and private treble damage actions. Section 2(a) bars direct or indirect discriminatory pricing where specified competitive injury may result. Certain affirmative defenses are allowed, notably cost justification for price differentials. Section 2(b) permits a seller to rebut a *prima facie* violation of Sections 2(a), (d), and (e) by showing that he acted in good faith to meet the equally low price, the services, or the promotional allowances of a competitor. Section 2(c) prohibits a seller from paying brokerage or commission or giving any discount in lieu of brokerage or commission to a buyer or to anyone acting for a buyer. It also prohibits the buyer from receiving the forbidden payment.

Section 2(d) prohibits a seller from making any payment to a customer as compensation for services or facilities provided by the buyer

---

89. 295 U.S. 495 (1935).

90. S.Res. 224, 70th Cong., 1st Sess. (1928); FTC Chain Stores—Final Report on the Chain Store Investigation, S.Doc. No. 4, 74th Cong., 1st Sess. (1935).

in connection with the processing, handling, resale, or offering for resale of the goods purchased unless such payment is available on proportionably equal terms to all other competing customers. Section 2(e), a companion provision, prohibits the furnishing of services or facilities by the seller to a customer unless accorded to competing customers on proportionably equal terms. Section 2(f) forecloses a buyer from knowingly inducing or receiving a discriminatory price prohibited by Section 2(a).

Section 3, the Borah-Van Nuys Bill, which was added as an amendment to the Clayton Act along with the Robinson-Patman Act, provides criminal sanctions for certain discriminatory pricing and other predatory pricing practices. It forbids a knowing discrimination in a discount or an allowance not available to a purchaser's competitors for sales of goods of like grade, quality, and quantity. It forbids geographical price discrimination for the purpose of destroying competition or eliminating a competitor. Finally, it forbids sales at "unreasonably low prices" for predatory purposes. The penalty provided is a fine of not more than $5,000, or imprisonment of not more than one year, or both.

Chapter Two

Government Implementation of the Antitrust Laws

11. The Antitrust Division of the Department of Justice

The primary responsibility for enforcing the antitrust laws lies with the Antitrust Division of the Department of Justice, which was formed in 1933. Therefore, some consideration should be given to the makeup of this important arm of the federal government. This division is headed by an assistant attorney general, appointed by the president, a chief deputy attorney general, and two deputy assistant attorneys general.

In Washington, D.C., the division has four enforcement or litigation sections—special litigation section, special trial section, general litigation section, and trial section. Additionally, it has a number of specialized sections—three dealing with regulated industries and one each dealing with judgments, patents, foreign trade, appeals, and legal evaluation. There are also three sections with broader responsibilities—covering economic policy, policy planning, and legislation—as well as an office of operations. Most important to the division are the field offices—located in Atlanta, Chicago, New York, San Francisco, Cleveland, Los Angeles, Philadelphia, and Dallas—which handle the bulk of the government's antitrust litigation. The average field office has twenty to twenty-five lawyers supervised by a chief and an assistant chief. The field offices have geographic jurisdiction, whereas the Washington enforcement or litigation sections have specific product jurisdiction.

As of 1977, the Antitrust Division had 418 lawyers, 820 total personnel, and a budget of nearly $30 million. Ten years before there were 322 attorneys, 614 total personnel, and a budget of $7.2 million. Most of this growth came during the years 1973 to 1977 and indicates the division's growing presence in the antitrust enforcement area. Of the over 400 lawyers in the division, two thirds are under thirty-five and many are involved in their first major trial.

At the present time, a major portion of the division's efforts are directed toward price fixing. Some eighty to ninety grand juries around the country are engaged in price-fixing investigations alone. Since violations of the antitrust laws have been made a felony, the division has uniformly pressed for stiffer fines and sentences. The division's philosophy concerning sentencing was expressed by the then Assistant Attorney General Donald I. Baker:

Judges seem to have traditionally gone soft on price fixers because they were often "nice" people, because their crime often did not produce a highly visible public loss, because they were not physically dangerous to society, and because jail did not seem to offer much hope for rehabilitation. I was convinced and still am—that we sentence the price fixer to jail not for his own good so much as to deter the next person who might fix prices from doing so.[1]

12. Initiating antitrust investigations

It should be noted that the primary source of information leading to an antitrust investigation by the Antitrust Division is the business community itself. It is estimated that some two thirds of the three dozen or so complaints received each week by the division come from disgruntled businessmen complaining about the tactics of others. Some of these complaints are presented formally through legal counsel, while others are submitted in letter form or in person by the busi-

1. Testimony of Assistant Attorney General Donald I. Baker, Senate Judiciary Antitrust Subcommittee on "Oversight of Antitrust Enforcement," 813 Antitrust & Trade Reg. Rep., (BNA) May 12, 1977, at E-5.

nessman himself. Because of the increasing number of complaints originating with businessmen, it is advisable for any corporation or businessman seeking to avoid a potential investigation to respond to letters or complaints received from suppliers or customers making accusations having antitrust overtones.

Not infrequently businessmen involved in price fixing or some other antitrust violation make disclosures to the division in an effort to "clear the air" or perhaps exonerate themselves before it is too late.[2] Also, consumers who feel victimized by alleged antitrust violators regularly send complaints either to the division, members of Congress, or other agencies, which are then forwarded to the division.[3]

Other primary sources of information leading to a preliminary investigation are other agencies of government, particularly the Federal Trade Commission, the Securities Exchange Commission, and the various banking agencies. Potential antitrust violations may be uncovered in congressional hearings or in congressional committee reports, which are then referred to the division. Newspaper articles in the *Wall Street Journal* and the *New York Times,* as well as in local papers, provide leads concerning reorganizations, mergers, and interlocking directorates, all of which are of interest to the division.

The division, pursuant to presidential order,[4] receives from all federal departments, agencies, or instrumentalities all identical bids, involving the federal government, on purchases and sales exceeding $10,000. These bids must be reported to the division within twenty days of award or rejection.

Another source of information comes from antitrust lawsuits filed by private parties, so-called treble damage actions. The plaintiff in filing an antitrust treble damage action is required to provide an extra copy of his complaint, which is forwarded to the Antitrust Division for its review.

The division has a Business Review Procedure, whereby private businesses may obtain review of proposed transactions, such as mergers and acquisitions, and a statement of whether the division antici-

2. Williams, Investigations by the Department of Justice, A.B.A. Section of Antitrust Law 50 (1965).

3. Anyone seeking to file a complaint may send it to the Antitrust Division, Department of Justice, Washington, D.C.

4. 26 Fed.Reg. 3555 (April 24, 1961) (Executive Order 10936).

pates initiating enforcement proceedings.[5] Information received under this procedure can lead to a further preliminary inquiry by the division into potential violations.

The division may also launch a preliminary inquiry as a result of studies conducted by its own sections, such as the Economic Section,

---

5. 28 C.F.R. §1.50 (1979), provides: "Although the Department of Justice is not authorized to give advisory opinions to private parties, for several decades the Antitrust Division has been willing in certain circumstances to review proposed business conduct and state its enforcement intentions. This originated with a 'railroad release' procedure under which the Division would forego the initiation of criminal antitrust proceedings. The procedure was subsequently expanded to encompass a 'merger clearance' procedure under which the Division would state its present enforcement intention with respect to a merger or acquisition; and the Department issued a written statement entitled 'Business Review Procedure.' This is a revision of that statement, as amended.

1. A request for a business review letter must be submitted *in writing* to the assistant attorney general, Antitrust Division, Department of Justice, Washington, D.C. 20530.
2. The Division will consider only requests with respect to proposed business conduct, which may involve either domestic or foreign commerce.
3. The Division may, in its discretion, refuse to consider a request.
4. A business review letter shall have no application to any party which does not join in the request therefor.
5. The requesting parties are under an affirmative obligation to make full and true disclosure with respect to the business conduct for which review is requested. Each request must be accompanied by all relevant data including background information, complete copies of all operative documents and detailed statements of all collateral oral understandings, if any. All parties requesting the review letter must provide the division with whatever additional information or documents the division may thereafter request in order to review the matter. Such additional information, if furnished orally, shall be promptly confirmed in writing. In connection with any request for review the division will also conduct whatever independent investigation it believes is appropriate.
6. No oral clearance, release, or other statement purporting to bind the enforcement discretion of the division may be given. The requesting party may rely upon only a written business review letter signed by the Assistant Attorney General in charge of the Antitrust Division or his delegate.
7. (a) If the business conduct for which review is requested is subject to approval by a regulatory agency, a review request may be considered before agency approval has been obtained only where it appears that exceptional and unnecessary burdens might otherwise be imposed on the party or parties requesting review, or where the agency specifically requests that a party or parties request review. However, any business review letter issued in these as in any other circumstances will state only the department's present enforcement intentions under the antitrust laws. It shall in no way be taken to indicate the department's views on the legal or factual issues that may be raised before the regulatory agency, or in an appeal from the regulatory agency's decision. In particular, the issuance of such a letter is not to be represented to mean that the Division believes that there are no anticompetitive consequences warranting agency consideration.
(b) The submission of a request for a business review, or its pendency, shall in no way alter any responsibility of any party to comply with the Premerger Noti-

fication provisions of the Antitrust Improvements Act of 1975, 15 U.S.C. 18A, and the regulations promulgated thereunder, 16 C.F.R., Part 801.

8. After review of a request submitted hereunder the Division may state its present enforcement intention with respect to the proposed business conduct, decline to pass on the request, or take such other position or action as it considers appropriate. Ordinarily, however, the Division will state a present intention not to bring a *civil* action only with respect to mergers, acquisitions, or similar arrangements.

9. A business review letter states only the enforcement intention of the Division as of the date of the letter, and the Division remains completely free to bring whatever action or proceeding it subsequently comes to believe is required by the public interest. As to a stated present intention not to bring action, however, the Division has never exercised its right to bring a criminal action where there has been full and true disclosure at the time of presenting the request.

10. (a) Simultaneously upon notifying the requesting party of and Division action described in paragraph 8, the business review request, and the Division's letter in response shall be indexed and placed in a file available to the public upon request.

    (b) On that date or within thirty days after the date upon which the Division takes any action as described in paragraph 8, the information supplied to support the business review request and any other information supplied by the requesting party in connection with the transaction that is the subject of the business review request, shall be indexed and placed in a file with the request and the Division's letter available to the public upon request. This file shall remain open for one year, after which time it shall be closed and the documents either returned to the requesting party or otherwise disposed of, at the discretion of the Antitrust Division.

    (c) Prior to the time the information described in subparagraphs (a) and (b) is indexed and made publicly available in accordance with the terms of that subparagraph, the requesting party may ask the division to delay making public some or all of such information. However, the requesting party must: (1) specify precisely the documents or parts thereof that he asks not to be made public, (2) state the minimum period of time during which nondisclosure is considered necessary; and (3) justify the request for nondisclosure, both as to content and time, by showing good cause therefor, including a showing that disclosure would have a detrimental effect upon the requesting party's operations or relationships with actual or potential customers, employees, suppliers (including suppliers of credit), stockholders, or competitors. The Department of Justice, in its discretion, shall make the final determination as to whether good cause for nondisclosure has been shown.

    (d) Nothing contained in subparagraphs (a), (b) and (c) shall limit the Division's right, in its discretion, to issue a press release describing generally the identity of the requesting party or parties and the nature of action taken by the Division upon the request.

    (e) This paragraph reflects a policy determination by the Justice Department and is subject to any limitations or public disclosure arising from statutory restrictions, executive order, or the national interest.

11. Any requesting party may withdraw a request for review at any time. The Division remains free, however, to submit such comments to such requesting party as it deems appropriate. Failure to take action after receipt of documents or information, whether submitted pursuant to the procedure or otherwise, does not in any way limit or estop the Division from taking such action at such time thereafter as it deems appropriate. The Division reserves the right to retain documents submitted to it under this procedure or otherwise and to use them for all purposes of antitrust enforcement."

or the division chief may request a preliminary inquiry into a particular industry activity, such as a sudden increase in prices in one sector of the economy. Finally, the division, in carrying out the provisions of a prior civil judgment, may uncover potential new antitrust violations when inspecting company files as permitted in the prior judgment.

13. The preliminary inquiry—its nature and scope

The purpose of the preliminary inquiry is to determine whether a full-scale investigation should be commenced. The division exercises some caution in this regard because of its limited resources and because businessmen not infrequently make unjustifiable complaints for the desired purpose of subjecting a competitor to a full-scale investigation. The preliminary inquiry includes (1) studying public information about the company or companies named, (2) reviewing division files for similar complaints in the past or to ascertain if an investigation is already started, (3) checking with the Federal Trade Commission to avoid duplication of effort, (4) interviewing the person making the charges for more information, (5) interviewing other persons affected by the alleged illegal conduct, and (6) checking with the Economic Section of the division to see if it has made any studies of normal competitive patterns of the industry involved.

After completing the preliminary inquiry, the division will evaluate whether the conduct reported has sufficient impact on the economy to warrant a field investigation.

14. The field investigation

The field investigation is normally conducted by the Federal Bureau of Investigation, also a part of the Department of Justice, although division attorneys might on occasion assist in such an investigation. This investigation may involve an examination of a target company's files and records and informal interviews with its employees and officers if consent is given. It is the policy of the FBI that such interviews be without the presence of counsel, and transcripts of conversations be denied.

A question arises as to the degree of cooperation one should exercise when contacted by the FBI or division attorneys. Granting such an interview and turning over files for investigation are purely voluntary, and any adverse evidence uncovered may be the prelude to a full grand jury investigation. Thus, there is little to be gained and much to lose by much cooperation.

As a general rule there are only a few instances in which the granting of an interview or file search may be warranted and then only in the presence of counsel. For example, if the target of the investigation is convinced, after consultation with counsel, that no violation has occurred but rather the complaint was made as a result of some misunderstanding, an interview may be helpful in disposing of the matter. Immediately after the interview a memorandum should be prepared with the assistance of counsel to record the important matters covered.

It should be noted that when an interview is granted, it is absolutely essential that truthful answers be given. Normally, statements are not made under oath, although a party may be requested to sign a transcribed statement under oath. In either case a false statement can lead to very serious consequences, including a felony indictment.[6]

15. Good housekeeping considerations—retention of documents

In the normal antitrust price-fixing case brought by the Antitrust Division, the defendants' or industry documents can constitute the most incriminating evidence the division will offer at trial. These documents are obtained from company files either voluntarily during the preliminary investigation or pursuant to subpoena or civil investigative demand. A question arises as to whether all incriminating documents must be indefinitely retained awaiting government inspection.

There is no federal law that requires a company to preserve documents merely because they may be of interest to the Antitrust

6. 18 U.S.C. §1001 (1976), provides: "Whoever, in any matter within the jurisdiction of any department or agency of the United States knowingly and willfully falsifies, conceals or covers up by any trick, scheme, or device a material fact, or makes any false, fictitious or fraudulent statement or representation, or makes or uses any false writing or document knowing the same to contain any false, fictitious or fraudulent statement or entry, shall be fined not more than $10,000 or imprisonment not more than five years, or both." Section 1001 imposes penalties regardless of whether the statements were made under oath. A false unsworn statement to the FBI bears the same consequences as a sworn statement.

Division at some future date. Thus, it is recommended that periodic examination of files be made to determine whether there are documents evidencing an illegal course of conduct. If such documents are found, a question arises as to what should be done with these documents other than to correct the conduct that they evidence. Many factors should be weighed before a decision is made to destroy them.

If a document appears to have antitrust significance only when read out of context of the underlying transactions, a memorandum explaining its business background could be attached to the document. It then can be safely returned to the files. An incriminating document that cannot be so explained can be destroyed if the following conditions are met: (1) there are no recordkeeping laws or rules of sound business practices that require the preservation of the document and (2) at the time the document is found, the company is not being investigated by the Antitrust Division and has no reason to believe the division is contemplating such an investigation.

Although the destruction of documents in the above circumstances may be legal and, from the company's standpoint, desirable, there can be adverse results. A random disposal of documents may raise the inference that they were deliberately destroyed to cover an antitrust violation. This inference is less likely if they were destroyed as part of a long-established document–retention-destruction procedure. Theoretically, the judge and jury are not supposed to draw such inferences. As a practical matter, however, if such conduct is brought to their attention, the risk exists that they might draw inferences of guilt, which could tip the scales in favor of conviction.

Under the following circumstances documents may not be destroyed:

1. The Antitrust Division has already served the company with process requiring the production of documents.
2. No process has been served, but the company has good reason to believe such service of process is imminent.
3. The company has already volunteered, during the course of an informal investigation by the division, to produce the documents for the division to inspect.

Destruction of documents called for in a civil investigative demand (CID) served by the Antitrust Division is a criminal act carrying a fine of $5,000, or imprisonment not more than five years, or both.[7] Similarly, the destruction of documents called for in a subpoena *duces tecum* served by the grand jury is a criminal act carrying the same penalty.[8]

Destruction of documents prior to being served with a CID or a grand jury subpoena, when service of such process is known to be imminent, might arguably lead to a violation of the obstruction-of-justice statute.[9] Or, if a company during an informal investigation by the Antitrust Division agrees to produce certain documents and removes a number of the documents called for, there arises the risk of criminal sanctions pursuant to the "false statement" statute.[10]

16. Cooperating with the FBI and the Antitrust Division

It is, of course, desirable and even patriotic to cooperate with all branches of government. However, "ignorant" cooperation with the

7. 18 U.S.C. §1505 (1976), provides in part: "Whoever, with intent to avoid, evade, prevent, or obstruct compliance, in whole or in part, with any civil investigative demand duly and properly made under the Antitrust Civil Process Act, willfully withholds, misrepresents or removes from any place, conceals, covers up, destroys, mutilates, alters, or by other means falsifies any documentary material which is the subject of such demand; or attempts to do so or solicits another to do so . . . shall be fined not more than $5,000, or imprisoned not more than five years, or both."

8. 18 U.S.C. §1503 (1967), the obstruction-of-justice statute, provides: "Whoever corruptly, or by threats or force, or by any threatening letter or communication endeavors to influence, intimidate, or impede any witness, in any court of the United States or before any United States magistrate or other committing magistrate, or any grand jury or petit juror, or officer in or of any court of the United States, or officer who may be serving at any examination or any other proceeding before any United States magistrate or other committing magistrate, in the discharge of his duty, or injures any party or witness in his person or property on account of his attending or having attended such court or examination before such officer, magistrates, or other committing magistrate, or on account of his testifying or having testified to any matter pending therein, or injures any such grand or petit juror in his person or property on account of any verdict or indictment, assented to by him, or on account of his being or having been such juror, or injures any such officer, magistrate, or other committing magistrate in his person or property on account of the performance of his official duties, or corruptly or by threats or force, or by any threatening letter or communication, influences, obstructs, or impedes, or endeavors to influence, obstruct or impede, the due administration of justice, shall be fined not more than $5,000 or imprisoned not more than five years, or both."

9. 18 U.S.C. §1503 (1976).

10. 18 U.S.C. §1001, provides: "Whoever, in any matter within the jurisdiction of any department or agency of the United States knowingly and willfully falsifies, conceals or covers up by any trick, scheme, or device a material fact, or makes any false, fictitious or fraudulent statement or entry, shall be fined not more then $10,000 or imprisoned not more than five years, or both."

FBI and the Antitrust Division at the investigatory stage can lead to very serious consequences. Thus, permitting employees to communicate directly with investigators could lead to the uncovering of serious violations of which management is ignorant. An individual voluntarily turning over documents to the government may waive his privilege against self-incrimination with respect to those documents. Any immunity from prosecution based on incriminating matters contained in the documents is lost. Any attorney-client privilege is also lost, and the documents themselves, which become property of the government, might show up before the Federal Trade Commission or at congressional hearings.

When a company is contacted by government investigators seeking cooperation, it should be remembered that they normally have already accumulated a significant amount of evidence. Testimony and documents voluntarily given, however innocuous standing alone, when combined with the government's evidence could establish an overall course of illegal conduct. Thus, the best and safest course of conduct when a company is contacted by the FBI or Antitrust Division is to do nothing until counsel has been contacted and the overall matter discussed. Common sense forbids allowing employees to talk to the FBI or division attorneys without counsel present. For one thing, no transcript of the conversation will be kept, so that unless counsel is present, it is impossible for him to learn specifically what evidence the government investigators have obtained.

The first notice a company will have that an investigation has begun is a letter from the division requesting the firm to voluntarily supply certain information. The letter may request the company to compile certain statistical information, provide information about company policies and procedures, explain certain activities about which the division has received complaints, or make available certain documents for inspection. Such a letter should be brought to counsel's immediate attention, for although no response is required, a properly drafted response might place the company in a favorable light and ward off further involvement. A refusal to reply may only invite further government inquiry and formal process.

Working through an attorney at this initial stage will enable the company to respond in the most effective way possible. Counsel will normally contact the division directly and inquire specifically as to what is sought and where the target of the investigation centers.

Although the division is not prone to disclose too much, an attorney sensitive to antitrust matters is better equipped to sense where the government is going and what the dangers to the company are. If documents are to be produced, counsel will make certain that the investigators have specifically described in writing those they wish to examine. Furthermore, counsel will examine the documents before they are produced, retain the originals and give the investigators photostatic copies, remove those documents covered by the attorney-client privilege, and categorize all documents turned over.

17. The formal civil antitrust investigation

After the preliminary investigation is completed, the Antitrust Division will then decide whether or not to proceed with a formal civil or criminal investigation. If criminal sanctions are sought, a special grand jury, which is discussed subsequently, will be impaneled. If the division proceeds with a civil investigation, the Antitrust Civil Process Act will be utilized.[11] This act permits the government to obtain documentary evidence and request written interrogatories (written questions) or oral testimony during the course of the investigation.

The most important investigative tool provided to the division under the act is the Civil Investigative Demand (CID). The assistant attorney general in charge of the Antitrust Division may issue a CID whenever he has reason to believe that any natural person or legal entity has in his possession documents or information relevant to a civil antitrust investigation. The CID must state the nature of the conduct constituting or possibly resulting in an alleged antitrust violation. It must describe the documentary material sought with definiteness and certainty so that the recipient of the CID may fairly identify what is sought. The CID must provide a reasonable return date in order to give the recipient time to assemble the material and must identify the custodian to whom the material is to be made available.

The CID demanding answers to written interrogatories must similarly describe with definiteness and certainty the subject matter to be answered, give the date or dates on which the answers are to be submitted, and identify the custodian to whom the answers are to be

11. 15 U.S.C. §§1311–1314 (1976).

submitted. Similarly, if oral testimony is required, the CID must give the date, time, and place at which the testimony is to begin, as well as identify the investigator conducting the questioning.

There are limits to what the division can request in a CID. One limitation is the Fourth Amendment prohibition against unreasonable search and seizure; another is the Fifth Amendment privilege against self-incrimination. A Fourth Amendment violation occurs when:

1. There is no reasonable relation between the documents called for and the purposes of the investigation.
2. The CID does not specify with reasonable particularity the things to be produced.
3. The request for records does not cover a reasonable time period.
4. The information requested is already in the division's possession or the information sought repeatedly requires the person to recanvas its files.

Similarly, if the information sought would violate the Fifth Amendment right against self-incrimination or the attorney-client privilege, it is privileged and need not be produced. However, the Fifth Amendment right against self-incrimination applies only to natural persons; it does not extend to corporations. Corporations as well as natural persons do have the right to assert the attorney-client privilege.[12]

18. The federal grand jury—an overview

Perhaps the most powerful weapon in the government's investigative arsenal is the grand jury. It is the primary means by which the government uncovers antitrust violations. In order for the government to successfully investigate complex antitrust violations, often involving millions of documents and numerous witnesses, the division must be able to present this mass of evidence before a single body for evalu-

---

12. Under the attorney-client privilege, a corporation or natural person may prevent the disclosure of any communication made to counsel for the purpose of obtaining legal assistance. The right to prevent such disclosure is accorded under the law in order to encourage clients to be completely honest in their conversations with counsel. *See* United States v. United Shoe Mach. Corp., 89 F.Supp. 357, 358–359 (D.Mass. 1950).

ation. As opposed to FBI interviews and voluntary examination of documents, the grand jury is a body mandated by the Constitution; it has the power to subpoena documents and compel the testimony of witnesses.[13]

In testimony before the Senate Judiciary Antitrust Subcommittee, former Assistant Attorney General Donald I. Baker indicated the extent to which federal grand juries are being utilized in the antitrust area:

> Between 35 and 40% of the division's resources are continuously devoted to the task of conducting investigations, as distinct from conducting litigation, pursuing regulatory matters or accomplishing non-case related tasks. At the present time, the bulk of these resources are assigned to grand jury investigations. As has been recently noted, the Division has over 100 grand jury investigations in progress. This is an affirmative choice, designed to make maximum use of the increased deterrent impact of the Sherman Act felony sanctions enacted by Congress in December, 1974. Consequently, there has been a 30% increase in the number of pending antitrust grand juries over the pre-felony period. In [fiscal year] 1976, almost 2,000 attorney days were spent in grand jury investigations.[14]

The grand jury meets in secret sessions, and the only outside persons present are the assistant U.S. attorneys who assist in conducting the investigation. It is an *ex parte* rather than an adversary proceeding; neither the targeted companies nor their attorneys have a right to be present. There is no cross-examination of witnesses inasmuch as the targeted companies cannot have representatives at the hearing. While witnesses appearing before the grand jury are normally ques-

---

13. *See* Kastigar v. United States, 406 U.S. 441, 443 (1972).

14. 803 BNA Antitrust & Trade Regulation Reporter, May 12, 1977 at E-6. The dramatic increase in grand jury indictments in recent years illustrates the increased use of grand jury investigations.

Grand Jury Indictments 1958–1978

Year	Parties Indicted	Year	Parties Indicted	Year	Parties Indicted
1958	34	1965	41	1972	24
1959	61	1966	43	1973	42
1960	66	1967	70	1974	84
1961	18	1968	48	1975	82
1962	129	1969	28	1976	105
1963	61	1970	14	1977	88
1964	67	1971	34	1978	103

tioned by the government attorneys, grand jurors can and do ask questions.

Pursuant to federal rules, the number of grand jurors sitting on a case can be no fewer than sixteen nor more than twenty-three. No matter how many jurors are sitting, an indictment requires the vote of at least twelve members. A quorum of sixteen grand jurors is required to be present at all hearings, but not all jurors voting to indict need be present at every hearing.

A grand jury may not sit for a period longer than eighteen months. In busy judicial districts there may be a number of grand juries conducting separate antitrust investigations.[15]

The vast power of the grand jury stems from its ability to compel the attendance of witnesses. The grand jury's subpoena power is found in Rule 17(a) of the Federal Rules of Criminal Procedure.[16]

---

15. Grand jurors are generally selected from voter registration lists or the list of actual voters within the judicial district or division. Certain groups of persons or occupational classes are exempt from serving, such as members of the armed services, members of fire or police departments, public officers in the executive, legislative, and judicial branches of the state and federal government. In general, a person is qualified to act as a grand juror unless he

1. is not a citizen of the United States eighteen years old who has resided for a period of one year within the judicial district;
2. is unable to read, write, and understand the English language with a degree of proficiency sufficient to fill out satisfactorily the juror qualification form;
3. is unable to speak the English language;
4. is incapable, by reason of mental or physical deformity, to render satisfactory jury service; or
5. has a charge pending against him for the commission of, or has been convicted in a state or federal court of record of a crime punishable by imprisonment for more than one year and his civil rights have not been restored by pardon or amnesty. 28 U.S.C.A. §1861 (1968).

The clerk of the court draws, at random, from a master jury wheel the names of as many potential jurors as needed and then mails each a "jury qualification form." From the responses, a determination is made of the eligibility of each to act as a juror. The names of all persons drawn from the master jury list found to be qualified are placed in the qualified juror wheel. When a grand jury is to be impaneled, the names of a specified number of prospective jurors are drawn therefrom and summoned.

16. Rule 17(a) of the Federal Rules of Criminal Procedure provides: (a) For attendance of Witnesses; Form; Issuance. "A subpoena shall be issued by the clerk under the seal of the court. It shall state the name of the court and the title, if any, of the proceeding, and shall command each person to whom it is directed to attend and give testimony at the time and place specified therein. The clerk shall issue a subpoena signed and sealed and otherwise in blank to a party requesting it, who shall fill in the blanks before it is served. A subpoena shall be issued by a United States magistrate in a proceeding before him, but it need not be under seal of the Court." Rule 17(d) provides that a subpoena may be served by the Marshal, by his deputy or by any other person who is not a party and who is not less than 18 years of age. Service of a subpoena shall be made by delivering a copy to the person named and by tendering him a fee for one day's attendance and the mileage allowed by law.

Witnesses anywhere in the United States can be subpoenaed and required to appear before the grand jury.[17]

The courts have developed certain rules concerning the proper use of the subpoena: it must not be overly broad[18] or unreasonable in its scope; the documents requested must be material and relevant to the investigation being conducted; the demand must cover a reasonable period of time; the subpoena must describe the documents sought with sufficient particularity; the burden of complying with the subpoena must not be too great; and the subpoena cannot be used to secure privileged information. However, because antitrust investigations invariably involve great amounts of records, either by reason of the size of the corporations involved or the industry being investigated, greater latitude has been extended in the use of subpoenas. Courts have noted that the scope of antitrust subpoenas is, by necessity, greater than that of other types of criminal cases: antitrust conspiracies are seldom capable of proof by direct testimony; rather, they must be inferred from the conduct of the parties, which may be meaningful only if a pattern of activity over a number of years is studied.[19]

The burden of complying with a subpoena *duces tecum* can at

17. Rule 17(e)(1) of the Federal Rules of Criminal Procedure provides: "A subpoena requiring the attendance of a witness at a hearing or trial may be served at any place within the United States."

18. A valid subpoena *duces tecum* may only request documents which are material and relevant to the investigation being conducted. "The requirement of relevance is satisfied by a showing that there was a relation between the documents which must be produced and the purpose of the inquiry." *In re* Grand Jury Subpoena Duces Tecum, 203 F.Supp. 575, 578 (S.D.N.Y. 1961). In addition to being relevant, the documents sought must be material to the grand jury's investigation: "Relevance and materiality necessarily are terms of broader content in their use as to a grand jury investigation than their use as to evidence in a trial. They must be given practical meaning in relation to the functions which a grand jury is designed to serve and to the realities which are necessary as any expeditious carrying on of its operations. Thus, a grand jury has no catalog of what books and papers exist and are involved in a situation with which it is attempting to deal, nor will it ordinarily have any basis for knowing what their character or contents immediately are. It can therefore hardly be expected to be able to designate or call for what its exact needs may ultimately turn out to be. And since the path which it is entitled to travel in its search for probable cause has no general limits except those of reasonableness on the entirety of the situation being pursued, it obviously has a right, as against the objection of unreasonable search and seizure, to a fair margin of reach and material in seeking information, not merely direct but also as a matter of possible light in seemingly related aspects whose significance it is seeking to uncover. Some exploration or fishing necessarily is inherent and entitled to exist in documentary productions sought by a grand jury." Schwimmer v. United States, 232 F.2d 855, 862–63 (8th Cir. 1956), *cert. denied* 352 U.S. 833 (1956).

19. United States v. Household Goods Movers Investigation, 184 F.Supp. 689, 690 (D.D.C. 1960).

times be onerous, yet the courts, for the most part, have required compliance notwithstanding substantial cost to the party subpoenaed. The U.S. Supreme Court has noted that "there is in fact a public obligation to provide evidence . . . and that this obligation persists no matter how financially burdensome it may be. . . . The personal sacrifice involved is a part of the necessary contribution to the welfare of the public."[20]

Although motions to quash subpoenas on the ground that they are oppressive and burdensome, both in terms of man-hours and costs required for compliance, have found limited success, one case is of interest and should be noted. In *In re Grand Jury Subpoena Duces Tecum,*[21] the grand jury was convened to investigate the motor carrier industry. The Southern Motor Carriers Rate Conference, Inc. (SMCRC) objected to the burden and expense of being required to produce and copy the subpoenaed documents, the assembling and copying of which would consume approximately 125,700 to 243,294 man-hours at an estimated cost of $908,811.00 to $1,759,015.62. Furthermore, SMCRC stated that it was a nonprofit organization with a gross income of $3,261,581, gross expenses of $3,251,947, and a balance of $9,634. To substantiate the claim that the volume of materials sought was excessive, SMCRC produced photographs of some of the file cabinets containing the subpoenaed documents. SMCRC argued that the subpoena constituted a taking of property in violation of its due process rights under the Fifth Amendment. The court determined that it was virtually impossible for SMCRC to comply with the subpoena at its own expense. However, the court refused to quash the subpoena, but rather required SMCRC to produce the documents, provided that the government advanced the costs to be incurred in inspecting, assembling, and photocopying.[22]

20. Hurtado v. United States, 410 U.S. 578, 589 (1973).

21. 405 F.Supp. 1192 (N.D.Ga. 1975).

22. Courts have refused to quash subpoenas as oppressive when the government has taken some step to reduce the burden on the party subpoenaed. In United States v. Continental Bank & Trust Co., 503 F.2d 45 (10th Cir. 1974), the court found that the subpoena in question was not unreasonably burdensome in light of the government's offer to provide the personnel and equipment required to locate and copy the needed documents. In United States v. Dauphin Deposit Trust Co., 385 F.2d 129 (3d Cir. 1967), *cert. denied,* 390 U.S. 921 (1968), the Third Circuit Court of Appeals held that a subpoena *duces tecum* was not unreasonable when it did not require the transportation of any records, and the bank could comply merely by providing access to its records to federal agents who would supply their own copying equipment. The court expressed "no doubt that the recipient of a summons has a duty of cooperation and that at least up to some point must shoulder the financial burden of cooperation." *Id.* at 130.

This decision indicates that the matter of responding to a subpoena should not be undertaken by a layman, but rather should be handled by a lawyer trained in the antitrust field. When a subpoena is too broad or unreasonable, an attorney is better equipped to negotiate with government counsel to cut down its scope to a manageable size. In addition, allowing an attorney to participate at this initial stage has the advantage of familiarizing the attorney with the facts so that he can better evaluate future strategy.

Interrelated with the prohibition against subpoenas being unreasonably broad in scope is the requirement that the subpoena *duces tecum* be limited to a reasonable time span. In *Application of Certain Chinese Family Benevolent and District Associations,*[23] the subpoenas, with few exceptions, asked for "all lists, rolls, or other records of membership of the association during the period of the association's existence. . . ." The existence of the organizations comprising the association ranged from one to sixty-one years. The sweeping and all-inclusive nature of the subpoenas, both as to time and subject matter, was challenged as an unreasonable search and seizure in violation of the Fourth Amendment. The court recognized that producing the documents in question was not burdensome in and of itself. However, the court quashed the subpoena on the ground that

> it is the demand for all the records without regard to time or to the purpose of the inquiry which creates the problem. . . . The broad demand smacks . . . of the fishing expedition which was condemned [by the Supreme Court] in *Federal Trade Commission* v. *American Tobacco Co.*[24]

When a corporation is subpoenaed, the corporate agent delivering the documents to the grand jury should be knowledgeable as to the search conducted so that he can answer any questions relative to the search. A subpoena served upon a particular corporate officer, such as the president, places upon him the responsibility either to present

23. 19 F.R.D. 97 (N.D. Cal. 1956).

24. The courts have generally sustained subpoenas *duces tecum* covering long periods of time. *In re* Grand Jury Subpoena Duces Tecum addressed to Provision Salesmen and Distributors Union, Local 627, 203 F.Supp. 575 (S.D.N.Y. 1961) (eighteen years—records related only to a single public event); In re United Shoe Machinery Corp., 73 F.Supp. 207 (D.Mass. 1947) (twenty-seven years—the subpoena pointed out with particularity the documents sought); Petition of Borden Co., 75 F.Supp. 857 (N.D.Ill. 1948) (twenty years notwithstanding the fact that the company had been subject to repeated investigations by the Antitrust Division and a previous subpoena caused the production of ten truckloads, approximately fifty tons of paper, to be delivered).

himself before the grand jury or to send an officer or responsible representative of the corporation to respond to the requirements of the subpoena. Failure to so respond will subject the subpoenaed officer to personal liability for contempt of court.

Ordinarily, production of documents is not required where such production would cause the violation of a foreign criminal law. In *Societe Internationale* v. *Rogers,*[25] the U.S. Supreme Court held that a large number of banking records did not have to be produced where their disclosure would violate Swiss penal laws and might lead to the imposition of criminal sanctions on those responsible for disclosure. Furthermore, the Court noted, the Swiss Federal Attorney had deemed disclosure of the records a violation of a provision of the Swiss Bank Law, which related to the secrecy of banking records.

19. Appearing before the grand jury as a witness

Appearing before the grand jury as a witness is often a more traumatic experience than appearing at a trial. The grand jury proceedings are, by statute, conducted in secrecy, and no person may be present other than the witness, the court reporter, the government attorneys, and the jurors themselves. While the grand jury is voting on the indictment, no one may be present other than the jurors. All testimony taken is kept secret and may not be disclosed until much later in the criminal proceedings and then only when a particularized need for disclosure has been demonstrated.

Unlike a regular trial, the witness must face the grand jury alone, without the presence or assistance of an attorney, and is subjected to questioning by several government attorneys and the jurors themselves. Because the function of the grand jury is to determine if there is probable cause to believe that a crime has been committed rather than determining liability for a crime, a witness who may be targeted as a potential defendant has no right to confront other witnesses who testify against him, no right to cross-examine other witnesses, and no right to offer evidence in his own defense. A witness before the grand jury may not even be warned that he has a constitutional right to remain silent.

Any person subpoenaed to appear before the grand jury should

25. 357 U.S. 197 (1957).

immediately confer with counsel. The Antitrust Division generally has subpoenas issued two or three weeks in advance of the scheduled appearance, and witness testimony is normally heard three days per week. Counsel will generally contact the government attorney in charge to confirm the actual date the witness is to appear or set a new date if the witness, for good cause, is unavailable on the date set.

Once subpoenaed, the primary goal of the witness should be to obtain immunity from subsequent prosecution before appearing before the grand jury. The witness who feels he has nothing to hide or has done nothing illegal and therefore testifies without immunity is simply asking for trouble. The risk is simply too great that another witness or a forgotten document has disclosed incriminating evidence. Generally, the government will not oppose the granting of immunity to witnesses it has subpoenaed; therefore, failure to seek and receive immunity is simply forfeiting an important constitutional protection.

The procedure for obtaining "use immunity" under the Organized Crime Control Act of 1970[26] is for the witness to invoke his Fifth Amendment privilege against self-incrimination and refuse to testify before the grand jury. This is normally accomplished by counsel sending a written statement to the Antitrust Division that the witness will not testify without the court granting immunity. If the government agrees not to oppose the grant, the witness is brought before the court and inquiry is made as to whether he is invoking his Fifth Amendment rights. Once confirmed, the court issues an order granting the requested immunity.

It should be noted that the Fifth Amendment privilege against

26. 18 U.S.C.A. §§6001–6005 (1970). Prior to December 15, 1970 (the effective date of the Organized Crime Control Act), once a subpoenaed witness gave testimony to the grand jury substantially touching the offense alleged, the witness was granted "transactional immunity," that is, he could not be prosecuted for the conduct disclosed. This very broad grant of immunity extended not only to testimony that would provide sufficient evidence for subsequent prosecution, but also "clue" evidence that could be used as a "link" in the chain of evidence necessary to such prosecution. The Witness Immunity Act as part of the Organized Crime Control Act of 1970, however, repealed the prior law. Under the new act the witness is not granted "transactional immunity." The act only provides that "no testimony or other information compelled under the order (or any information directly or indirectly derived from such testimony or other information) may be *used* against the witness." This statutory expression defines what has become known as "use" and "derivative use" immunity. Under the new act, a witness given "use" immunity can still be prosecuted so long as the government makes no use whatsoever of the testimony or documentary evidence the witness was compelled to produce. Such a result could never have occurred under the prior immunity law.

self-incrimination extends only to individuals and cannot be invoked by corporations. Likewise, a corporation may not claim the privilege on behalf of an individual, nor may an individual protest that a corporation's compliance with a subpoena issued for the production of corporate papers would tend to incriminate him.

Whether a witness is the target of a grand jury investigation is always an important consideration. The government is under no obligation to inform a witness that he is the target of an investigation. However, if the government opposes the granting of immunity to a witness, he can assume that he is such a target. When immunity is denied, the witness must still appear before the grand jury. He must then invoke his Fifth Amendment privilege against testifying on a question-by-question basis.

Whether immunity is granted or not, sufficient time should be allotted with counsel for careful preparation. The following points should be discussed with counsel:

1. The witness should be informed of what a grand jury is and the physical setting of the grand jury room. He should be informed of the identity of the persons who are authorized to be in the grand jury room. The presence of an unauthorized person in the grand jury room is grounds for quashing any indictment the grand jury hands down.

2. The witness should be informed of the sequence of events that will occur once he is before the grand jury—the oath, background questions concerning identity, personal background, education and employment, and the intensive interrogation.

3. When the witness has not received immunity, the witness should only identify himself and then claim his privilege for all further questions. Answering additional questions may constitute a "waiver" of the witness' Fifth Amendment protection.[27]

4. The witness should be informed that he has the right to confer with counsel during the course of his examination.[28] Counsel should remain available immediately outside the grand jury

27. Disclosure of a fact waives the privilege as to details. Rogers v. United States, 340 U.S. 367 (1951).

28. The witness, if he so desires, has the right to consult with counsel after each and every question is asked. United States v. George, 444 F.2d 310, 315 (6th Cir. 1971). It is up to the witness to request the right to consult with counsel, and the government is under no obligation to inform the witness of the right.

room so that such a conference can take place if the witness so elects. Any time the witness is confused by a question or is being harassed or abused by government counsel during the course of the questioning, he should feel free to request a recess to confer with counsel.[29]

5. Those conversations between the witness and his attorney may not be inquired into by the government or grand jurors because they are privileged under the attorney-client privilege. Should a question be asked concerning such conversations, the witness should either refuse to answer or ask for a recess to consult with counsel.

6. In answering questions, the witness should not speculate or answer hypothetical questions, even when requested to do so by the government attorneys. If the witness has a legitimate uncertainty about an answer, he may qualify his answer with the words to the effect of, "to the best of my knowledge" or "to the best of my present recollection." If, however, counsel for the government presses for a definitive answer on an uncertain point, the witness should request a recess to consult with counsel.

7. If the government attorney prefaces a question by referring to a document or to prior testimony of another witness, the witness should ask to examine the document or the transcript so that he is thoroughly familiar with the statement used before answering. In this regard, the witness should be alert to the possibility that the statement upon which a question is based is being used out of context.

8. In general, the witness must listen carefully to each question without interrupting and weigh his answers. He should demand the right to furnish his answers without interruption by the government attorney or the grand jurors. The witness should realize, however, that obvious evasiveness or rambling will not be tolerated by either the prosecutor or the grand jury.

9. An important part of the witness' grand jury appearance is the

---

29. The government attorneys may not harass or badger a witness by shouting at him or asking grossly insulting or prejudicial questions. The Department of Justice has directed that its attorneys are to treat the witness with courtesy. *See* Antitrust Div., Dep't of Justice, *Antitrust Grand Jury Practice Manual* (CCH) 158–59 (1976). Extreme behavior on the government's part will necessitate going before the court for a protective order.

debriefing session with the witness' own counsel after his testimony has been completed.[30] Such information is essential for the subsequent preparation for trial or negotiations with the government in attempting to settle the matter. The information needed during the debriefing session includes (a) a description of what was (and, equally important, what was not) asked, particularized by subject matter covered and the nature of the questions asked as to each, (b) the names of all persons, companies, or trade associations mentioned in either the questions or answers, (c) which documents the government attorneys showed the witness or referred to during the questioning and the inquiry made as to each document, and (d) any references to prior testimony read from the transcript and the nature of the resulting questions.

20. The criminal charge and pleas

Inasmuch as violations of Sections 1 and 2 of the Sherman Act prior to January 1974 were misdemeanors, that is crimes punishable by a fine or by imprisonment of one year or less, criminal actions under the antitrust laws could be commenced on information alone. Unlike the indictment, the information is prepared and filed solely by the government, but has the same effect as an indictment in initiating the criminal action. Since 1974, however, violations under Sections 1 and 2 of the Sherman Act are felonies and must be prosecuted by indictment, which can be returned only by a grand jury, unless the defendant waives the indictment, in which case the government may proceed by information.

An indictment is returned by a grand jury upon the concurrence of twelve or more grand jurors. The indictment, as well as the information, must clearly apprise the defendant of the nature of the charges against him. The prosecution is required to provide the defendant with a "plain, concise, and definite written statement of the essential facts constituting the offense charged."[31] However, the indictment or information need not set out all the essential elements

30. Because a witness may testify for several days, it is suggested that during each break an effort be made to record what occurred in the just completed session. Thus, the lapse of several days will not result in losing important testimony.

31. Fed.R.Crim.P. 7(c) (1976).

of the offense if they are necessarily implied in the language actually used.

When an accused party is first brought before the court at the arraignment, he may plead not guilty, guilty, or nolo contendere. A nolo contendere, or "no contest" plea, if accepted by the court in its discretion, is of particular significance in the antitrust laws. Section 5 of the Clayton Act[32] provides that a final judgment or decree rendered in a civil or criminal proceeding brought by the United States under the antitrust laws finding that a defendant has violated said laws "shall be prima facie evidence against such defendant in any action or proceeding" brought by private citizens, or the United States, to recover civil damages. In other words, if a plea of guilty or a judgment of guilty after trial is entered in a criminal case, that determination of guilt can be used in a civil treble damage action brought by private citizens injured by the illegal conduct in question as evidence of guilt. Because the criminal judgment establishes a *prima facie* case, the plaintiff need not offer any other evidence other than the judgment in presenting his case. The judgment, standing alone, shifts the burden to the defendant to establish that he did not engage in the illegal conduct. If, however, the defendants in a criminal case plead nolo contendere and it is accepted by the court, the judgment entered, which carries the same penalties as a conviction or a plea of guilty, cannot be used in subsequent treble damage actions brought by private citizens or a civil damage action brought by the government. It is for this reason that defense attorneys make every effort, in a difficult case, to encourage the court to accept pleas of nolo contendere, whether or not they are opposed by the government.

21. Other criminal provisions

In addition to crimes set forth in Sections 1 and 2 of the Sherman Act, Section 14 of the Clayton Act[33] also sets forth criminal acts that are subject to fine and imprisonment. A violation of Section 14 is a misdemeanor and subjects the offender to a fine not exceeding $5,000, or imprisonment for a period not exceeding one year, or both.

32. 15 U.S.C. §16.
33. 15 U.S.C. §24.

This statute provides that whenever a corporation violates any of the penal provisions of the antitrust laws, such violations shall also be deemed those of the individual directors, officers, or agents who authorized, ordered, or did any of the illegal acts charged.

This criminal provision, which has very seldom been used by the government, was intended by Congress "to be a reaffirmation of the Sherman Act's basic penal provisions and a mandate to prosecutors to bring all responsible persons to justice." Any corporate officer or agent who *knowingly* participates in effectuating an illegal contract, combination, or conspiracy, whether he authorizes, orders, or helps perpetuate the crime and whether or not he acts in a representative capacity, may be prosecuted either under Section 14 of the Clayton Act or the more stringent Sections 1 or 2 of the Sherman Act. Unlike the Sherman Act, however, prosecution under Section 14 of the Clayton Act will lie only if the corporation itself is in violation of the antitrust laws. Thus, where the officer acts solely in his individual capacity so that his conduct cannot be attributed to the corporation, Section 14 will not apply.[34]

A second criminal statute, which has very seldom been used by the government, is Section 3 of the Robinson-Patman Act,[35] which provides for a fine of not more than $5,000, or imprisonment of not more than one year, or both. The first clause of the statute imposes sanctions against any seller who knowingly discriminates in sale of goods by offering secret discounts, rebates, allowances, or advertising service charges that are not made available to competitors of the recipient. The second clause proscribes territorial price discriminations employed for predatory purpose of destroying competition or eliminating a competitor. The third clause outlaws the sale of goods at unreasonably low prices for the purpose of destroying competition or eliminating a competitor.

Unlike other provisions of the Robinson-Patman Act, Section 3 has been seldom invoked against business interests primarily because private litigants cannot sue under that provision for treble damages,

---

34. *See* Von Kalinowski, *Antitrust Laws and Trade Regulations,* Vol. 3, §102.02.

35. 15 U.S.C. §13a. Section 3 of the Robinson-Patman Act is an enactment of the Borah-Van Nuys bill, which was passed by Congress, as a compromise measure, at the same time as the Robinson-Patman Act.

and the government, in the few cases it has commenced, has been fairly unsuccessful in obtaining convictions under the statute.[36]

It is clear, from a criminal standpoint, that the primary concern of the businessman must be Sections 1 and 2 of the Sherman Act. Section 14 of the Clayton Act and Section 3 of the Robinson-Patman Act simply do not create sufficient exposure of criminal liability to warrant deep concern.

36. *See* United States v. National Dairy Products Corp., 372 U.S. 29 (1963), where the Supreme Court upheld the constitutionality of the statute.

Chapter Three

Violations of Section 1 of the Sherman Act

The great bulk of antitrust litigation commenced by both the government and private parties falls within Section 1 of the Sherman Act. This statute speaks in the most general of terms, yet out of it have emerged narrowly defined activities that are condemned as violations of the Sherman Act. The Supreme Court has held that price fixing, territorial allocations of the market, group boycotts, and tie-in agreements are *per se* violations of Section 1 of the Sherman Act; that is, if the specific conduct is shown to have been committed, there can be no defense or argument that the activity was reasonable and did not restrain trade and commerce. In explaining the *per se* doctrine of liability under Section 1 of the act, Justice Black stated that there

> are certain agreements or practices which because of their pernicious effect on competition and lack of any redeeming virtue are conclusively presumed to be unreasonable and therefore illegal without elaborate inquiry as to the precise harm they have caused or the business excuse for their use. This principle of *per se* unreasonableness not only makes the type of restraints which are proscribed by the Sherman Act more certain to the benefit of everyone concerned, but it also avoids the necessity for an incredibly complicated and prolonged economic investigation into the entire history of the industry involved, as well as

57

related industries, in an effort to determine at large whether a particular restraint has been unreasonable—an inquiry so often wholly fruitless when undertaken. Among the practices which the courts have heretofore deemed to be unlawful in and of themselves are price fixing, *United States* v. *Socony-Vacuum Oil Co.,* 310 U.S. 150, 210; division of markets, *United States* v. *Addyston Pipe & Steel Co.,* 85 F. 271, *aff'd* 175 U.S. 211; group boycotts, *Fashion Originators' Guild of America* v. *Federal Trade Commission,* 312 U.S. 457; and tying arrangements, *International Salt Co.* v. *United States,* 332 U.S. 392.[1]

In the following sections the four *per se* violations are discussed with primary emphasis on the case law.

Price Fixing—Horizontal

22. Horizontal price fixing

As noted in Chapter 2 the Department of Justice's primary interest in the criminal enforcement of the Sherman Act has focused on Section 1—horizontal or industry-wide price fixing. Industry price fixing is described as horizontal, as distinguished from vertical, price fixing, in that it involves the fixing of prices by *competitors* on the same (horizontal) level of competition. Vertical price fixing, conversely, involves, for example, an agreement between a manufacturer and its distributors that fixes the price at which those distributors will resell the product to the retail trade. This question is covered subsequently.

Because price fixing is a *per se* violation, it does not matter if the purpose of the agreement or arrangement was to raise prices, lower prices, or merely stabilize prices. If there is price fixing, it violates Section 1 of the Sherman Act. In *United States* v. *Socony-Vacuum Oil Co., Inc.,*[2] five individuals and twelve corporations, including most of the major integrated oil companies operating in the Midwest, were convicted of price fixing. The defendant companies sold 83 percent of all gasoline sold in the Midwest in 1935. The conviction arose out of an effort of the defendants to "stabilize" indirectly the price of gasoline, which had become severely depressed beginning in 1926.

1. Northern Pac. Ry. Co. v. United States, 356 U.S. 1, 5 (1958).
2. 310 U.S. 150, (1940).

Due to overproduction of crude oil, the price of gasoline had dropped to a low of 2⅛ cents per gallon. Independent refiners with little storage capacity began to dump "distress" gasoline on the market for whatever price they could receive. In June 1933, in an attempt to help alleviate the surplus problem, Congress passed the National Industrial Recovery Act which authorized the president to forbid interstate shipment of "hot oil" produced in violation of state proration laws. The act also allowed the president to approve codes of fair competition, and in August 1933 the NRA Petroleum Code was approved, with the secretary of interior designated as administrator.

The secretary of interior appointed a Petroleum Administrative Board that included oil company executives, as well as a Planning and Coordination Committee. The task of this committee, as set forth by the secretary, was "to stabilize the oil industry on a profitable basis." The secretary appointed one of the defendants, Arnott, a vice-president of Socony-Vacuum, as Chairman of the Marketing Committee of the Planning and Coordination Committee. In response to ravaging price wars, the secretary purported to authorize Arnott to designate committees, negotiate and hold public hearings when local price wars developed, and "in a cooperative manner to stabilize the price level to conform to that normally prevailing in contiguous areas where marketing conditions are similar."

Arnott appointed a General Stabilization Committee and over fifty local committees pursuant to the secretary of interior's directions. The General Stabilization Committee, which included all of the individual defendants, met and discussed industry problems and decided on the need for "a firm market in the tank car market." A Tank Car Stabilization subcommittee was formed that established the mid-continental buying program in March 1935. Under this program each major oil company was assigned one or more "dancing partners," which were independent refiners from whom the assigned major oil concern would buy surplus gasoline. Each major oil company stated the amount of surplus oil it could take. Surveys were made to identify the location and amounts of distress gasoline, and each major oil company automatically continued buying from its assigned "dancing partners." Once established the program worked "smoothly and fairly automatically," with little need for communication between the oil producers. The Supreme Court noted that third-grade gasoline rose from 3½ cents per gallon on March 6, 1935, to 4¾ cents per gallon in early June as a result of the purchases made by the major oil companies from their "dancing partners."

In affirming the convictions the Supreme Court first noted that Congress' delegation of power to the president to prohibit "hot oil" shipments was unconstitutional as declared in an earlier case. However, the Tank Car Stabilization Committee continued to meet after this determination by the Court. The Court next held that the purpose of the Tank Car Stabilization Committee was to raise market prices. Finally, the Court rejected altogether as irrelevant the argument that the only intent of the defendants was to cure competitive abuses or evils which were destroying the market. The Court stated:

> Thus for over forty years this Court has consistently and without deviation adhered to the principle that price-fixing agreements are unlawful per se under the Sherman Act and that no showing of so-called competitive abuses or evils which those agreements were designed to eliminate or alleviate may be interposed as a defense.[3]

There was no dispute that defendants' actions raised the price of gasoline; however, it was clear that the increased price was a reasonable one. Yet the Court stated that the

> reasonableness of prices has no constancy due to the dynamic quality of the business facts underlying price structures. Those who fixed reasonable prices today would perpetuate unreasonable prices tomorrow, since those prices would not be subject to continuous administrative supervision and readjustment in light of changed conditions.[4]

An agreement to keep prices down is just as illegal as agreeing to raise prices. In *Kiefer-Stewart Co.* v. *Joseph E. Seagram & Sons, Inc.*,[5] plaintiff was a wholesale liquor distributor in the state of Indiana who sued Joseph E. Seagram & Sons and Calvert Distilling Company, a wholly owned subsidiary of Seagram. On October 23, 1946, governmental regulation of liquor prices administered by the Office of Price Administration terminated. Eight days later, wholesalers in Indiana met to discuss the termination of OPA prices and a majority thereafter raised their wholesale prices. However, Seagram reached a company decision on November 6, 1946, that it

3. *Id.* at 218
4. *Id.* at 221
5. 340 U.S. 211 (1951).

would not raise prices and would continue to sell at the old OPA prices. The cooperation of all wholesalers to hold prices in line was requested, and when the Indiana wholesalers, including plaintiff, failed to roll back their prices, shipments were suspended. On February 3, 1947, all Indiana wholesalers, except plaintiff, returned to the OPA price structure, and shipments were resumed to them.

In October 1946 Calvert, a wholly owned subsidiary of Seagrams, offered plaintiff a distributorship and negotiations began. The parties discussed plaintiff's increased prices and Seagram's announced policy. The Calvert representatives stated that Calvert still wanted plaintiff as a distributor, in spite of its position on prices. On November 19, 1946, plaintiff's president received a telephone call from Calvert's central division informing him that Calvert "had to go along with Seagram," and consequently, it could not ship the Calvert products that had been allocated to plaintiff because of plaintiff's pricing policy. It was at this time that officials at Seagram had communicated with officials at Calvert with reference to sales to plaintiff.

The district court found there was price fixing, but the court of appeals reversed and ruled that Seagram and Calvert's price policy was neither in restraint of trade nor an impairment of competition. Indeed, the court held that lower prices were a benefit to the consumer and competition. The U.S. Supreme Court reversed the court of appeals, holding that an agreement among competitors to fix maximum resale prices of their products was as much a *per se* violation as fixing minimum prices:

> For such agreements, no less than those to fix minimum prices, cripple the freedom of traders and thereby restrain their ability to sell in accordance with their own judgment. . . . "Under the Sherman Act a combination formed for the purpose and with the effect of raising, depressing, fixing, pegging, or stabilizing the price of a commodity in interstate or foreign commerce is illegal *per se*."[6]

The *Kiefer-Stewart* case raises a number of red flags for the businessman. First, it makes cogently clear that intent and purpose in fixing prices will not be considered by the courts even if the price fixing seeks to lower prices and thus benefit the public directly. If prices are agreed upon among competitors, nothing further need be

6. *Id.* at 213, citing United States v. Socony-Vacuum Oil Co., 310 U.S. 150, 223 (1940).

proven to establish a violation. Second, as discussed subsequently in this book, price fixing can exist between subsidiary corporations or a parent corporation and its wholly owned subsidiary. Careful consideration must be given by the executive employed by a conglomerate organization or large corporate enterprise of possible price fixing within the organizational structure. This particular area of liability is expanding and creating ever-increasing vulnerability to the business executive. Third, price fixing that involves or affects distributors is a popular area for antitrust enforcement. Distributors as a group are particularly prone to filing complaints with the government or filing lawsuits when they feel they are being improperly treated by their suppliers. They have gained a unique degree of sophistication as to their rights under the antitrust laws, thereby making them a prolific source of litigation. It is advisable to go that extra mile with the recalcitrant distributor before punishing or terminating him.

Stabilization of prices even at a lower level is likewise a *per se* violation regardless of the reasons for such action. As in *Socony-Vacuum,* it constitutes a violation of Section 1 of the Sherman Act though done for the purpose of saving the industry or smaller members of the industry. For example, in *United States* v. *Container Corp. of America,*[7] a civil action brought by the United States, defendants were eighteen of the fifty-one producers in the southeastern part of the United States manufacturing corrugated containers for use by industry. The defendants accounted for about 90 percent of the container production in that region. The industry was one in which entry was relatively easy, costing no more than $50,000 to $75,000. Customers of the defendants were highly price conscious and typically obtained several bids before placing an order, and they tended to shift rapidly from one source of supply to another. Elasticity of demand was low because container costs were a small part of the customer-buyers' total production costs and because their needs were fixed by their own production needs. During the prior eight years the industry had grown from thirty firms and forty-nine plants to fifty-one firms with ninety-eight plants. Although total sales had doubled as a result of increased demands, growth capacity of the industry far exceeded the growth in demand, thereby creating excess capacity. Significantly, prices tended downward during the relevant period of the lawsuit.

7. 393 U.S. 333 (1969).

The trial court found that before determining the price to be quoted to a particular customer, each defendant "was naturally interested in all pertinent marketing information applicable to such account" in order to accurately determine the pricing alternatives available to the customer. "Usually such information was obtained from the defendants' own records of prior sales, or from the purchaser involved." However, the court noted that "on occasion, purchasers furnished the defendants with incomplete, inaccurate or misleading information as to prices offered by competing suppliers, and it was only on these occasions that a competitor was consulted with respect to price information."[8] Defendants were in no way required by agreement or otherwise to supply such pricing information when requested, although it was the practice that when such a request was made, the recipient would reciprocate.

The evidence clearly established that the corrugated container industry was highly competitive and that prices continued declining, in spite of the illegal conduct alleged. On the basis of this evidence the trial court found for the defendants, holding that in all instances the price information, from whatever source, merely permitted the recipient to make its independent pricing decision, and that the gathering of price information from competitors enabled the defendants to "prevent the perpetration of fraud upon them" by buyers deliberately misquoting the price of a competitor, which information they were free to act upon or not as they chose.[9]

The U.S. Supreme Court reversed, concluding that the exchange of pricing information "seemed to have the effect of keeping prices within a fairly narrow ambit. . . . The result . . . was to stabilize prices though at a downward level."[10] The Court stressed the fact that production capacity increased at a faster rate than the growth of demand. It also stressed that knowledge of a competitor's price usually meant matching it, not undercutting it. The Court stated:

> Price information exchanged in some markets may have no effect on a truly competitive price. But the corrugated container industry is dominated by relatively few sellers. The product is fungible and the competition for sales is price. The demand is inelastic, as buyers place orders only for immediate, short-run needs. The exchange of price

8. 273 F.Supp. 18, 59 (1967).
9. *Id.* at 61.
10. 393 U.S. at 336.

data tends toward price uniformity. For a lower price does not mean a larger share of the available business but a sharing of the existing business at a lower return. Stabilizing prices as well as raising them is within the ban of §1 of the Sherman Act. As we said in *United States* v. *Socony-Vacuum Oil Co.,* . . . "in terms of market operations stabilization is but one form of manipulation." The inferences are irresistible that the exchange of price information has had an anticompetitive effect in the industry, chilling the vigor of price competition.[11]

Under the Robinson-Patman Act, discussed subsequently, a statutory defense to the charge that a seller has sold at discriminatory prices is that the lower price was charged to meet an equally low price of a competitor. To establish this defense, *sellers have not infrequently,* upon request, shared their prices with competitors. However, this exchange of pricing information, though valid as a means to establish the meeting-competition defense, has now been held to constitute *per se* price fixing under Section 1 of the Sherman Act.

In *United States* v. *United States Gypsum Co.,*[12] the defendants—six corporations and eleven individuals, including the chairman of the board and executive vice-president of U.S. Gypsum; the chairman of the board and vice-president for sales of National Gypsum; the president of Georgia-Pacific; the president, vice-president, and general manager of Kaiser-Gypsum; the president of Celotex; and the chairman of the board and president of Flintkote—were indicted for price fixing on the ground that they engaged in the practice of telephoning a competing manufacturer to determine the price being currently offered on gypsum to a specific customer, a form of interseller price verification. The indictment charged that the defendants

> telephoned or otherwise contacted one another to exchange and discuss current and future published or market prices and published or standard terms and conditions of sale and to ascertain alleged deviations therefrom.[13]

Defendants defended on the ground that price verification was necessary in order to establish their "meeting competition" defense under the Robinson-Patman Act.

Under this defense a seller must establish that it had a good-faith

11. *Id.* at 337.
12. 438 U.S. 422 (1978).
13. *Id.* at 428.

belief, rather than an absolute certainty, that its price concession was being offered to meet an equally low price offered by a competitor. Casual reliance on uncorroborated reports of buyers or sales representatives without further investigation is not sufficient to make the requisite showing of good faith. Faced with this construction of Section 2(b), the defendants engaged in interseller price verification in order to identify precisely the price they desired to meet. In some instances this was required for the added reason that the buyer was untruthful and interseller verification was the only means available for invoking defendants' Section 2(b) defense in good faith. However, the Supreme Court rejected these arguments, holding that any exchange of pricing information, whether for price verification under Section 2(b) of the Robinson-Patman Act or not, was subject to the close scrutiny of Section 1 of the Sherman Act:

> To recognize even limited "controlling circumstance" exception for interseller verification in such circumstances would be to remove from scrutiny under the Sherman Act conduct falling near its core with no assurance, and indeed with serious doubts, that competing antitrust policies would be served thereby. In *Automatic Canteen* v. *FTC,* 346 U.S. 61, 74, 73 S.Ct. 1017, 1024, 97 L.Ed. 1454 (1953), the Court suggested that as a general rule the Robinson-Patman Act should be construed so as to insure its coherence with "the broader antitrust policies that have been laid down by Congress"; that observation buttresses our conclusion that exchanges of price information—even when putatively for purposes of Robinson-Patman Act compliance— must remain subject to close scrutiny under the Sherman Act.[14]

The *Gypsum* decision ably demonstrates that the Sherman Act is the cornerstone of antitrust enforcement and that any conflict between it and other laws will be resolved in favor of Sherman Act enforcement. This is particularly true where the Sherman Act violation charged is price fixing. Certain exemptions from Sherman Act coverage are written into the law, as discussed in Chapter 8, but they are strictly applied and construed.

There are many and varied forms of horizontal price-fixing arrangements, which the courts have found to be illegal. For example, a manufacturer can be the illegal conduit for "indirect" horizontal price fixing among its distributors. In *United States* v. *General*

14. *Id.* at 458–59.

Motors Corporation,[15] suit was brought against General Motors Corporation, which manufactures, among other things, the Chevrolet line of cars and trucks, and three associations of Chevrolet dealers in and around Los Angeles, California. Each dealer was franchised pursuant to the terms of a Dealer Selling Agreement. Beginning in the 1950s "discount houses" began selling new cars to the public at allegedly bargain prices. The sources of supply of these cars were twelve of the eighty-five franchised Chevrolet dealers in Los Angeles. By 1960, sales by the discount houses had reached the point that the nonparticipating franchised dealers were feeling the "pinch."

At an association meeting on June 28, 1960, the franchised dealers agreed to submit their complaint to General Motors. The latter reacted by contacting each dealer and eliciting a promise that it would not sell Chevrolet vehicles to the discounters and also by hiring private investigators to police the dealers, the cost of which was financed in part by the dealer associations. Thereafter, when a dealer was suspected of selling to discounters, a "shopper," posing as a discounter, was sent to purchase a car and then confronted the dealer with the car, the sales documents, and a tape recording of the transaction. In every case the embarrassed dealer repurchased the car, often at a loss, and promised to discontinue the practice.

The Supreme Court ruled that the conduct in question had an indirect effect upon prices, in that it eliminated the lower discounter prices from the market, and therefore was a *per se* violation of Section 1 of the Sherman Act. The Court stated:

> We note, moreover, that inherent in the success of the combination in this case was a substantial restraint upon price competition—a goal unlawful *per se* when sought to be effected by combination or conspiracy.... And the *per se* rule applies even when the effect upon prices is indirect....
>
> There is in the record ample evidence that one of the purposes behind the concerted effort to eliminate sales of new Chevrolet cars by discounters was to protect franchised dealers from real or apparent price competition.... [T]here is evidence in the record that General Motors itself was not unconcerned about the effect of discount sales upon general price levels.
>
> The protection of price competition from conspiratorial restraint is

15. 384 U.S. 127 (1966).

an object of special solicitude under the antitrust laws. We cannot respect that solicitude by closing our eyes to the effect upon price competition of the removal from the market, by combination or conspiracy, of a class of traders [discounters]. Nor do we propose to construe the Sherman Act to prohibit conspiracies to fix prices at which competitors may sell, but to allow conspiracies or combinations to put competitors out of business entirely.[16]

In a second case, *Plymouth Dealers' Ass'n of Northern California* v. *United States,*[17] a Plymouth dealers' association was indicted under the Sherman Act for price fixing. The only illegal conduct alleged was that the association printed and published a retail price list and circulated it to its members.[18] This list set the retail price for Plymouth cars at $2,340, which was higher than the manufacturer's suggested retail price, which was $2,130. Members agreed to use the association's suggested retail price, which meant only that dealers discounted off that price rather than the manufacturer's suggested retail price. However, the court found there was a *per se* price-fixing violation, inasmuch as the dealers had agreed on a suggested retail price off of which they discounted:

> The competition between the Plymouth dealers and the fact that the dealers used the fixed uniform list price in most instances only as a starting point, is of no consequence. It *was* an agreed starting point; it had been agreed upon between competitors; it was in some instances in the record respected and followed; it had to do with, and had its effect upon prices.[19]

23. Price fixing through trade associations

Trade association meetings are a most fertile arena for price-fixing discussions and thus of great interest to the government. Government and grand jury investigations immediately focus in on such meetings and in particular the social activities connected therewith, for common experience suggests that it is in the "casual conversations" at trade association meetings that prices are frequently discussed and

16. *Id.* at 147–48.

17. 279 F.2d 128 (9th Cir. 1960).

18. There was no allegation that this price list was adhered to, that it was utilized to fix prices, or that it did actually fix prices.

19. 279 F.2d at 132.

illegally fixed. It goes without saying that such communications must be avoided at all costs. However, trade associations can expose the businessman to different kinds of price fixing not as obvious to the layman as the motel room "conversation."

In *American Column & Lumber Co.* v. *United States,*[20] one third of the 365 hardwood lumber producers, members of an unincorporated organization called the American Hardwood Manufacturers' Association, produced one third of the total hardwood produced in the United States, although operating only 5 percent of the mills. A committee of the association developed an "Open Competition Plan," the purpose of which was "to disseminate among members accurate knowledge of production and market conditions so that each member may gauge the market intelligently instead of guessing at it; to make competition open and above board instead of secret and concealed; to substitute, in estimating market conditions, frank and full statements of our competitors for the frequently misleading and colored statements of the buyer."

The plan required each member to make six reports to the secretary: (1) a daily report of all sales, "[t]he reports to the exact copies of orders taken," (2) a daily shipping report, with exact copies of the invoices, (3) a monthly production report, (4) a monthly stock report (inventory at first of month), (5) price lists, to be filed as soon as made, and (6) inspection reports, to be made out by a service of the association. The plan provided for inspectors to examine stocks of the members from time to time. All of the reports were subject to audit, and penalties resulted from failure to report.

Upon receiving this information the secretary of the association was required to send each member the following: (1) a monthly summary showing the production of each member, (2) a weekly report giving every sale, the price, and the name of the purchaser, (3) a weekly report of all shipments, (4) a monthly report showing the inventory of stock on hand of each member, (5) a monthly summary of the price lists received from the members (and immediate transmittals of any changes), and (6) a market report letter giving an "analysis of the market conditions." Meetings were to be held monthly, but in practice were held more often.

The Supreme Court found that the conduct of the association and

20. 257 U.S. 377 (1921).

its members "constituted a combination and conspiracy in restraint of interstate commerce within the meaning of the Anti-Trust Act of 1890."[21] The Court noted that before meetings a questionnaire was sent out to members from which a statistician compiled an estimate of the condition of the market, "actual and prospective," which was distributed to the members attending each meeting and mailed to those not present. Eleven questions were asked, three of which provided:

> 4. What was your total production of hardwood during the last month? What do you estimate your production will probably be for the next two months?
> 10. Do you expect to shut down within the next few months on account of shortage of logs or for any other reason? If so, please state how long you will be idle.
> 11. What is your view of market conditions for the next few months and what is the general outlook for business? State the reasons for your conclusion.

The Court further noted that the only thing lacking in the "scheme to make it a familiar type of the competition suppression organization is a definite agreement as to production and prices." However, this was supplied

> by the disposition of men "to follow their most intelligent competitors," especially when powerful; by the inherent disposition to make all the money possible, joined with the steady cultivation of the value of "harmony" of action; and by the system of reports, which makes the discovery of price reductions inevitable and immediate. The sanctions of the plan obviously are financial interest, intimate personal contact, and business honor, all operating under the restraint of exposure of what would be deemed bad faith and of trade punishment by powerful rivals.[22]

The Court concluded that the "purpose of the organization, and especially of the frequent meetings, was to bring about a concerted effort to raise prices regardless of cost or merit, and so was unlawful, and that members were soon entirely satisfied that the Plan was 'carrying out the purpose for which it was intended.'"[23]

21. *Id.* at 412.
22. *Id.* at 399.
23. *Id.* at 409.

In a second case, *Maple Flooring Mfrs. Ass'n.* v. *United States*,[24] the Supreme Court reached the opposite result. There the defendants included the Maple Flooring Manufacturers' Association, an unincorporated trade association, twenty-two corporate members accounting for 70 percent of the industry, and several individuals. The following are the activities of the association about which the government complained:

1. The computation and distribution among the members of the association of the average cost to association members of all dimensions and grades of flooring.
2. The compilation and distribution among members of a booklet showing freight rates on flooring from Cadillac, Michigan, to between 5,000 and 6,000 points of shipment in the United States.
3. The gathering of statistics, which at frequent intervals are supplied by each member of the association to the secretary of the association, giving complete information as to the quantity and kind of flooring sold and prices received by reporting members, and the amount of stock on hand, which information is summarized by the secretary and transmitted to members without, however, revealing the identity of the members in connection with any specific information thus transmitted.
4. Meetings at which the representatives of members congregate and discuss the industry and exchange views as to its problems.

It was conceded by the defendants that the dissemination of information as to cost of the product and as to production and prices would tend to bring about uniformity in prices through the operation of economic law. Although the parties at one point did discuss market prices at their meetings, this practice had been discontinued. Past prices were fully detailed in statistical reports, but there were no discussions of future prices.

The Supreme Court stated the issue was whether there was a combination existing by virtue of the association, which had the necessary tendency to cause direct and undue restraints on competition. The Court noted that the dissemination of pertinent information concerning any trade or business tends to stabilize that trade or business and

---

24. 268 U.S. 563 (1925).

to produce uniformity of price and trade practice:

> Exchange of price quotations of market commodities tends to produce uniformity of prices in the markets of the world. Knowledge of the supplies of available merchandise tends to prevent overproduction and to avoid the economic disturbances produced by business crises resulting from overproduction. But the natural effect of the acquisition of wider and more scientific knowledge of business conditions, on the minds of the individuals engaged in commerce and its subsequent effect in stabilizing production and price, can hardly be deemed a restraint of commerce, or, if so, it cannot, we think, be said to be an unreasonable restraint, or in any respect unlawful.[25]

The Supreme Court then pronounced guidelines of conduct governing trade associations:

> We decide only that trade associations or combinations of persons or corporations which openly and fairly gather and disseminate information as to the cost of their product, the volume of production, the actual price which the product has brought in past transactions, stocks of merchandise on hand, approximate cost of transportation from the principal point of shipment to the points of consumption as did these defendants and who, as they did, meet and discuss such information and statistics without however reaching or attempting to reach any agreement or any concerted action with respect to prices or production or restraining competition, do not thereby engage in unlawful restraint of commerce.[26]

This case has been widely criticized and its present vitality questioned, particularly in light of the Supreme Court's decision in *United States* v. *Container Corporation of America*,[27] discussed *supra*. Subject to particular criticism are two of the programs—the circulation of average production costs data and of a book showing freight rates from selected cities in the producing area to other parts of the country. The first suggests to all producers that prices should be sufficiently set above these costs to allow marginal firms to operate profitably. The second encourages producers to set freight rates computed from selected cities rather than from actual plant locations, thereby inviting a basing point pricing system.[28]

25. *Id.* at 582.
26. *Id.* at 586.
27. 393 U.S. 333 (1969).
28. Sullivan, Antitrust 269 (1977).

The fine line between trade association price fixing and lawful conduct is best demonstrated by a comparison of two cases, *Sugar Institute, Inc.* v. *United States,*[29] and *Tags Mfrs. Institute* v. *Federal Trade Commission.*[30] In the first case fifteen sugar refining companies marketing 70 to 80 percent of all refined sugar in the United States held a series of meetings in 1927 to discuss elimination of undesirable industry practices, including secret price concessions, which at least one of the members felt constituted discriminatory pricing in violation of Section 2 of the Clayton Act. As a result of these meetings the Sugar Institute, a trade association, was formed and proposed a "Code of Ethics," which was submitted to the Department of Justice. After certain suggested changes were made, the code was adopted. The basic principle of the code stated that "All discriminations between customers should be abolished. To that end, sugar should be sold only upon open prices and terms publicly announced." Most sugar was sold pursuant to the trade practice called "moves" that took place when a refiner made a public announcement that at a fixed time, it would change its selling price to a certain figure, and a grace period was allowed to buy in at the lower price. If other refiners did not also announce a similar "move," it did not go forward. The Code of Ethics did not change this basic practice, but it did require each company to adhere, without deviations or secret concessions, to the announcement of a change in price. Prior to the code, secret concessions were a common practice.

The Supreme Court concluded that the above plan constituted a violation of Section 1 of the Sherman Act:

> The unreasonable restraints which defendants imposed lay not in advance announcements, but in the steps taken to secure adherence, without deviation, to prices and terms thus announced. It was that concerted undertaking which cut off opportunities for variation in the course of competition however fair and appropriate they might be.[31]

In the *Tags Mfrs. Institute* case, the Federal Trade Commission charged the association, whose members sold approximately 95 percent of the tag products sold in the United States, as well as officers of the association and thirty-one tag manufacturers, with a conspir-

29. 297 U.S. 553 (1936).
30. 174 F.2d 452 (1st Cir. 1949).
31. 297 U.S. at 601.

acy to restrain price competition and fix uniform prices. The scheme challenged was that all members would submit to one Baxter, the secretary-treasurer and executive director of the association, their complete price lists and would report to Baxter each subsequent revision no later than the close of the business day following publication. Each member also agreed to report the prices, terms, and conditions of each sale or contract made. It was provided that members were not limited in any way in establishing their prices, and reporting such prices did not constitute a representation or pledge to adhere to those prices. Baxter disseminated all such information both to the members of the association and the general public. Also, duplicates of all invoices were to be forwarded to Baxter, but Baxter, in disseminating the information, was not to disclose customer names.

Because a manufacturer could put into effect at any time new prices or make off-list sales without prior notice to Baxter—its only obligation being to report the transaction—the circuit court found no violation. The court noted that

> the issuance of a price list may be said to be an "announcement of future prices." The nature of price lists has not changed under the Tag Industry Agreements from what it has historically been in the industry. The price list is subject to change without notice, and may be freely revised at any time. Even while a particular price list is extant, the manufacturer is free to make sales at off-list prices. . . . Once a price list has been issued to the trade it necessarily becomes pretty much public property. There is certainly nothing secret about it. It would be no great feat for a manufacturer to obtain copies of his competitors' price lists. The Tag Industry Agreement merely facilitates the assembling of such data.[32]

Comparing the two cases, it is clear that a mere sharing of price changes in advance through a trade association will not run afoul of the Sherman Act, but anything that suggests an agreement implemented by a code of ethics or otherwise to adhere to those prices once announced will constitute a price-fixing violation. More particularly, where there is no commitment to comply with published prices, where individual transactions are not identified, where information goes to buyers as well as sellers, and where no audit procedure, common analysis, or exhortation is associated with price reporting, the

32. 174 F.2d at 463.

reporting system of the trade association will be treated as serving an informative function to seller and buyer alike and not as conspiratorial action for purposes of Section 1 of the Sherman Act.[33]

In analyzing a trade association reporting system the courts will look to the purpose and effect of the program and to related conduct of the members for any indication of collusive purpose. For example, in *United States* v. *American Institute of Certified Public Accountants, Inc.,*[34] a consent decree was entered that prohibited an association of accountants from publishing a code of ethics containing a provision prohibiting members from submitting competitive bids for accounting services. Similarly, in *United States* v. *American Institute of Architects,*[35] an association of architects was prohibited by a consent decree from adopting any plan, program, or course of action that prohibited members from submitting price quotations for architectural services.

Trade associations have acted in other ways that have led courts to rule that a price-fixing conspiracy has resulted. For example, in *United States* v. *Gasoline Retailers Association, Inc.,*[36] a trade association made up of gasoline station operators was indicted along with a labor union and its chief negotiator on the charge that the defendants conspired to stabilize retail gasoline prices in the Calumet region of Illinois and Indiana in order to end reoccurring price wars. In furtherance thereof, the defendant union and individual station operators included in their labor contracts clauses that prohibited major-brand station operators from displaying the retail price of gasoline on the station premises by any manner other than the price computing device on the gasoline pump, and banned the use of premiums or trading stamps by station operators in connection with retail sales. Operators not selling major-brand gasoline were not required to adhere to the advertising ban since they needed to advertise their lower price in order to compete, but they did agree not to give trading stamps. The differential between the majors and the independents was 3 cents per gallon, which the union and trade association agreed was proper. Of the 206 dealers in the trade association, 146 signed the union contracts in question.

33. Sullivan, Antitrust 268–69 (1976).
34. 1972 Trade Cases ¶74,007 (D.C. 1972).
35. 1972 Trade Cases ¶73,981 (D.C. 1972).
36. 285 F.2d 688 (7th Cir. 1961).

The court found that the "basic objective of defendants' conspiracy was stabilization of retail gasoline prices" and keeping "price wars" out of the area. Because premium offers and trading stamps added to the price wars, they were also eliminated. In finding a *per se* violation, the court stated:

> The continuing agreement among the defendants and the coconspirators that the "major brand" and "independent brand" station operators would refrain from either advertising or giving premiums, including trading stamps in connection with the retail sales of gasoline, and that the "major brand" stations would refrain from advertising retail prices excepting at sites of the stations by the regular price computing gasoline pumps is a *per se* violation of the Sherman Act.[37]

The court found in *United States* v. *Nationwide Trailer Rental System*[38] that a nonprofit corporation made up of one-way trailer rental businesses violated Section 1 of the Sherman Act, because the lease form put out by the association and voluntarily used by its members included a rate charge for overtime use of trailers. Although the association put out the form only for voluntary use by members, the fact that all members used it and followed the overtime rates printed therein made the court conclude that "while not fixing a rigid price," it was "a tampering with prices as is forbidden by the Sherman Act."[39]

24. Following a price leader

Following the prices of a price leader is not in itself a violation of Section 1 of the Sherman Act. Thus, when a price leader raises prices, others in the industry may follow that lead without violating the Sherman Act. Mere "conscious parallelism" in pricing, as it is called, is not in itself a violation of the law; something more must be shown to prove that the price was more the result of conspiratorial or concerted action. The case of *Interstate Circuit, Inc.* v. *United States*[40] best illustrates the pitfalls the businessman can encounter in this area of price leadership.

In *Interstate Circuit* certain of the defendants distributed about

37. *Id.* at 691.
38. 156 F.Supp. 800 (D.Kan. 1957), *aff'd* 355 U.S. 10 (1957).
39. 156 F.Supp. at 805.
40. 306 U.S. 208 (1939).

75 percent of the first-class feature films exhibited in the United States in the 1930s. Two of the defendants, Interstate and Colsolidated, operated movie theaters in Texas and New Mexico and were affiliated with Paramount Pictures Distribution Co., Inc. The defendant Interstate operated forty-three first-run and second-run theaters located in six Texas cities and had almost a complete monopoly on first-run theaters in those cities. It also operated twenty-two subsequent-run theaters in the same areas. The defendant Consolidated operated sixty-three theaters in Texas and New Mexico. The remaining defendants distributed movies to the movie theater exhibitors such as Interstate and Consolidated. On July 11, 1934, one O'Donnell, the manager of Interstate and Consolidated, sent a letter to each distributor defendant, stating that as a condition to Interstate's exhibition of a distributor's films two conditions had to be met. First, that in selling films to subsequent-run theaters, the distributors were to make certain that "A" films were not exhibited at an admission price of less than 25 cents for adults in the evenings. Second, that "A" pictures that were exhibited at night at an admission of 40 cents or more were not to be exhibited in conjunction with another feature picture under the so-called double-feature policy.

After discussions individually with Interstate, each of the distributor defendants agreed to the conditions. Although there was no direct evidence of conspiracy among the distributors, the Supreme Court concluded that such a conspiracy to fix prices could be inferred from circumstantial evidence of parallel conduct: (1) each distributor was advised that the others were asked to participate; (2) each knew that cooperation was essential to the plan; (3) each knew that the plan, if carried out, would result in a restraint of commerce; and (4) knowing this, each distributor participated in the plan. The Court stated that the circumstantial evidence not only warranted but virtually demanded a finding of conspiracy:

> It taxes credulity ... that the several distributors would ... have accepted and put into operation with substantial unanimity such far reaching changes in their business methods without some understanding that all were to join.[41]

The Court also stated:

> It is elementary that an unlawful conspiracy may be and often is formed without simultaneous action or agreement on the part of con-

41. *Id.* at 223.

spirators. . . . Acceptance by competitors, without previous agreement, of an invitation to participate in a plan, the necessary consequence of which, if carried out, is restraint of interstate commerce, is sufficient to establish an unlawful conspiracy under the Sherman Act.[42]

The Court suggested that when a substantial change in conduct occurs among the parties in question at or about the same time and the new course of action is uniform, concerted action has been established. Buttressing this analysis of *Interstate Circuit* is the case of *American Tobacco Co.* v. *United States.*[43] During the depression, low-priced cigarettes, the so-called "ten-cent brands," started to take an increased share of the market at the expense of the high-priced (fifteen-cent) brands produced by the "big three" producers—American Tobacco Company, R. J. Reynolds, and Liggett Meyers Tobacco Company. The latter companies, which did not use and had not previously bid for cheap tobacco and which seldom bid against each other even for tobacco of the quality they did use, all began to bid when cheap tobacco was offered at auction. This caused the price of the cheap tobacco to go up. At the same time the big three cut prices on their own brands. Later, after the market share of the cheap brands declined, the majors again raised their prices. On this evidence the big three were convicted. The Supreme Court observed that the common course of conduct of the defendants was sufficient to warrant the finding of "a unity of purpose or a common design."

In *United States* v. *Paramount Pictures, Inc.,*[44] the Supreme Court found that a conspiracy existed, predicated on evidence that five vertically integrated companies, which made, distributed, and exhibited movies, specified the same minimum admission prices in licenses, used the same clearances between first-run and second-run theaters and the same "block booking" practices, and imposed substantially identical terms, with reference to a variety of complex matters, on nonintegrated exhibitors with which they dealt. Based on this evidence the conclusion was warranted that concert of action was both contemplated and executed by the five.

In the above cases, there was evidence from which the courts could infer that a conspiracy existed. However, when there is nothing more than consciously parallel conduct the courts have expressed reluc-

42. *Id.* at 226–27.
43. 328 U.S. 781 (1946).
44. 334 U.S. 131 (1948).

tance to infer a conspiracy. Justice Clark stated in *Theatre Enterprises, Inc.* v. *Paramount Film Distributing Corp.,*[45] "'conscious parallelism' has not yet read conspiracy out of the Sherman Act entirely." In that case plaintiff, the owner and operator of a suburban neighborhood theater, sued nine motion picture producers—including Paramount, RKO, Twentieth Century-Fox, Warner Bros., and Columbia Pictures—alleging that the defendants had violated Section 1 of the Sherman Act by conspiring to restrict first-run pictures to downtown Baltimore theaters, thereby confining suburban theaters to subsequent runs. There was no direct evidence of an illegal agreement, and the defendants offered evidence that their business behavior toward plaintiff was motivated by independent business considerations. The jury returned a verdict for the defendants, and the Supreme Court affirmed.

Similarly, in *United States* v. *National Malleable & Steel Castings Co.,*[46] the evidence showed that a group of small manufacturers followed National's prices because they were "constrained" to do so, in that the product in question, couplers, were exactly alike and completely interchangeable and fungible. The evidence also demonstrated that each defendant sold to the same small group of customers that were represented by astute purchasing agents who would not pay a higher price to a small manufacturer. Each defendant did not follow National's prices until they were announced to the world. On this record the court concluded that defendants' "conscious parallelism" was not the result of conspiratorial conduct but the existence of strong and informed competition.

Any number of cases can be cited wherein the courts have found that conscious parallelism "resulted from competitive factors and not conspiracy."[47]

---

45. 346 U.S. 537, 541 (1954).

46. 1957 Trade Cases ¶68,890 (N.D.Ohio 1957), *aff'd per curiam,* 358 U.S. 38 (1958).

47. In First Nat'l Bank v. Cities Serv. Co., 391 U.S. 253 (1968), the Supreme Court affirmed a judgment for the defendant over plaintiff's contention that a "parallel refusal to deal" permitted an inference of conspiracy. The Court held that divergent business interests among the alleged conspirators, together with the lack of demonstrable benefit to defendant from the claimed conspiracy, made an inference of conspiracy impermissible.

In Esco Corp. v. United States, 340 F.2d 1000, 1007 (9th Cir. 1965), the court discussed the following hypothesis in an effort to clarify some of the problems in this area: "Let us suppose five competitors meet on several occasions, discuss their problems, and one finally states—'I won't fix prices with any of you, but here is what I am going to do—put the price of my gidget at X dollars; now you all do what you want.' He then leaves the meeting. Com-

Mere price leadership is not sufficient to establish a violation. Thus, one court announced the so-called "plus factor" test, that is, common action such as price uniformity plus some additional factor demonstrating complicity. In *C-O-Two Fire Equipment Co.* v. *United States*,[48] three manufacturers of fire extinguishers were indicted for price fixing, in that all three maintained identical prices in the market. There was no direct evidence of conspiracy; however, the three defendants were members of the Fire Extinguishers Manufacturers Association, one committee of which was the Carbon Dioxide Committee at whose meetings, the court determined, there was ample opportunity to discuss and agree on prices and pricing policies. The defendants argued there was no direct evidence of what transpired at these meetings, but the trial court found that the opportunity to discuss prices was "one in a series of 'plus factors' which, when standing alone and examined separately, could not be said to point directly to the conclusion that the charges of the indictment were true beyond a reasonable doubt, but which, when viewed as a whole, in their proper setting, spelled out that irresistible conclusion."[49]

Defendants next argued that the standardization of the product was the cause of uniform prices and not a conspiracy. The court rejected this, stating that "such standardization of a product that is not naturally standardized facilitates maintenance of price uniformity." In summarizing all of the "plus factors" that led the court to find a price-fixing agreement, the court stated:

> As before stated, that question is not whether identical prices throughout the industry *in and of itself* establishes a conspiracy. We would be deciding the unnecessary to answer that question. Here, however, we have in addition to price uniformity, the other so-called plus factors

---

petitor number two says—'I don't care whether number one does what he says he's going to do or not; nor do I care what the rest of you do, but I am going to price my gidget at X dollars.' Number three makes a similar statement—'My price is X dollars.' Number four says not a word. All leave and fix 'their' price at 'X' dollars.

"We do not say the foregoing illustration *compels* an inference in this case that competitors' conduct constituted a price-fixing conspiracy, *including an agreement to so conspire*, but neither can we say, as a matter of law, that an inference of no agreement is compelled. As in so many other instances, it remains a question for the trier of fact [jury or judge] to consider and determine what inference appeals to it (jury) as most logical and persuasive, after it has heard all the evidence as to what these competitors had done before such meeting, and what actions they took thereafter, or what actions they did not take."

48. 197 F.2d 489 (9th Cir. 1952), *cert. denied*, 344 U.S. 892 (1952).

49. *Id*. at 493.

hereinbefore treated. They include a background of illegal licensing agreements containing minimum price maintenance provisions, an artificial standardization of product, a raising of prices at a time when a surplus existed in the industry, and a policing of dealers to effectuate the maintenance of minimum price provisions in accordance with price lists published and distributed by the corporate defendants, including appellant C-O-Two. Other factors which convinced the trial court, beyond a reasonable doubt, that the conspiracy did in fact exist, as charged, were the use of a delivered price system which resulted in price identity to the customer for the products sold, regardless of where they were manufactured, and the submitting of identical bids to public agencies. We think that the facts are not only consistent with the guilt of appellants, but also inconsistent with any other reasonable hypothesis.[50]

The plus factor may be conduct of the defendants that is inconsistent with decisions independently arrived at. For example, in *Milgram* v. *Loew's Inc.,*[51] the defendants were movie distributors that refused to license first-run feature films to plaintiff, a drive-in theater. In finding concerted or joint action the court stated that the starting point of its analysis was the "complete unanimity with which all the distributors refused to license features on a first run to plaintiff." The court next found that the defendants were putting into effect a general program, not just as to plaintiff, uniformly followed by all defendants, which was to relegate all drive-ins to second-run status. The court then noted that each defendant acted in contradiction to its own self-interest, for each refused to license plaintiff even though the latter offered to pay a higher price for first-run movies. The court stated:

> This uniformity in policy forms the basis of an inference of joint action. This does not mean, however, that in every case mere consciously parallel business practices are sufficient evidence, in themselves, from which a court may infer concerted action. Here we add that each distributor refuses to license features on first run to a drive-in even if a higher rental is offered. Each distributor has thus acted in apparent contradiction to its own self-interest. This strengthens con-

50. *Id.* at 497.
51. 192 F.2d 579 (3rd Cir. 1951), *cert. denied,* 343 U.S. 929 (1952).

siderably the inference of conspiracy, for the conduct of the distributors is, in the absence of a valid explanation, inconsistent with decisions independently arrived at.[52]

The inference of illegality arising from conscious parallel conduct can be overcome by demonstrating that there is an independent business justification for the allegedly concerted conduct. Evidence demonstrating the innocence of parallel conduct might include a common problem confronting various manufacturers or that there are a small number of manufacturers producing a standardized product. A time lapse between actions taken by various parties is also probative evidence.

In *Pevely Dairy Co.* v. *United States,*[53] the trial court found a conspiracy on evidence that two dairy companies charged identical prices, with the one following the other immediately when a price change was made. The court of appeals reversed, noting that the product was identical and standardized, due to natural causes and health requirements applicable to processing. Defendants also had substantially identical cost structures because each paid the same government-controlled price for raw milk and the same wages, which resulted from bargaining with the same union. In this setting, the court concluded that identity of prices was well-nigh inevitable. The court stated:

> We are clear that mere uniformity of prices in the sale of a standardized commodity such as milk is not in itself evidence of a violation of the Sherman Anti-trust Act. It is to be observed too that the price changes in question were not simultaneous. Neither were the changes uniformly initiated by the same appellant. When a change was made by one of the appellants a like change was made by the other in a few days following. It is conceded that there was no direct proof of any agreement between the appellants for the fixing of prices. In fact, the evidence is undisputed that every price change was made, not as the result of any understanding or agreement, but because of economic factors, and the same economic factors prompting a change by one of the appellants were equally applicable to the other.[54]

---

52. *Id.* at 583.
53. 178 F.2d 363 (8th Cir. 1949), *cert. denied,* 339 U.S. 942 (1950).
54. *Id.* at 369.

Wall Products Co. v. *National Gypsum Co.,*[55] found that there was no direct evidence that the defendants National Gypsum Company and Kaiser Gypsum Company knew in advance that United States Gypsum Company was going to withdraw all price exceptions and strictly adhere to published prices. However, the consciously parallel conduct of National and Kaiser following U.S. Gypsum's lead was held to constitute conspiratorial conduct by tacit understanding. In that case, there had been communications between the defendants that something had to be done about depressed prices. When U.S. Gypsum made its announcement, the other two major sellers followed with the identical announcements of withdrawing all price exceptions and adherence to published prices. There was even adherence to unannounced changes in policy and practices implemented by U.S. Gypsum. The court stated that when the major competitive sellers in an industry composed of few sellers of a homogeneous product engage in policies and practices that have for their objective the stopping·of declining prices and deviations from terms of sale and when those practices are parallel in detail (even as to unannounced policies and practices) and are so interdependent that adherence thereto on the part of all such major competition is essential to the achievement of their objective, such "interdependent conscious parallel action may well constitute a tacit understanding by 'acquiescence—coupled with assistance' to effectuate a price fixing agreement."[56]

Price Fixing—Vertical

25. Vertical price fixing, a per se violation

One of the more difficult areas of the law is determining the extent to which a manufacturer or seller may influence the resale prices of its customers. As a general proposition, vertical price fixing—that is, dictating to distributors the prices which they will charge to their customers—like horizontal price fixing, is a *per se* violation of Section 1 of the Sherman Act. However, the extent to which the man-

---

55. 326 F.Supp. 295 (N.D. Cal. 1971).
56. *Id.* at 316.

ufacturer may influence those prices has been a sensitive area, perhaps still unresolved by the courts.

The question of resale price maintenance first arose in *Dr. Miles Medical Co.* v. *John D. Park & Sons Co.,*[57] a case involving a manufacturer of trademark proprietary medicines, manufactured pursuant to secret formulas. The plaintiff manufacturer had consignment contracts with over 400 jobbers and wholesalers and 25,000 retail stores, under which plaintiff set both the wholesale and retail prices of its products. Each wholesaler and jobber convenanted that they would not sell to a retailer unless licensed by the plaintiff and that they would not sell below the minimum price dictated by plaintiff. Each retailer was required to sign a contract foreclosing them from selling to anyone who sought to resell the product at less than the standard price set forth in the agreement. Plaintiff, seeking an injunction to enjoin such conduct, sued a wholesaler that refused to abide by plaintiff's prices and that induced other wholesalers to similarly breach their agreements with plaintiff.

The contracts in question were held to be illegal and a violation of Section 1 of the Sherman Act. The plaintiff manufacturer argued that because a manufacturer may make and sell as it chooses, it may also affix the conditions as to the use of the article, including the price at which its customers may dispose of it. In rejecting this argument the Supreme Court held that the instant plan had the same adverse effect on the public as an agreement among wholesalers and jobbers themselves fixing the prices at which they would resell. "The complainant [plaintiff] having sold its products at prices satisfactory to itself, the public is entitled to whatever advantage may be derived from competition in the subsequent traffic."[58] This case thus established the basic premise that a manufacturer could not dictate the resale prices of its customers.

In a second case, the U.S. Supreme Court began defining what a manufacturer could do in influencing the resale prices of its customers. In *United States* v. *Colgate & Co.,*[59] the defendant was indicted for distributing among its customers letters, telegrams, circulars, and lists showing the uniform prices to be charged and urging

57. 220 U.S. 373 (1911).
58. *Id.* at 409.
59. 250 U.S. 300 (1919).

its customers to adhere to those prices. It investigated and placed on "suspended lists" those customers not adhering to its suggested prices, informing them that it would not sell to offending customers. Any customer placed on the suspended list had to promise that future sales would be at the established prices. The Supreme Court held that such conduct was not a violation of Section 1 of the Sherman Act. The Court noted:

> In the absence of any purpose to create or maintain a monopoly, the act does not restrict the long recognized right of trader or manufacturer engaged in an entirely private business, freely to exercise his own independent discretion as to parties with whom he will deal. And of course, he may announce in advance the circumstances under which he will refuse to sell. . . . "A retail dealer has the unquestioned right to stop dealing with a wholesaler for reasons sufficient to himself, and may do so because he thinks such dealer is acting unfairly in trying to undermine his trade." . . . In *Dr. Miles Medical Co.* v. *Park & Sons Co., supra,* the unlawful combination was effected through contracts which undertook to prevent dealers from freely exercising the right to sell.[60]

The *Colgate* doctrine affirms the principle that a manufacturer or seller may suggest resale prices without more and subsequently refuse to sell to a distributor or retailer failing to follow those suggested prices. The difficulty of applying the *Colgate* doctrine is twofold: first, how do you determine when "suggestion" ends and "coercion" begins? For example, the activities condoned in the *Colgate* case itself, if they occurred today, would undoubtably amount to "coercion" and thus *per se* price fixing. Second, trial of the issue of "suggestion" versus "coercion" frequently creates a confrontation between the sworn testimony of the distributor against that of a salesman or employee of the manufacturer or seller, the one claiming that he was threatened and thereby coerced, and the other affirming that his words or conduct were only intended to suggest. Quite clearly, there must be very careful monitoring of salesmen and employees dealing with a recalcitrant distributor that may have to be terminated to assure that they are not exceeding the premissible bounds of *Colgate.*

Subsequent cases have shed some light on what the boundary of

60. *Id.* at 307–08.

Colgate is. In *Federal Trade Commission* v. *Beech-Nut Packing Co.*,[61] the defendant initiated its "Beech-Nut policy" pursuant to which it issued circulars, price lists, and letters setting forth both wholesale and retail prices. The defendant requested and insisted that the selected jobbers, wholesalers, and retailers sell only at the suggested prices and only to customers who were reselling at the suggested prices. The defendant made clear that any customer not adhering to this policy would be refused the products in question. The defendant maintained a card file listing whether wholesalers and retailers were price cutters and therefore ineligible to purchase the products in question. A terminated distributor or retailer could be reinstated with the assurance that it would thereafter sell at the suggested prices and refuse to sell to others that did not maintain those prices.

The Supreme Court first noted that the "Beech-Nut Policy" was not within the ambit of the *Colgate* doctrine, for if a customer failed to adhere to the suggested prices, he was reported to the defendant either by special agents or other dealers enlisted by defendant to maintain the suggested prices. The errant customer was also enrolled as an "Undesirable Price Cutter," which meant he could receive no more of the defendant's products until he gave satisfactory assurance of compliance. In answer to the contention that there was no evidence of an agreement to fix prices, the Court stated:

> The specific facts found show suppression of the freedom of competition by methods in which the company secures the cooperation of its distributors and customers, which are quite as effectual as agreements express or implied intended to accomplish the same purpose.[62]

It is clear that a formal written agreement as in the *Dr. Miles* case is not required. It is enough if there is an implied understanding of cooperation between the manufacturers and wholesalers and retailers. This understanding can be established by the conduct of the parties rather than by actual words. In *United States* v. *Parke Davis and Company*,[63] the defendant made some 600 pharmaceutical products that were sold through a catalog that contained a "Net Price Selling

61. 257 U.S. 441 (1922).
62. *Id.* at 455.
63. 362 U.S. 29 (1960).

Schedule." The catalog stated that it was Parke Davis' continuing policy to deal only with drug wholesalers who observed that schedule and who sold only to drug retailers authorized by law to fill prescriptions. In the summer of 1956, two retailers advertised defendants' vitamin products below the suggested minimum price listed in the wholesalers' "Net Price Selling Schedule." In order to ensure that wholesalers would stop selling to those retailers, Parke Davis visited the wholesalers and told them, in effect, that not only would Parke Davis refuse to sell to wholesalers who did not adhere to the policy announced in its catalog, but also that it would refuse to sell to wholesalers who sold Parke Davis products to retailers who did not observe the suggested minimum retail prices. Each wholesaler interviewed was informed that his competitors were also being apprised of this. The wholesalers without exception indicated a willingness to go along with the program.

The Court, in finding that this scheme went beyond that permitted under the *Colgate* doctrine, stated that when a manufacturer's actions go beyond mere announcement of its suggested prices and the simple refusal to deal and it employs other means that effect adherence to its resale prices, a violation of the Sherman Act has been shown. Whether "an unlawful combination or conspiracy is proved is to be judged by what the parties actually did rather than by the words they used."[64] The Court noted:

> Parke Davis did not content itself with announcing its policy regarding retail prices and following this with a simple refusal to have business relations with any retailers who disregarded that policy. Instead Parke Davis used the refusal to deal with wholesalers in order to elicit their willingness to deny Parke Davis products to retailers and thereby gain the retailers' adherence to its suggested minimum retail prices.[65]

The extent to which the *Colgate* doctrine has been diluted and retail price maintenance schemes held illegal is demonstrated by *Albrecht* v. *Herald Co.*[66] There, the defendant published the *Globe-Democrat,* a morning newspaper distributed in the St. Louis area by independent carriers who bought the papers at wholesale and sold them at retail. The carriers, who covered 172 home delivery routes,

64. *Id.* at 44.
65. *Id.* at 45.
66. 390 U.S. 145 (1968).

had exclusive territories and were subject to termination if their prices exceeded the suggested maximum price established by the defendant. Plaintiff owned one such route and until 1961 adhered to the suggested price. In 1961, plaintiff raised his price to home customers above the printed maximum price, and after several warnings from defendant, was informed that defendant, by offering customers the established suggested price, was going to compete for plaintiff's customers.

Letters were then sent to subscribers on plaintiff's route who were notified that defendant would deliver at the lower price. Defendant also hired an independent concern to solicit customers away from plaintiff through telephone calls and house-to-house solicitation. As a result, 300 of plaintiff's 1,200 customers switched to defendant, and defendant again threatened to stop doing business with plaintiff altogether if he continued to charge the higher price. Defendant transferred the 300 customers to another carrier who knew that defendant would not tolerate overcharging and understood that he might have to return the route if plaintiff abandoned his pricing practices. Subsequently, defendant offered to return plaintiff's customers as long as he charged the suggested price. Plaintiff then sued, and defendant terminated him as a carrier.

Relying on the *Parke Davis* decision, the Supreme Court found that defendant had violated Section 1 of the Sherman Act. The Court noted that the agreements between the defendant and the outfit soliciting plaintiff's customers and the second carrier constituted a "combination" sufficient to satisfy the Sherman Act. In answer to the argument that the alleged price fixing was intended to keep prices down, not raise them, the Court stated:

> Maximum and minimum price fixing may have different consequences in many situations. But schemes to fix maximum prices, by substituting the perhaps erroneous judgment of a seller for the forces of the competitive market, may severely intrude upon the ability of buyers to compete and survive in that market. Competition, even in a single product, is not cast in a single mold. Maximum prices may be fixed too low for the dealer to furnish services essential to the value which goods have for the consumer or to furnish services and conveniences which consumers desire and for which they are willing to pay. Maximum price fixing may channel distribution through a few large or specially advantaged dealers who otherwise would be subject to signifi-

cant nonprice competition. Moreover, if the actual price charged under a maximum price scheme is nearly always the fixed maximum price, which is increasingly likely as the maximum price approaches the actual cost of the dealer, the scheme tends to acquire all the attributes of an arrangement fixing minimum prices. It is our view, therefore, that the combination formed by the respondent in this case to force petitioner [plaintiff] to maintain a specified price for the resale of the newspapers which he had purchased from respondent [defendant] constituted, without more, an illegal restraint of trade under §1 of the Sherman Act.[67]

26. Vertical price fixing through agency or consignment agreements

In 1926 the Supreme Court ruled that if a product is sold by consignment, that is, title to the goods remains in the manufacturer until purchased by the consumer, resale price maintenance was not illegal. In *United States* v. *General Electric Co.,*[68] General Electric devised a three-pronged distribution system for its incandescent electric lights: sales made directly to large customers by General Electric itself, which handled all negotiations and deliveries from its own factories and warehouses; sales made to large consumers pursuant to contracts negotiated by agents of General Electric (designated "B" agents) with deliveries made from stock in the custody of the agents; sales made to general consumers by agents (designated "A" agents).

The B agents were under one-year contracts with General Electric, which provided that the company was to maintain on consignment in the custody of the agent a stock of lamps, the sizes, types, classes, quantity, and length of time in stock to be determined by General Electric. B agents were required to distribute lamps to A agents as directed, to sell lamps to any consumer at prices set by General Electric, and to sell and deliver lamps to any consumer under contract with General Electric at the prices and terms fixed by the company. These agents paid all expenses in the storage, cartage, transportation, handling, sale, and distribution of lamps. The agents paid over to the company all receipts, less the agent's commission, for all lamps sold by him.

67. *Id.* at 152–53.
68. 272 U.S. 476 (1926).

In holding that the fixing of prices by General Electric was not a violation of Section 1 of the Sherman Act, the Court noted that there was a true agency-consignment relationship, as evidenced by the fact that General Electric retained title to the lamps until sold to customers, as well as assumed all risks of loss due to fire, flood, and declining prices.

Almost forty years later, in *Simpson* v. *Union Oil Company of California,*[69] the Supreme Court all but overruled the *General Electric* case on a fact situation, which was at most superficially distinguishable. In the *Simpson* case, plaintiff operated a Union Oil gasoline station pursuant to a lease and consignment agreement. Under the consignment agreement title to gasoline remained in Union Oil until sold to the consumer. While the defendant paid all property taxes on all gasoline in the possession of the plaintiff, Simpson did carry personal liability and property damage insurance covering the consigned gasoline and was responsible for all losses of the consigned gas, save for specified acts of God. Plaintiff Simpson was compensated by a minimum commission and paid all costs of his operation. The selling price of the consigned gasoline was fixed by Union Oil, and when Simpson sold at prices below the established price his lease was not renewed, and he lost his gasoline station.

The Supreme Court found that Union Oil Company's maintenance of retail prices through the consignment device was a *per se* violation of Section 1 of the Sherman Act: "To allow Union Oil to achieve price fixing in the vast distribution system through this 'consignment' device would be to make legality for antitrust purposes turn on clever draftsmanship. We refuse to let a matter so vital to a competitive system rest on such easy manipulation."[70] In so stating, the Supreme Court limited the *General Electric* case to the patent situation.

The *Simpson* court does not altogether eliminate consignment agreements and the right of the manufacturer to sell at prices it fixes through consignment agents. However, where the consignment agent displays many of the indicia of an independent businessman and bears many of the risks normally borne by the entrepreneur, the *Simpson* rule may well apply. This is particularly true, as in *Simp-*

69. 377 U.S. 13 (1964).
70. *Id.* at 24.

son, where the system is comprehensive and adopted by others in the industry as well as by the defendant. The alternative to *Simpson* is for the manufacturer or seller to integrate forward, and then it has unbridled control over retail prices; this is exactly what many oil companies are doing today in establishing company-operated gasoline stations.

27. "Suggested" resale prices may constitute vertical price fixing

A number of other resale maintenance schemes have been scrutinized by the courts and are worth considering. One practice that came under attack, in *Bailey's Bakery, Ltd.* v. *Continental Baking Company,*[71] involved the sale of bakery products to stores with the retail or consumer price, printed on the package, set by the manufacturer. Plaintiff, a competing bakery, argued that placing a preprinted price on the bread forced retail stores to sell at that price, thereby constituting a *per se* price-fixing violation. The court rejected this argument, holding that the preprinted price on the package without more did not violate the Sherman Act. The preprinted price, unilaterally arrived at by the manufacturer, was intended to protect the public and keep down the price of bread in Honolulu, Hawaii. Furthermore, the preprinted price did not deprive retailers of their right to exercise their own free judgment as to "whether to sell defendants' products at all or to sell defendants' products at any price they chose."[72] As long as the preprinted price was not below the retailers' costs or the wholesale price below plaintiff's or defendant's costs, there was no violation. Significantly, no coercion was asserted by defendant against retailers to sell at the preprinted prices.

In *Engbrecht* v. *Dairy Queen Company,*[73] plaintiff, a Dairy Queen franchise, alleged that Dairy Queen was guilty of price fixing because (1) defendant each year issued weight specification cards that had imprinted on them the prices charged in stores owned by defendants, (2) defendant placed advertisements in *Life* magazine in 1955 and

71. 235 F.Supp. 705, 721 (D.Hawaii 1964), *aff'd per curiam* 401 F.2d 182 (9th Cir. 1968), *cert. denied* 393 U.S. 1086 (1969).
72. *Id.* at 722.
73. 203 F.Supp. 714 (D.Kans. 1962).

1956 advertising 15-cent and 16-cent sundaes, and (3) defendant distributed handbills giving the price of items on sale days. Plaintiff argued that by advertising these prices to consumers, franchisees were coerced to sell Dairy Queen products at the price fixed. The court found no violation because the evidence established that plaintiff did in fact fix his own retail prices.

The extent to which a manufacturer can advertise prices in areas serviced not by the manufacturer, but by its independent distributors, without identifying the prices as suggested prices is not clear. If the market structure is such that the distributor is foreclosed as a practical matter from going above the advertised price, then such a price announcement might contain elements of coercion, thereby establishing a price-fixing violation. Quite clearly, the safest course for the manufacturer to follow is to identify the price as a "suggested price," thereby eliminating any element of coercion.

Manufacturers, such as those in the food industry, distributing through independent distributors, face unique problems in dealing with large chain grocery stores that operate on a regional basis. In such cases the chain store will have a regional buyer purchasing food products for any number of its retail stores. He naturally will seek a single price from the food manufacturer, yet the latter may be selling its products through a number of independent distributors in the chain store's region. Two questions arise: can the manufacturer deal directly with the chain store buyer and set a uniform price at which the manufacturer's distributors will sell? And should it consult with the distributors first in reaching a price?

The answer to both of the these questions must be in the negative. As long as the manufacturer has chosen to distribute through independent distributors, it cannot interfere in the price they charge the chain stores. To do so amounts to a fixing of wholesale prices, not by coercion as in other cases, but by actual agreement or conspiracy with the chain stores. Furthermore, the manufacturer cannot confer with its distributors to fix their wholesale prices, for this is outright price fixing.

The plaintiff in *Greene* v. *General Foods Corporation*[74] was an independent food distributor for General Foods Corporation, selling among other things Maxwell House Coffee. Plaintiff sold to large

74. 517 F.2d 635 (5th Cir. 1975).

institutional accounts as well as smaller local accounts. For both types of accounts plaintiff purchased the products from General Foods and resold it. Plaintiff was free to charge the local accounts any price he desired; however, as to the large institutional accounts the price was set by General Foods. At all times, General Foods' institutional accounts prices were lower than what plaintiff charged the local accounts. General Foods argued that it had a right to set the prices of products sold to the institutional accounts because they were customers of General Foods and not plaintiff.

However, the court rejected defendant's argument, stating that General Foods "makes no pretense to ownership of the goods that are ultimately sold to the" institutional accounts, but instead "concedes that title to these rests in the independent distributor."[75] The court concluded that the seller-buyer relationship was between the independent distributor and the institutional accounts, and General Foods' interference in the price structure constituted resale price maintenance in violation of Section 1 of the Sherman Act.

The dangers inherent in the *Green* decision lie not only with the manufacturer, but also with the large chain store or institutional buyer. If the latter is participating in a scheme to fix the price of its suppliers—the independent distributors—through a third party—the manufacturer—it might also be found in violation of Section 1. In many instances, in entering a Consolidated Foods type of price agreement, the institutional buyer may not be cognizant of the nature of the manufacturer's distribution system and wrongly believe that the manufacturer is the seller and the distributors merely delivery agents. Thus, there may be some duty of inquiry.

Territorial Allocation of the Market

28. Horizontal territorial allocation of the market—a per se violation

Recognizing at an early date that price fixing could lead to severe consequences, businessmen turned to other means to bring "competitive stability" into the market. One instrument was the division of

75. *Id.* at 657.

the market among competitors so that each would have a protected area in which to sell. Agreements or arrangements to share the market have taken different forms, from an outright granting of exclusive territories, to allocating fixed percentages of available business to each producer, or allotting customers to each seller. Techniques have varied to effectuate market sharing; for example, competitors may agree to limit the hours of plant operation, thereby in effect sharing the market on the basis of production capacity, or they may channel all their business through a common sales agency with authority to impose production quotas or apportion orders, thereby creating an allocation of the market.

The theory of market sharing is one of "live and let live." Each producer will receive its share of the market, and although price fixing or price control may not be a part of the arrangement, prices tend to become uniform, and effective price competition, responding to economic changes, is lost. Market sharing limits those firms capable of expanding and protects the least efficient producers at a greater cost to the public.

The first case holding that a territorial allocation of the market violated the Sherman Act was *Addyston Pipe & Steel Co.* v. *United States.*[76] There, six manufacturers of cast-iron pipe, who supplied about two thirds of the markets in which they competed, formed a trade association through which they "reserved" certain cities for a particular member. When a city was "reserved" to a particular member, the other members submitted bids as high as the selected bidder requested, in order to give the appearance of active competition among the defendants. The Supreme Court found that such conduct violated Section 1 of the Sherman Act in that competitors had divided the market between them, thereby eliminating competition.

It was not until 1950, however, that the Supreme Court announced that territorial allocations of the market among competitors or potential competitors were *per se* violations of the Sherman Act. In *Timken Roller Bearing Co.* v. *United States,*[77] the defendant Timken Roller Bearing, an Ohio corporation, owned 30 percent of the outstanding shares of British Timken, Ltd., and with one Dewar, an English businessman, all the stock of Societe Anonyme Francaise

76. 175 U.S. 211 (1899).
77. 341 U.S. 593 (1951).

Timken (French Timken). All three companies were engaged in the business of manufacturing and selling antifriction bearings. In 1928 the three entered "agreements" regulating the manufacture and sale of antifriction bearings under the "Timken" trademark. Each company was granted an exclusive area of the world in which it would manufacture and sell Timken bearings. It was also agreed that joint efforts would be made to eliminate outside competition and that the three would participate in cartels to restrict imports to and exports from the United States. Finally, the three agreed to sell at prices fixed by the parties in each of the respective areas. Defendant argued that the restrictions were ancillary to its right to license the trademark "Timken."

The Supreme Court rejected this argument, holding that the trademark provisions in the agreements were secondary to the primary purpose of allocating trade territories between potential competitors, even though there existed a parent subsidiary relationship. The Court therefore found that Section 1 of the Sherman Act had been violated.

The more recent case of *United States* v. *Sealy, Inc.*[78], further emphasized that any kind of allocation of territories among potential competitors will run afoul of the Sherman Act even if those competitors are licensed by a common licensor. In that case Sealy licensed thirty independent manufacturers of mattresses and bedding products to manufacture said products under the "Sealy" trademark. Pursuant to the license agreement Sealy agreed not to license any other person to manufacture or sell in an assigned territory, and the licensee manufacturer agreed not to manufacture or sell Sealy products outside the designated area, although the latter could sell its private label products wherever it chose. Although at first blush the allocation appeared to be vertical, the Supreme Court concluded that it was horizontal among the licensee manufacturers because they in fact owned the stock of Sealy, controlled its board of directors, and directed its affairs. Thus, the Court held that the Sealy arrangement amounted to a horizontal allocation of the Sealy mattress market among potential competitors, a *per se* violation of the Sherman Act.

Sealy's problems, however, did not end with this case, for it was subsequently sued in a private treble damage action brought by a

78. 388 U.S. 350 (1967).

disgruntled manufacturer licensee. In *Ohio-Sealy Mattress Co.* v. *Sealy, Inc.,*[79] decided some ten years after the original *Sealy* case, a licensed manufacturer requested permission from Sealy to open new plants, thereby resulting in the manufacturer selling in territories assigned to other manufacturers. Sealy refused, and the manufacturer sued for treble damages. Sealy argued that the territories granted were not exclusive but rather areas of "primary responsibility" in which Sealy agreed not to assign any other manufacturers.

The court affirmed a jury verdict against Sealy, finding that there was a horizontal territorial allocation. The court of appeals' decision was based on the fact that Sealy refused to allow a licensed manufacturer to open additional plants in areas that would result in spillover sales in another manufacturer's territory, and because Sealy required a manufacturer selling in another territory to pay an additional royalty on such sales. Not only did Sealy lose again, but it ended up paying $10,444,556 in damages to the manufacturer that sued.

A third leading case is *United States* v. *Topco Associates, Inc.*[80] The defendant Topco was a cooperative association of approximately twenty-five small- and medium-sized regional supermarket chains that operated stores in some thirty-three states. Each chain of stores operated independently from the others. Topco's sole function was to act for its members as a purchasing agent of some one thousand different food and related nonfood items, most of which were distributed under brand names owned by Topco. All the stock of Topco was owned by the individual members, with the common stock, the only stock having voting rights, being equally distributed. The board of directors of Topco was made up of executives from the member stores.

All members of Topco signed an agreement with Topco in which the latter designated the territory in which each member could sell Topco-brand products. No member could sell these products outside the licensed territory. New members had to be approved by an affirmative vote of 75 percent of the association's membership, except in those instances in which an existing member closest to the new applicant's area or any member within one hundred miles voted

79. 585 F.2d 821 (7th Cir. 1978), *cert. denied* 9999 U.S. S. Ct. 1267 (1979).
80. 405 U.S. 596 (1972).

against membership, in which case an 85 percent approval of members was required.

In answer to the charge that exclusive territories had been created, Topco argued that because of its small size it was only through the granting of exclusive territories that the system could remain viable and compete against the giant chain stores. The Supreme Court ruled, however, that because a horizontal allocation of the market was a *per se* violation, the reasons for the allocation would not be considered. In reversing the district court and holding that a *per se* violation had been committed, the Supreme Court stated:

> The District Court determined that by limiting the freedom of its individual members to compete with each other, Topco was doing a greater good by fostering competition between members and other large supermarket chains. But, the fallacy in this is that Topco has no authority under the Sherman Act to determine the respective values of competition in various sectors of the economy. On the contrary, the Sherman Act gives to each Topco member and to each prospective member the right to ascertain for itself whether or not competition with other supermarket chains is more desirable than competition in the sale of Topco-brand products. Without territorial restrictions, Topco members may indeed "[cut] each other's throats." C.f. *White Motor Co.,* . . . 372 U.S. at 278, . . . (Clark, J. dissenting). But we have never found this possibility sufficient to warrant condoning horizontal restraints of trade.[81]

The Supreme Court also noted that it was a *per se* violation to allocate customers among competitors as well as territories.

29. Vertical allocation of the market

A more difficult question has arisen in the courts as to whether a vertical allocation of the market should be treated as a *per se* violation of Section 1 of the Sherman Act. A vertical allocation of the market occurs when a manufacturer sells products to its distributors and in order to protect their market positions grants to each an exclusive territory in which to sell. Thus, the allocation is between distributors at the secondary level and is not between manufacturers at the primary or horizontal level.

81. *Id.* at 610–11.

The Supreme Court in *United States* v. *Arnold, Schwinn & Co.*[82] held that allocating territories and customers among distributors was just as much a *per se* violation of the Sherman Act as an allocation of the market among competitors (horizontal). In the *Schwinn* case, a bicycle manufacturer, which in the 1950s had 25 percent of the bicycle market, saw its market position deteriorate to 13 percent of the market in the 1960s due to the influx of such mass merchandisers as Sears and Montgomery Ward. To combat this deterioration in the market, Schwinn granted exclusive territories to each of its distributors and by agreement foreclosed each from selling outside their assigned territories or to customers other than Schwinn franchised retail stores.

The Supreme Court held this to be *per se* illegal, stating that "[u]nder the Sherman Act, it is unreasonable without more for a manufacturer to seek to restrict and confine areas or persons with whom an article may be traded after the manufacturer has parted with dominion over it. . . . Such restraints are so obviously destructive of competition that their mere existence is enough."[83]

Ten years later, in 1977, the Supreme Court overruled *Schwinn* in *Continental T.V., Inc.* v. *GTE Sylvania Incorporated,*[84] and ruled that a vertical allocation of the market and customers was not a *per se* violation of the Sherman Act, and therefore a court could hear evidence concerning the business reasons for such allocation. In this case, Sylvania, due to a decrease in its share of the television market to a relatively insignficant 1 to 2 percent, eliminated its wholesale organization and began selling directly to a few select retailers. Sylvania's marketing strategy was that by limiting the retailers in a given area, it would attract more agressive and competent retailers to handle its products. Under the franchise agreement each retailer was permitted to sell only from the location stated in the agreement.

Continental was one such selected retailer, who under the new plan had prospered for a period of time. When sales began softening, Sylvania granted a second location franchise in Continental's area, over Continental's strong protest. Continental then canceled a large order and gave it to Phillips, one of Sylvania's competitors. Subse-

---

82. 388 U.S. 365 (1967).
83. *Id.* at 379.
84. 433 U.S. 36 (1977).

quently, Continental requested the right to sell in another area, and this request was denied. Thereafter, the relationship further deteriorated, and Continental was terminated as a franchisee. In a claim (counterclaim) against Sylvania, Continental pleaded that the agreements prohibiting the sale of Sylvania products by franchises other than at specified locations was a *per se* violation of Section 1 of the Sherman Act. At trial Continental received a verdict for $591,505, which was trebled, as required by law, to $1,774,515.

The Supreme Court ruled with Sylvania and overruled the *Schwinn* case. It held that when a manufacturer vertically limits competition between its distributors by allocating exclusive territories or customers, competition with other manufacturers (interbrand competition) can be enhanced, thus promoting rather than diminishing overall competition in the marketplace. The Court stated:

> Vertical restrictions promote interbrand competition by allowing the manufacturer to achieve certain efficiencies in the distribution of his products. These "redeeming virtues" are implicit in every decision sustaining vertical restrictions under the rule of reason. Economists have identified a number of ways in which manufacturers can use such restrictions to compete more effectively against other manufacturers. . . . For example, new manufacturers and manufacturers entering new markets can use the restrictions in order to induce competent and aggressive retailers to make the kind of investment of capital and labor that is often required in the distribution of products unknown to the consumer. Established manufacturers can use them to induce retailers to engage in promotional activities or to provide service and repair facilities necessary to the efficient marketing of their products. Service and repair are vital for many products, such as automobiles and major household appliances. The availability and quality of such services affect a manufacturer's goodwill and the competitiveness of his product.[85]

Although not a *per se* violation of the Sherman Act, a violation may still exist if the restraint is an unreasonable one. Thus, if a major manufacturer grants exclusive distributorships for the purpose of eliminating competition between distributors and thereby increasing its already dominant position in the market, such a restriction would undoubtedly be treated as unreasonable, in violation of the Sherman Act.

85. *Id.* at 54–55.

In *In re The Coca-Cola Company*,[86] the Federal Trade Commission brought an action against the Coca-Cola Company and others charging them with dividing up the United States among independent Coca-Cola bottlers, thereby establishing exclusive territories and eliminating intrabrand competition. The commission noted that the Coca-Cola Company at the turn of this century sold its rights to bottle Coca-Cola and licensed the "Coca-Cola" trademark, in perpetuity, to private investors who as independent businessmen operated their own bottling facilities within assigned territories. At this time, the Coca-Cola Company itself produced no bottled soft drinks, but entered this field at a later date when it acquired the bottling rights of some independent bottlers. Complaint counsel contended that because the Coca-Cola Company was a bottler in certain areas, there was a horizontal allocation of the market among potential competitors in the bottling and selling of Coca-Cola products, including Coca-Cola, Tab, Sprite, Fresca, Fanta, and Mr. Pibb. Thus, they argued, there was a *per se* violation of the law.

In its opinion the Federal Trade Commission rejected this theory of liability and held, instead, that because the initial franchising was vertical in nature—that is, the franchiser, the Coca-Cola Company, was not a bottler when it set up the exclusive territories for the independent bottlers—its mere subsequent acquisition of certain territories did not alter this vertical arrangement. Although vertical, the commission still ruled that the territorial division was "unreasonable," in violation of the law:

> While the territories in which Coca-Cola and the allied products are sold are not devoid of interbrand competition, nevertheless Coca-Cola and allied products prices have great competitive significance in the marketplace. Moreover the record amply demonstrates that respondents' [Coca-Cola's] territorial restrictions constitute a serious impediment to free market forces and diminish competition in the manufacture, distribution, and sale of several important soft drink product lines. The record also shows that intrabrand competition would invigorate price competition which would be likely to produce lower wholesale prices for Coca-Cola and the allied products. . . . By suppressing the development of intrabrand competition in the sale of these products packaged in bottles and cans, the restrictions have, over the years, distorted the competitive dynamics of the industry and have disrupted

86. 3 *Trade Reg. Rep.* (CCH) ¶21,509, appeal docketed, No. 78-1364 (D.C.Cir. April 24, 1978).

the natural economic forces which would have, in the absence of restraints, caused an evolution in the geographic market boundaries of respondents' bottlers.[87]

It should be noted that Coca-Cola today has both a vertical and horizontal relationship with its distributor bottlers. As a manufacturer it sells the secret formula syrup to the bottlers (vertical relationship), and as a bottler itself it operates on the same level with its licensed independent bottlers (horizontal). A question then arises as to whether or not this "dual distribution" setup should be treated as a *per se* violation. As just noted the commission said no because the vertical relationship was more predominant. But there are a number of cases that hold that in a dual distribution case the *per se* rule will apply when there is an exclusive allocation of the market among distributors.

30. The manufacturer competing against its distributors

One note of caution to manufacturers seeking to create exclusive territories for their distributors arises when the manufacturer is also distributing its own products in competition, or potential competition, with its distributors. If the manufacturer is competing with its distributors and thus has both a vertical and horizontal relationship with them,[88] a "dual distribution" setup, a territorial or customer allocation will constitute a *per se* violation of the Sherman Act. A classic example of this is found in the Holiday Inns franchise setup.

In *American Motor Inns, Inc.* v. *Holiday Inns, Inc.*,[89] Holiday Inns granted to franchisees the right to construct and operate Holiday Inns. However, pursuant to the franchise agreement, franchisees could operate only at the specific sites designated. When a prospective franchisee sought to obtain a new inn, Holiday Inns sent a letter ("radius letter") to the three existing franchisees nearest the pro-

---

87. *Id.* at

88. The relationship is vertical because the manufacturer is selling its products to the distributors. It is also horizontal because as a distributor, the manufacturer is competing or is in potential competition with its distributors. See, Fortuna Aviation, Inc., v. Beech Aircraft Corporation, 432 F.2d 1080 (7th Cir. 1970). Interphoto Corporation v. Minolta Corporation, 295 F.Supp. 711 (S.D.N.Y. 1969), *aff'd* 417 F.2d 621 (2d Cir. 1969).

89. 521 F.2d 1230 (3d Cir. 1975).

posed location. If any of the three objected, this was given great weight as to whether the new franchise would be given. Also, Holiday Inns owned and operated its own motels in areas that it designated "company towns." No franchisee could operate an inn in those areas, and each, pursuant to the franchise agreement, was barred from operating a non-Holiday Inns motel anywhere in the United States. Thus, in the "company towns" Holiday Inns foreclosed all competition from its franchisees, who were unable to obtain a Holiday Inns franchise there and were also foreclosed from operating a non-Holiday Inns motel there.

Plaintiff in this case, the largest Holiday Inns franchisee with some forty-eight motels, sought to open an additional motel adjacent to the passenger terminal at the Newark, New Jersey, airport. Plaintiff was refused because the three nearest franchisees objected. Plaintiff sued Holiday Inns, arguing that the franchise arrangement was a horizontal allocation of the market and therefore a *per se* violation of Section 1 of the Sherman Act. The court agreed on the ground that Holiday Inns, as an operator of motels itself, was in competition with its franchisees, and thus creating exclusive territories was a *horizontal* allocation. The court stated:

> Acts by a franchisor, such as HI [Holiday Inns, Inc.] that create otherwise unreasonable restraints of trade are not insulated from the antitrust laws by the fact that such company functions as a franchisor as well as a motel operator. . . .
>
> In the present case, since HI, in one of its capacities, was dealing on the same market level as its franchisees, its contracts that, in effect, foreclosed such franchisees from operating either Holiday Inns or non-Holiday Inns in cities where HI operated an inn, except with HI's permission, constitute market allocation agreements among competitors. The district court therefore did not err in ruling that the combination of the non-Holiday Inn clause and the company-town policy constituted an unlawful restraint of trade.[90]

The Baskin-Robbins ice cream system was challenged on similar grounds in *Krehl* v. *Baskin-Robbins Ice Cream Company*.[91] In creating the Baskin-Robbins system, Baskin-Robbins divided up the United States into exclusive territories and then licensed various

90. *Id.* at 1253–54.
91. 78 F.R.D. 108 (C.D. Cal. 1978).

independent ice cream manufacturers to manufacture and sell Baskin-Robbins ice cream in each territory. Each manufacturer was also given the right to franchise, along with Baskin-Robbins, Baskin-Robbins ice cream stores in its territory. Baskin-Robbins retained for itself certain areas of the United States. The evidence established that as a manufacturer of ice cream Baskin-Robbins, except for the territorial restrictions, was in competition with each of the licensed manufacturers, inasmuch as ice cream was sold as far away as 900 miles from the various plants.[92] With four plants located in California, Texas, Kentucky, and Connecticut, Baskin-Robbins' potential area of sales overlapped that of each of the independent manufacturers.

The defendants argued that the territorial allocation was vertical with Baskin-Robbins at the top and therefore not a *per se* violation of the Sherman Act. The district court rejected the argument, holding that when a party acts in a dual role of both franchiser and competitor, a territorial allocation becomes *per se* illegal because it is horizontal in effect. Thus, when Baskin-Robbins divided up the United States among nine manufacturers, including itself, and granted each an exclusive territory to manufacture and sell Baskin-Robbins ice cream products, it horizontally eliminated competition between them, thereby violating Section 1 of the Sherman Act.

Boycotts and Concerted Refusals to Deal

31. Group boycotts—a per se violation

A businessman acting *unilaterally* may deal with whomever he selects to do business, and he may refuse to deal with whomever he chooses for reasons sufficient to himself.[93] If, however, one's refusal to deal with another is the result of an agreement with others who also agree not to deal with a particular party, a violation of Section 1 of the Sherman Act may arise.

---

92. From Baskin-Robbins Bryan, Texas, plant, Baskin-Robbins sold ice cream to its ice cream stores located in Europe.

93. This statement is the so-called Colgate Doctrine. United States v. Colgate & Co., 250 U.S. 300 (1919). It has severe limitations when one is in a monopoly position or the effect of the refusal is to fix resale prices.

The first case of importance discussing concerted refusals to deal is *Eastern States Retail Lumber Dealers' Ass'n.* v. *United States.*[94] In that case, a large number of retail lumber dealers organized themselves into associations, one of the aims of which was to stop wholesaler lumber companies from selling directly to the consumer. To this end the associations created "blacklists" naming each wholesaler who sold directly to consumers, and the only way a wholesaler could have his name removed from the list was to assure the associations that he would no longer deal in direct sales.

The Court noted that although there was no agreement among retailers that they would refrain from dealing with a blacklisted wholesaler and there was no penalty if they did, "he is blind indeed who does not see the purpose in the predetermined and periodical circulation of this report to put the ban upon wholesale dealers whose names appear in the list of unfair dealers trying by methods obnoxious to the retail dealers to supply the trade which they regard as their own."[95] The Court, in finding a violation of the Sherman Act, then discussed what the law does and does not permit:

> A retail dealer has the unquestioned right to stop dealing with a wholesaler for reasons sufficient to himself, and may do so because he thinks such dealer is acting unfairly in trying to undermine his trade. "But . . . when [parties] combine and agree that no one of them will trade with any producer or wholesaler who shall sell to a consumer within the trade range of any of them, quite another case is presented. An act harmless when done by one may become a public wrong when done by many acting in concert, for it takes on the form of a conspiracy, and may be prohibited or punished, if the result be hurtful to the public or to the individual against whom the concerted action is directed.[96]

A second case, *Fashion Originators' Guild of America, Inc.* v. *Federal Trade Commission,*[97] further demonstrates the illegality of group action. There, the Fashion Originators' Guild was an organization of firms that designed and manufactured women's dresses and the textiles used in making them. The designs were original, and as they

94. 234 U.S. 600 (1914).
95. *Id.* 608–09.
96. *Id.* at 614.
97. 312 U.S. 457 (1941).

entered the channels of trade other manufacturers systematically made copies that were sold at lower prices. The guild considered this unethical and immoral and labeled it "style piracy." The guild was formed to create a boycott of these pirate manufacturers by having its members agree to refuse to sell their products to retailers who sold garments purchased from these manufacturers. As a result of these efforts, approximately 12,000 retailers throughout the country signed agreements to "cooperate" with the guild boycott program, many only because they were constrained by threats that guild members would not sell to them if they failed to yield to their demands.

Guild members argued that the boycott was a reasonable effort to protect the manufacturer, laborer, retailer, and consumer against "the devastating evils growing from the pirating of original designs." The Supreme Court refused, however, to consider evidence of reasonableness on the ground that the purpose and object of the combination was to destroy a rival method of competition, which the Court held was a *per se* violation of Section 1 of the Sherman Act.

Klor's Inc. v. *Broadway-Hale Stores, Inc.*[98] presents an entirely different type of group boycott, which the Court found was also a *per se* violation of the Sherman Act. Here, the plaintiff Klor's operated a retail store on Mission Street in San Francisco, California. Defendant Broadway-Hale Stores operated a chain of department stores, one of which was next door to Klor's. The stores competed in the sale of radios, television sets, refrigerators, and other household appliances. Klor's alleged that it was as well equipped as Broadway-Hale to handle all brands of appliances; nevertheless, manufacturers and distributors of such well-known brands as General Electric, RCA, Admiral, Zenith, Emerson, and others allegedly conspired among themselves and with Broadway-Hale either not to sell to the plaintiff or to sell to it at discriminatory prices and highly unfavorable terms. It further alleged that Broadway-Hale used its "monopolistic" buying power to bring about this situation. As a result of this boycott plaintiff lost substantial profits. In holding that the above allegations constituted a violation of the Sherman Act, the Supreme Court stated:

> Group boycotts, or concerted refusals by traders to deal with other traders, have long been held to be in the forbidden category. They

98. 359 U.S. 207 (1959).

have not been saved by allegations that they were reasonable in the specific circumstances, nor by a failure to show that they "fixed or regulated prices, parcelled out or limited production, or brought about a deterioration in quality." [cases cited] Even when they operated to lower prices or temporarily to stimulate competition they were banned. [cases cited][99]

Trade associations can become involved in a boycott or concerted refusal to deal and end up as a named defendant along with the individual company members. In *Radiant Burners, Inc.* v. *Peoples Gas Light and Coke Co.,*[100] the American Gas Association, Inc., which was a membership corporation, operated testing laboratories to determine the safety, utility, and durability of gas burners. It adopted a "seal of approval," which was affixed on gas burners passing its tests. Plaintiff Radiant Burners on two occasions submitted its burners for approval, but was refused although its gas burners were purported to be safer and more efficient than burners manufactured by competitors who were members of the association, and which had been approved. Because utility members of the association refused to provide gas for use in plaintiff's burners because they did not have the AGA "seal of approval," its burners were effectively excluded from the market, as its potential customers would not buy gas burners for which they could not obtain gas.

Plaintiff sued the association as well as its members, alleging that the American Gas Association's refusal to give its burners the AGA "seal of approval" was conspiratorially motivated by member manufacturers attempting to keep plaintiff's burners off the market. The Court had little difficulty in finding that a boycott had been pleaded, which if proved would constitute a *per se* violation.

Even the New York Stock Exchange has found itself enmeshed in an illegal boycott. In *Silver* v. *New York Stock Exchange,*[101] Harold J. Silver, of Dallas, Texas, entered the securities business by establishing a firm to handle municipal bonds and a second firm to trade in over-the-counter securities. Both firms were registered broker-dealers and members of the National Association of Securities Dealers, Inc. Because of the need to have instantaneous communications

99. *Id.* at 212.
100. 364 U.S. 656 (1961) (per curiam).
101. 373 U.S. 341 (1963).

with firms in the mainstream of the securities business, one firm obtained direct private telephone wire connections with the municipal bond departments of a number of securities firms (three of which were members of the New York Stock Exchange) and the other arranged for private wires to the corporate securities trading departments of ten member firms of the exchange, as well as the trading desks of a number of nonmember firms.

Pursuant to the requirements of the New York Stock Exchange's rules, all but one of the member firms that granted private wires to Silver's firms applied to the exchange for approval of the connections. During the summer of 1958 the exchange granted "temporary approval" for these connections, as well as for a direct teletype connection to a member firm in New York City and for stock ticker service to be furnished to Silver's firms directly from the floor of the exchange.

On February 12, 1959, without prior warning to Silver or his firms, the Exchange's Department of Member Firms decided to disapprove the private wire and related applications. Notice was sent to the member firms involved, instructing them to discontinue the wires, a directive that each member was required to follow by the Exchange's constitution and rules. By March 1959, the wires and ticker were all removed. As a result, Silver's concerns lost business and profits, and he therefore sued, alleging a boycott.

The Supreme Court held that removal of the wires by collective action of the exchange and its members constituted a *per se* violation of Section 1 of the Sherman Act. "The concerted action of the Exchange and its members here was, in simple terms, a group boycott depriving petitioners of a valuable business service which they need in order to compete effectively as broker dealers in the over-the-counter securities market."[102] The Exchange argued that by virtue of the Securities Exchange Act it was permitted to regulate itself and that such self-regulation was exempt from the ambit of the Sherman Act. The Court, however, rejected this argument, holding that the Exchange had exceeded its regulatory powers because its action to eliminate Silver was done capriciously and arbitrarily and without a hearing being afforded Silver. Under these circumstances there could be no exemption from the antitrust laws.

---

102. *Id.* at 347.

Another leading case in this area is *Associated Press* v. *United States,*[103] wherein Associated Press, a cooperative association composed of the publishers of more than 1,200 newspapers (in 1945), was in the business of collecting, assembling, and distributing news, which it obtained from employees of the association, employees of member newspapers, and employees of foreign news agencies. According to AP's bylaws, member newspapers were prohibited from selling news to nonmembers. Also, members could block from membership nonmember competitors. The Supreme Court noted that inability to buy news from the largest news agency or any one of its multitude of members could have most serious effects on the publication of competitive newspapers. "Trade restraints of this character, aimed at the destruction of competition, tend to block the initiative which brings newcomers into a field of business and to frustrate the free enterprise system which it was the purpose of the Sherman Act to protect."[104] Defendants' argument that because other news agencies sold news there could be no violation was rejected by the Court: "But the fact that an agreement to restrain trade does not inhibit competition in all of the objects of that trade cannot save it from the condemnation of the Sherman Act."[105]

32. Terminating a distributor—refusal to deal

Terminating a distributor can present serious Sherman Act problems. Under the *Colgate* doctrine, a seller has the unilateral right to refuse to deal with a distributor if based on sound business reasons and not pursuant to some agreement or conspiracy with others. Thus, individual refusals to deal have been upheld when based upon the failure of a distributor to adhere to the supplier's quality image,[106] when reliable security for payment has not been given or payments have not been made,[107] when the refusal was based on a chronic history of customer complaints,[108] when competitive products were sold

---

103. 326 U.S. 1, (1945).

104. *Id.* at 13–14.

105. *Id.* at 17.

106. D & M Distribs. Inc. v. Texaco, Inc., 1970 Trade Cas. ¶73,099 (C.D. Cal. 1970).

107. Hallmark Indus. v. Reynolds Metal Co., 1971 Trade Cas. ¶73,409 (N.D. Cal. 1970), *Mandamus denied sub nom.* Hallmark v. Peckham, 1971 Trade Cas. ¶73,577 (9th Cir.), *cert. denied,* 403 U.S. 932 (1971).

108. Bunty v. Shell Oil Co., 1872 Trade Cas. ¶74252 (D.Nev. 1972).

by a customer at lower prices,[109] when a customer would not enter into a five-year contract,[110] and when a manufacturer decided to perform its own distributing directly or establish exclusive outlets for its goods.[111]

In *Bushie* v. *Stenocord Corp.,*[112] Hamilton and Doris Bushie were engaged in selling at retail and servicing Stenocord office dictating machines in the Phoenix, Arizona, area, under a distributorship contract with defendant Stenocord. Stenocord decided to change its distribution system in Phoenix by selling and servicing through its own outlets rather than through distributors. The Bushies were therefore terminated as distributors. In their lawsuit, plaintiffs alleged that they had been a good distributor—this statement was not contested—and that their termination eliminated them from competition on Stenocord products, thereby restraining trade in violation of Section 1 of the Sherman Act. The court of appeals rejected this argument, stating that "a manufacturer may discontinue dealing with a particular distributor 'for business reasons which are sufficient to the manufacturer,' and adverse effect on the business of the distributor is immaterial in the absence of any arrangement restraining trade."[113]

In a second case, *Beverage Distributors, Inc.* v. *Olympia Brewing Co.,*[114] the court of appeals sustained a jury verdict that the termination of a beer distributor did not violate the law. There, the plaintiff was originally a wholly owned subsidiary of Safeway Stores and acted as a beer distributor for those stores only. In 1953, the defendant Olympia Brewing appointed plaintiff to distribute its Olympia beer to Safeway stores. Subsequently, employees of plaintiff bought out the company and with a change in management began selling Olympia beer to other customers in addition to the Safeway stores. With this announcement and subsequent sales, Olympia stopped filling plaintiff's orders, expressing concern that plaintiff's increased dis-

109. GAF Corp. v. Circle Floor Co., 329 F.Supp. 823 (S.D.N.Y. 1971), *aff'd,* 463 F.2d 752 (2d Cir. 1972) *cert. dismissed per stipulation,* 413 U.S. 901 (1973).

110. Daily Press, Inc. v. United Press Int'l., 412 F.2d 126 (6th Cir.), *cert. denied,* 396 U.S. 990 (1969).

111. Bushie v. Stenocord Corp., 460 F.2d 116 (9th Cir. 1972); Beverage Distrib., Inc. v. Olympia Brewing Co., 440 F.2d 21 (9th Cir.), *cert. denied,* 402 U.S. 906 (1971).

112. 460 F.2d 116 (9th Cir. 1972).

113. *Id.* at 119.

114. 440 F.2d 21 (9th Cir. 1971).

tribution created a quality control problem. Plaintiff's complaint contended that Olympia's refusal to deal was motivated by a desire to stop plaintiff from selling to customers other than the Safeway Stores. The court of appeals ruled with Olympia, holding that "a single manufacturer can select his own customers and sell to these and not to any others, at least where there are other and equivalent brands readily available."[115]

Although both the *Stenocord* and *Olympia* cases permitted the unilateral termination of distributors, a large body of case law has found such terminations illegal if the termination is intended to eliminate a price-cutter, to keep new competition out of the market, to create a monopoly, or to strengthen further an already dominant market position. Already discussed are the numerous resale price maintenance cases in which a manufacturer or seller terminated a distributor for failing to adhere to suggested resale prices, such as *Parke Davis, Albrecht* v. *Herald Co.,* and *Kiefer-Stewart Co.*[116] The courts have had little difficulty in finding that the termination was directly related to an illegal price-fixing scheme and thus illegal *per se* under Section 1 of the Sherman Act. Therefore, it is clear that when the distributor is a price-cutter or has sold at other than suggested prices, serious problems can arise in attempting to terminate him. If a salesman or agent of the manufacturer has in any way threatened the distributor because of his pricing practices, such threats can be the basis of an antitrust action brought to bar termination. The distributor will plead that termination is not for legitimate business reasons but as punishment for the distributor's failure to adhere to suggested prices.

When the manufacturer is in a monopoly or in a dominant market position, termination of distributors is no longer a legitimate unilateral matter, but has inherent illegal monopoly implications. For example, in *Eastman Kodak Co. of New York* v. *Southern Photo Materials Co.,*[117] plaintiff operated a photographic stock house in Atlanta, Georgia, and handled photographic materials and supplies, which it sold to photographers in the South. The defendant, Eastman Kodak, was engaged in the manufacture and sale of photographic apparatus and supplies, which it sold to plaintiff on the same terms

115. *Id.* at 32.
116. See *supra.*, pp. 85–88.
117. 273 U.S. 359 (1927).

that it sold to other distributors. In 1910, Kodak unsuccessfully attempted to purchase plaintiff's business, and thereafter refused to sell to plaintiff at the normal dealers' discount. Plaintiff sued under the Sherman Act, arguing that defendant's refusal to deal with plaintiff on terms similar to that afforded others was in furtherance of its purpose to monopolize interstate trade in photographic supplies.

The Court noted that Kodak's 70 to 80 percent control of the market plus its acquisition of a number of competitors and stock houses similar to plaintiff evidenced an intent to monopolize. Although there was no direct evidence that Kodak's refusal to sell to plaintiff was in pursuance of a purpose to monopolize, the evidence disclosed circumstances that supported a reasonable inference that Kodak's refusal was motivated by such a plan and was thus illegal.

In *Lorain Journal Co.* v. *United States*,[118] the defendant was the only newspaper publisher in Lorain, Ohio, selling some 13,000 copies daily. In 1948, the Elyria-Lorain Broadcasting Company began operating a radio station and soliciting the same advertisers as the *Lorain Journal.* The latter then initiated a plan whereby it refused to accept advertising from any person who advertised or was about to advertise over the radio station. The court found that Section 2 of the Sherman Act was violated, in that the *Lorain Journal's* refusal to deal with advertisers advertising over the radio station was part of an attempt to monopolize the dissemination of news and advertising in the Lorain, Ohio, area. "The publisher claims a right as a private concern to select its customers and to refuse to accept advertisements from whomever it pleases. . . . [However] the right claimed by the publisher is neither absolute nor exempt from regulation. Its exercise as a purposeful means of monopolizing interstate commerce is prohibited by the Sherman Act."[119]

A different question arises when a manufacturer terminates a distributor or refuses to deal with him at the request or pursuant to an agreement with a competing distributor. In *Cernuto, Inc.* v. *United Cabinet Corp.*,[120] plaintiff was made a distributor for defendant's cabinets used in home remodeling. The distributor agreement was for two years, but after only three months defendant informed plaintiff that it would cease supplying the latter with cabinets. Plaintiff

118. 342 U.S. 143 (1951).
119. *Id.* at 155.
120. 595 F.2d 164 (3d Cir. 1979).

asserted that this was the result of complaints from a competitor also selling defendant's cabinets in the same area that plaintiff was selling at discount prices. The court ruled that a *per se* violation had been demonstrated. The court stated that when a marketing decision is not made unilaterally by the manufacturer or seller, but because of pressure from another customer, that decision "must be scrutinized more closely than solely unilateral action might be." The court noted the distinction between unilateral action and that induced by a competitor:

> When a manufacturer acts on its own, in pursuing its own market strategy, it is seeking to compete with other manufacturers by imposing what may be defended as reasonable vertical restraints. . . . However, if the action of a manufacturer or other supplier is taken at the direction of its customer, the restraint becomes primarily horizontal in nature in that one customer is seeking to suppress its competition by utilizing the power of a common supplier. Therefore, although the termination in such a situation is, itself, a vertical restraint, the desired impact is horizontal and on the dealer, not the manufacturer, level.[121]

If pricing is the primary motive of the competing distributors' request, that is, the elimination of a price-cutter, there can be little doubt that the courts will find a *per se* violation. In the *Cernuto* case the court noted that although prices were not fixed, still the termination of plaintiff, who was a price-cutter, restrained "price movement and the free play of market forces."[122]

In *United States* v. *General Motors Corp.,*[123] "discount houses" began purchasing Chevrolet cars from authorized dealers and reselling them at discount prices. Several Chevrolet dealers' associations approached General Motors with a program to stop the discount houses, and this request was implemented. The Court found that the action of General Motors, initiated by the dealers, was concerted action designed to exclude discount competitors from the marketplace, a *per se* violation. The Court stated:

> [W]here businessmen concert their actions in order to deprive others of access to merchandise which the latter wish to sell to the public, we need not inquire into the economic motivation underlying their conduct. . . . Exclusion of traders from the market by means of combi-

121. *Id.* at 168.
122. *Id.* at 169.
123. 384 U.S. 127 (1966).

nation or conspiracy is so inconsistent with the free-market principles embodied in the Sherman Act that it is not to be saved by reference to the need for preserving the collaborators' profit margins or their system for distributing automobiles.[124]

Absent this pricing consideration, some cases have held that no violation has been committed even when termination was induced by a competing distributor. In *Packard Motor Car Co.* v. *Webster Motor Car Co.,*[125] suit was brought by a terminated Packard dealer against Packard for its termination induced by a rival dealer. The rival dealer was the largest Packard dealer in the Baltimore area and informed Packard that it would go out of business unless Packard gave it an exclusive franchise in Baltimore. The court ruled that since other cars on the market were "reasonably interchangeable by consumers for the same purposes,"[126] an exclusive contract for marketing Packards did not create a monopoly nor did the evidence show that a conspiracy existed between Packard and the favored dealer who made the request, in violation of Section 1 of the Sherman Act. One of the judges dissented in the case, stating that plaintiff's "elimination as a dealer resulted not from a unilateral decision by Packard in selecting its customers,"[127] but rather from a combination and conspiracy between Packard and the favored dealer to eliminate the latter's competitors.

In *Joseph E. Seagram & Sons, Inc.* v. *Hawaiian Oke & Liquors, Ltd.,*[128] plaintiff was the sole wholesale distributor in Hawaii for Calvert Distillers Company, Four Roses Distillers Company, and two of the products of Frankfort Distillers Company, all of which companies were owned by House of Seagram, Inc. Plaintiff was also the sole distributor for Barton Distilling Company. In May 1965 Calvert's president proposed to a nationwide distributor, McKesson & Robbins, Inc., that it become Calvert's distributor in Hawaii. McKesson & Robbins then approached Barton Distilling Company to inquire whether it could also become its exclusive distributor in Hawaii. An agreement was completed whereby McKesson & Robbins was to become the exclusive distributor in Hawaii for both the Calvert and

124. *Id.* at 146.
125. 243 F.2d 418 (D.C. Cir. 1957).
126. *Id.* at 420.
127. *Id.* at 421 (Bazelon, J. dissenting).
128. 416 F.2d 71 (9th Cir. 1969), *cert. denied,* 396 U.S. 1062 (1970).

Barton lines. The agreement also included the Four Roses and Frankfort lines as well. The switch was made by August 1965, and plaintiff was informed of its termination by all companies involved.

Plaintiff argued that the agreements between McKesson & Robbins and the Seagram companies (Calvert, Four Roses, Frankfort) and Barton constituted a *per se* boycott of the plaintiff. The court disagreed, stating "it is not a *per se* violation of the antitrust laws for a manufacturer or supplier to agree with a distributor to give him an exclusive franchise, even if this means cutting off another distributor."[129] Only if the boycott or refusal to deal (termination) was effectuated for anticompetitive purposes, such as putting one or more "discounters" or "price-cutters" out of business, or eliminating competitors, or impairing their ability to compete with the conspirators, or stabilizing the market or fixing prices, or enhancing an already existing monopoly, does a violation occur. The court found:

> Here, plaintiff presented no evidence whatever that either Seagram or Barton had any *anticompetitive* motive for terminating plaintiff as their distributor. There was no price fixing or other similar motives or demands or activities. There had been no anticompetitive practices imposed by either Seagram or Barton on plaintiff; none was imposed on McKesson; McKesson sought none. Of course McKesson wanted the part of the business that it got. But there is no evidence that either McKesson or any of the other defendants were primarily motivated by a desire to damage plaintiff or put it out of business.[130]

33. Practical considerations in terminating a distributor

It is clear from the above case analysis that terminating an existing distributor is not an easy task. Careful consideration must be given to any number of factors. First, there must be legitimate business reasons for the termination, such as dissatisfaction with the distributor's service to customers, poor payment record, failure to properly develop and expand the market. A satisfactory reason might be reorganization of the manufacturer's or seller's distribution system by reducing the number of distributors, with the expectation that concentration of business in the hands of fewer distributors will enhance each distributor's efforts in promoting and selling the products in

129. *Id.* at 76.
130. *Id.* at 78.

question, thereby increasing sales. Whatever the business reasons are for termination, they should be well documented with studies and reports over a period of months or longer.

Second, careful consideration should be given as to whether any element of pricing has entered the decision, such as the need to eliminate price-cutters or discounters. The presence of such a factor makes any termination most difficult in terms of defending against antitrust charges.

Third, if the distributor to be terminated is a price-cutter or discounter, exhaustive consideration must be given as to whether any salesman of the manufacturer or seller has threatened termination, either directly or by inference, if the distributor did not bring its prices in line. The difficulty of this task should not be underestimated, in view of the fact that salesmen and others who are directly in contact with distributors are not likely to make a full disclosure, either out of ignorance as to what constitutes a threat in legal terms or out of fear of reprisal from their employer if it became apparent that they had acted improperly. Trained outside antitrust counsel should be consulted and directed to interrogate sales personnel concerning any possible threats because of the seriousness of such evidence, if it exists, in blocking a termination.

Fourth, a careful investigation must be made to determine whether some other distributor has requested the termination so that it can gain an exclusive or a larger share of the market. In this regard, no communications should be made with the favored distributor until after notice of termination has been made. The natural inclination is to check with the favored distributor to determine if it is interested or in a position to take on greater volume or exclusive distribution. However, such communication can raise the inference that the termination was pursuant to an agreement between the manufacturer and the favored distributor and not as a result of unilateral action of the manufacturer.

Tie-In Arrangements

34. Tie-in agreements

Tie-in requirements are illegal *per se* under Section 1 of the Sherman Act. A tie-in exists when the seller declines to sell a desired product unless the buyer is also willing to purchase an additional product or products that are not as desirable or can be purchased from others at a lower price. The earlier tie-in cases involved patent owners or copyright owners who refused to sell or lease their patented or copyrighted products unless other products were also purchased.

In *International Business Machines Corporation* v. *United States*,[131] a case brought under Section 3 of the Clayton Act,[132] IBM leased its tabulating and computer machines upon the condition that the tabulating cards used in the machines would be purchased only from IBM. The reason given for this requirement was to ensure satisfactory performance of the machines, which could use only cards conforming to precise specifications as to size and thickness, and which were free from defects due to slime or carbon spots that cause unintended electrical contacts and consequent inaccurate results. The cards manufactured by IBM were electrically tested for such defects. A provision in the lease agreement provided that the lease would terminate if the lessee used a card not manufactured by IBM. The Court noted that approximately one third of IBM's annual income (in 1935) of $9,710,389 was derived from the sale of these cards.

The Court found the tie-in to be illegal on the ground that others were quite capable of manufacturing cards suitable for use in IBM's machines. The Court stated that IBM

> is not prevented from proclaiming the virtues of its own cards or warning against the danger of using, in its machines, cards which do not conform to the necessary specifications, or even from making its leases conditional upon the use of cards which conform to them. For aught that appears such measures would protect its good will, without the creation of monopoly or resort to the suppression of competition.[133]

International Salt Co. entered a similar lease arrangement with customers. International Salt was, at the time, the nation's largest producer of salt for industrial uses and in this connection owned patents on two machines used in the commercial utilization of salt. Under its lease agreements International Salt required lessees to purchase from it all unpatented salt and salt tablets consumed in the leased machines. The agreements also provided that if a competitor

131. 298 U.S. 131 (1936).
132. The same action could have been brought under Section 1 of the Sherman Act.
133. 298 U.S. at 139–40.

should offer salt at a lower price, the lessee could purchase such salt unless International Salt furnished the salt at an equal price.

Suit was brought by the government, *International Salt Co., Inc. v. United States,*[134] and the Supreme Court ruled that the tie-in arrangement was *per se* illegal as violative of Section 1 of the Sherman Act. The Court noted that the patents in question conferred only the right to restrain others from making, vending, or using the patented machines, but it did not confer the right to restrain use of, or trade in, unpatented salt. The Court also noted that the pricing provision, which permitted International Salt Co. to match a lower competitive price, did not cure the illegality of the tie-in because a competitor would have to undercut its price to have any hope of capturing the market, while International Salt could hold that market by merely meeting competition.

International Salt argued that since it remained under an obligation to repair and maintain the machines, it was reasonable to confine their use to its own salt because its high quality assured satisfactory functioning and lower maintenance costs. The Court answered this argument, stating that "a lessor may impose on a lessee reasonable restrictions designed in good faith to minimize maintenance burdens and to assure satisfactory operation ... [and] the lessee might be required to use only salt meeting such a specification of quality."[135] However, there was no showing by International Salt that others could not produce an equivalent salt or that its machines were "allergic to salt of equal quality produced by anyone except International."[136]

A different type of tie-in plan was used in the movie and television industry. Following World War II major distributors of copyrighted motion picture feature films conditioned the license or sale to television stations of one or more feature films upon the acceptance by the station of a package or "block of films" containing one or more unwanted or inferior films. In *United States v. Loew's, Inc.,*[137] the Supreme Court held that tying unwanted films to the desired feature films constituted a *per se* violation. The Court noted that tying arrangements

134. 332 U.S. 392 (1947).
135. *Id.* at 397–98.
136. *Id.* at 398.
137. 371 U.S. 38 (1962).

are an object to antitrust concern for two reasons—they may force buyers into giving up the purchase of substitutes for the tied product . . . and they may destroy the free access of competing suppliers of the tied product to the consuming market.[138]

As demonstrated by the *IBM, International Salt,* and *Loew's* decisions, the businessman must be alert to potential tie-in restrictions. Promotional programs to spur sales must be carefully scrutinized if they involve two or more products offered in a package or if they involve a desired or unique product in conjunction with one or more less desirable products. Tie-ins under Section 1 of the Sherman Act are not limited to products alone, but may encompass services as well. Thus, if a product is sold or leased on the condition that the seller be given exclusive rights to provide repair services, a tie-in restriction may be demonstrated.

35. Tie-in arrangements and franchising

In the last fifteen years, franchising has had a dramatic impact on business and the economy in general. The McDonalds, Burger Kings, Baskin-Robbins, Kentucky Fried Chickens, Arbys, Holiday Inns, Midases are as much a part of the American way of life as Chevrolet cars, Sears and Roebuck, and State Farm Insurance. The emergence of franchising brought with it a further tightening of the Sherman Act, aimed at protecting the public from the excesses of aggressive franchising programs. As franchising first emerged, a franchisee was required to purchase a complete package from the franchiser that included the complete store with all its equipment, furnishings, signs, utensils, etc., a sublease from the franchiser, as well as an agreement to purchase all food and supplies from the franchiser. Use of the trade name or franchise became the vehicle for franchisers to obtain substantial profits in many other areas that in themselves were not unique and were readily available in the marketplace at lower prices. By 1969, the courts stepped in and declared that if a franchiser licensed its trademark or franchised others to operate under its name, it could not require the licensees or franchisees to purchase numerous

138. *Id.* at 44–45.

other items from it which were readily available in the open market from others. The courts held that the trademark or franchise is the tying or desired product, and all other products including the equipment, lease, utensils, food items, etc. are tied products.

The first case of significance in the franchise area was *Siegel* v. *Chicken Delight, Inc.*[139] There, the defendant granted a royalty-free franchise to operate under the Chicken Delight trademark and trade name upon the condition that the franchisee purchase a specified number of cookers and fryers and purchase certain packaging supplies and mixes exclusively from Chicken Delight. The prices for these purchases were higher than comparable products sold by competing suppliers. The court noted that there were three requirements to establish an illegal tie-in: first, that there were two distinct items, a tying product and a tied product; second, that the tying product possessed sufficient economic power to compel the franchisee to purchase the tied products; and third, that interstate commerce must be affected, that is, the arrangement must have some effect on the flow of goods between the states.

On the first issue, Chicken Delight argued that its trademark and franchise licenses were not separate and distinct from the packaging, mixes, and equipment, and it asserted they were all essential components of the franchise system. It further argued that to "treat the combined sale of all these items as a tie-in for antitrust purposes . . . would be like applying the antitrust rules to the sale of a car with its tires or a left shoe with the right." The court rejected this argument, stating that whether an aggregation of separable items should be considered as one product or several for tie-in purposes depends upon whether such items are normally sold as a unit in the marketplace. The court concluded that the trademark was a separable item from the packaging, mixes, and equipment, for it reflected the goodwill and quality standards of the enterprise it identified and did not attach to the multitude of separate articles used in the operation of the licensed system or in the production of its end product.

On the second issue the court noted that the trademark in itself had sufficient economic power to compel franchises to accept the tied products, for unless franchisees agreed to Chicken Delight's terms, they could not operate under the Chicken Delight name with-

139. 448 F.2d 43, *cert. denied* 405 U.S. 955 (1972).

out the threat of a trademark infringement action. Thus, the economic power inherent in a franchise case is the fact that a franchisee either accepts the tie-in restrictions or it is foreclosed from using the name.

The third issue of interstate commerce was met, inasmuch as the equipment, packaging, and mixes were shipped in interstate commerce between the states. Chicken Delight also argued that it had to impose the tie-ins over the cookers and mixes in order to maintain quality control. However, the court rejected this defense on the ground that protection of goodwill fails when specifications as to the type and quality of product can be given or licensed to others to produce:

> The only situation, indeed, in which the protection of good will may necessitate the use of tying clauses is where specifications for a substitute would be so detailed that they could not practicably be supplied.[140]

The court thus concluded that a *per se* violation had occurred.

In *Krehl* v. *Baskin-Robbins Ice Cream Co.,*[141] twenty out of some 1,700 Baskin-Robbins ice cream stores sued Baskin-Robbins and nine ice cream companies licensed by Baskin-Robbins to manufacture its ice cream for franchise ice cream shops in assigned territories. Pursuant to the franchise agreements each franchisee purchased an entire store fully equipped with Baskin-Robbins equipment, furnishings, decorations, signs, etc., and was required to execute a sublease with Baskin-Robbins for use of the store premises. If the franchisee owned the property on which the store was to be constructed, he was required to grant a lease to Baskin-Robbins and take a sublease back. Additionally, each franchisee agreed to purchase his ice cream products only from the manufacturer assigned to the territory in which the franchisee was located. Plaintiffs pleaded that the trademark and franchise were the tying products and the tied products were the (1) ice cream products, (2) store leases, (3) equipment package, (4) supplies, and (5) advertising.

The court, in certifying a class action made up of all Baskin-Robbins stores, held that if the tying arrangement is found in the franchise agreement itself, it is presumed that franchisees were required

140. *Id.* at 51.
141. 78 F.R.D. 108 (C.D.Cal. 1978).

to purchase the tied products as a condition to obtaining the franchise. In the case of the ice cream products, the franchise agreement required the store owner to purchase his ice cream products from the manufacturer assigned to his territory. As to the leases and equipment, which were not mentioned as items that had to be purchased from Baskin-Robbins or a manufacturer, the court looked to the actual practices engaged in by the defendants and found that 100 percent of the franchisees purchased the completed store and took subleases from Baskin-Robbins. This, the court concluded, was conclusive evidence that franchisees were coerced into accepting these items as a condition to obtaining a Baskin-Robbins franchise. As to the supplies and advertising the court did not find that franchisees were required to purchase them from Baskin-Robbins or a source designated by it. Therefore, there was no tie-in.

The plaintiff franchisee in *Martino* v. *McDonald's System, Inc.,*[142] alleged that McDonald's required a prospective franchisee, as a condition to obtaining a McDonald's franchise, to lease or sublease from McDonald's the property underlying the restaurant. He also alleged that McDonald's required franchisees to purchase Coca-Cola as a condition of obtaining a franchise. McDonald's is a franchiser of over 4,000 fast-food drive-in restaurants, 25 percent of which are owned outright by McDonald's. In almost all cases McDonald's finds an appropriate site for a restaurant and purchases the property or takes a prime lease. It then supervises the planning and construction of the restaurant and subleases the property to the franchisees.

Plaintiff alleged that McDonald's would not license a franchise unless the franchisee also leased the property underlying the restaurant from it. This requirement forced franchisees to pay a higher rental than they would have had to pay in the absence of such a requirement. On the Coca-Cola tie-in, plaintiff argued that the franchise agreement required them to purchase only those supplies and foodstuffs that met McDonald's specifications and quality standards, and Coca-Cola was the only cola that McDonald's approved. On a motion to certify a class of McDonald's franchisees, the court agreed with plaintiff that a tie-in violation existed.

Perma Life Mufflers, Inc. v. *International Parts Corp.,*[143] is

---

142. 1979—1 Trade Cases ¶62,414 (N.D.Ill. 1979).
143. 392 U.S. 134 (1968).

another example of a franchising tie-in situation. There, the manufacturer of "Midas Mufflers" initiated, in 1955, a plan of promoting the sale of mufflers through extensive advertising and establishing a nationwide chain of franchised dealers. Each prospective dealer, in entering a franchise agreement, agreed to purchase all his mufflers and exhaust system parts from Midas, to honor the Midas guarantee on mufflers sold by any dealer, and to sell mufflers at resale prices fixed by Midas. The franchisee was also required to refrain from dealing with any of Midas' competitors. In exchange Midas gave the dealer permission to use the registered trademark "Midas" and the service mark "Midas Muffler Shops," and it promised to underwrite the cost of the muffler guarantee.

Plaintiffs were franchised Midas dealers and sued because of the illegal provisions in the contract, including those terms that (1) barred them from purchasing from other sources of supply, (2) prevented them from selling outside the designated territory, (3) required them to purchase other products from Midas in addition to the Midas mufflers, and (4) required them to sell at fixed retail prices. The case therefore had several *per se* violations: territorial allocation, tie-in, price fixing, and exclusive dealings.

The trial court dismissed the action because plaintiffs willingly participated in the plan and therefore could not complain. The court noted that the plaintiffs had "enthusiastically sought to acquire a Midas franchise with full knowledge of these provisions ... [and] had all made enormous profits as Midas dealers, had eagerly sought to acquire additional franchises, and had voluntarily entered into additional franchise agreements, all while fully aware of the restrictions they now challenge."[144] The Supreme Court reversed and held that a *per se* violation existed, and plaintiffs' willing participation in the program did not bar them from suing:

> The plaintiff who reaps the reward of treble damages may be no less morally reprehensible than the defendant, but the law encourages his suit to further the overriding public policy in favor of competition.[145]

As noted in the above cases, exposure to tie-in violations in this complex area of franchising is very real. Any franchising operation

144. *Id.* at 138.
145. *Id.* at 139.

today must not only comply with the antitrust laws, but also the franchising laws of the various states, which require complete disclosure of potential tie-in interests of the franchiser. For this reason, careful consideration must be given by an attorney to both the antitrust laws and the various franchising laws before a business is ready to venture into the land of franchising. The numerous antitrust lawsuits brought against many major franchise operations in the United States attest to the vulnerability of such an endeavor.

36. Tie-in restrictions in other cases

Although the greatest numbers of tie-in cases have arisen in the patent-copyright-trademark (franchise) areas, there have been a number of other areas where tie-in violations have been found to exist. The leading case in this category is *Northern Pacific Railway Company* v. *United States.*[146] In 1864 and 1870 Congress granted the predecessor of the Northern Pacific Railway approximately forty million acres of land in several Northwestern states and territories to facilitate its construction of a railroad line from Lake Superior to Puget Sound. In general terms, this grant consisted of every alternate section of land in a belt twenty miles wide on each side of the track through states and forty miles wide through territories. The granted lands were of various kinds; some contained great stands of timber, some iron ore or other valuable mineral deposits, some oil and natural gas, while still other sections were useful for agriculture, grazing, or industrial purposes.

By 1944 the railroad had sold about 37,000,000 acres of its holdings, but had reserved mineral rights in 6,500,000 acres. In a large number of these sales contracts and lease agreements, the railroad had inserted a "preferential routing" clause that compelled the grantee or lessee to ship over its lines all commodities produced or manufactured on the land, provided that its rates (and in some instances its service) were equal to those of competing carriers. The Supreme Court ruled that these "preferential routing" clauses constituted an illegal tie-in in violation of Section 1 of the Sherman Act. The Court first defined a tying arrangement as follows:

> For our purposes a tying arrangement may be defined as an agreement by a party to sell one product but only on the condition that the buyer

146. 356 U.S. 1 (1958).

also purchase a different (or tied) product, or at least agrees that he will not purchase that product from any other supplier. Where such conditions are successfully exacted competition on the merits with respect to the tied product is inevitably curbed. Indeed "tying agreements serve hardly any purpose beyond the suppression of competition. . . ." They deny competitors free access to the market for the tied product, not because the party imposing the tying requirements has a better product or a lower price but because of his power or leverage in another market. At the same time buyers are forced to forego their free choice between competing products. For these reasons "tying agreements fare harshly under the laws forbidding restraints of trade."[147]

The Court further noted that tying arrangements are *per se* illegal whenever a party has sufficient economic power with respect to the tying product to appreciably restrain free competition in the market for the tied product and a not insubstantial amount of interstate commerce is involved. In the patent, copyright, and trademark areas the economic power is presumed because the tying product is the patent, the copyright, or trademark that can be obtained pursuant to law from only the owner. Thus, if one wishes to sell or use such a product, the patent, copyright, or trademark owner has the economic power to impose the tied product upon the purchaser. In the *Northern Pacific* case economic power was not presumed, and the Court examined the evidence. The Court concluded that economic power was demonstrated "by virtue of [Northern Pacific's] extensive landholdings which it used as leverage to induce large numbers of purchasers and lessees to give it preference, to the exclusion of its competitors, in carrying goods or produce from the land transferred to them."[148]

A second important case in this area is *Fortner Enterprises, Inc. v. United States Steel Corp.*,[149] where the plaintiff charged that United States Steel and its wholly owned subsidiary, U.S. Steel Homes Credit, conspired to effectuate an illegal tying arrangement. The tying arrangement was that as a condition of obtaining a loan from U.S. Steel Homes Credit for the purchase and development of certain land in the Louisville, Kentucky, area a borrower had to agree to erect prefabricated houses manufactured by U.S. Steel on each of the lots purchased with the loan proceeds. Plaintiff claimed

147. *Id.* at 5–6.
148. *Id.* at 7.
149. 394 U.S. 495 (1969).

that the prefabricated materials supplied by U.S. Steel were at unreasonably high prices. Thus, the tying product was the loan of money and the tied products were the prefabricated houses. Defendants argued that there was no economic power in the loan of money on favorable terms that would force the borrower to accept the purchase of the tied products. In other words, there were any number of other sources of money other than U.S. Steel Home Credit. However, the Supreme Court stated that in order to demonstrate market power it is unnecessary to prove monopoly power, only that the defendant has the power to raise prices in the tied product or impose other burdensome terms with respect "to any appreciable number of buyers within the market."[150]

Defendants also argued that the granting of credit to purchase prefabricated houses does not constitute an illegal tie-in because "every sale on credit in effect involves a tie." They argued that offering favorable credit terms is simply a form of price competition equivalent to offering a comparable reduction in the cash price of the tied product. The Court rejected this argument since the granting of credit was made by one corporation and the sale of the tied products by another.

After the case was tried, the Supreme Court considered the case a second time and this time, on the facts presented, found there was no illegal tie-in.[151] Plaintiffs argued that because U.S. Steel Homes Credit gave 100-percent loans, a "unique" product was created, which in itself, because of this uniqueness, evidenced economic power to force purchases of the prefabricated houses. The Court observed that "[u]niqueness confers economic power only when other competitors are in some way prevented from offering the distinctive product themselves." Such barriers may be legal when the product is patented or copyrighted. When credit terms are unique "because the seller is willing to accept a lesser profit—or to incur greater risks— than its competitors, that kind of uniqueness will not give rise to any inference of economic power in the credit market." The Court concluded:

> The usual credit bargain offered to Fortner proves nothing more than a willingness to provide cheap financing in order to sell expensive

150. *Id.* at 504.
151. United States Steel Corp. v. Fortner Enterprises, Inc., 429 U.S. 610 (1977).

houses. Without any evidence that Credit Corp. had some cost advantage over its competitors—or could offer a form of financing that was significantly differentiated from that which other lenders could offer if they so elected—the unique character of its financing does not support the conclusion that petitioners [U.S. Steel] had the kind of economic power which Fortner had the burden of proving in order to prevail in this litigation.[152]

Texaco ran into an entirely different type of problem in the case of *Federal Trade Commission* v. *Texaco, Inc.*[153] Nearly 40 percent of the Texaco dealers in the late 1960s leased their stations from Texaco. These dealers typically held a one-year lease that was subject to termination at the end of any year on a ten-day notice. At any time during the year, Texaco could terminate a lease without advance notice "if in Texaco's judgment any of the 'house-keeping' provisions of the lease, relating to the use and appearance of the station, are not fulfilled." The contract under which Texaco dealers received their vital supply of gasoline and other petroleum products also ran from year to year and were terminable on a thirty-day notice.

Texaco entered a contract with B.F. Goodrich Company that provided that the latter would pay to Texaco a commission of 10 percent on all purchases of Goodrich tires, batteries, and accessories (TBA) by Texaco service station dealers. In return Texaco agreed to promote the sale of Goodrich products to Texaco dealers. During the five-year period 1952 to 1956, $245,000,000 of Goodrich and Firestone products sponsored by Texaco were purchased by dealers, for which Texaco received about $22,000,000 in commissions.

Because Texaco salesmen constantly reminded the dealers to purchase Goodrich products—although Texaco did not threaten termination of leases if dealers did not cooperate with the program as other oil companies had done—combined with the short-term leases pursuant to which dealers operated, the Court was convinced that the system was inherently coercive and thus illegal:

> The sales commission system for marketing TBA is inherently coercive. A service station dealer whose very livelihood depends upon the continuing good favor of a major oil company is constantly aware of the oil company's desire that he stock and sell the recommended brand

152. *Id*. at 622.
153. 393 U.S. 223 (1968).

of TBA. Through the constant reminder of the Texaco salesman, through demonstration projects and promotional materials, through all of the dealer's contacts with Texaco, he learns the lesson that Texaco wants him to purchase for his station the brand of TBA which pays Texaco 10 percent on every item the dealer buys. With the dealer's supply of gasoline, his lease on his station, and his Texaco identification subject to continuing review, we think it flies in the face of common sense to say, as Texaco asserts, that the dealer is "perfectly free" to reject Texaco's chosen brand of TBA. Equally applicable here is this Court's judgment in *Atlantic* [*Atlantic Refining Co.* v. *Federal Trade Commission*[154]] that "It is difficult to escape the conclusion that there would be little profit in paying substantial commissions for oil companies were it not for their ability to exert power over their wholesalers and dealers." 381 U.S., at 376[155]

37. Reciprocal arrangements

A reciprocal contract is a form of tying arrangement. It provides that the seller of a product, as a condition of the sale, will agree to purchase a second product back from the original purchaser. Thus, B purchases a product from A on the condition that A will purchase a second product from B or its subsidiary. In other words, purchasing power is used to generate sales in a second product. Reciprocity may take several forms, direct or subtle. It may be systematic and pursuant to a definite understanding or agreement, it may be the result of coercion, or it may be purely unilateral or voluntary.

In *United States* v. *General Dynamics Corp.,*[156] General Dynamics, a diversified industrial enterprise with net sales in excess of $1.5 billion, acquired Liquid Carbonic Corporation, a producer of gaseous, liquid, and solid carbon dioxide, with net sales in excess of $35 million, more than $18 million of which was attributable to the sale of carbon dioxide. General Dynamics purchased from some 80,000 suppliers approximately $500 million annually. Liquid Carbonic accounted for between 35 and 40 percent of total sales in the domestic carbon dioxide market, and it stood first in the industry. After the merger a special program was initiated whereby a list was compiled of major suppliers of General Dynamics, which also purchased prod-

154. 381 U.S. 357 (1964).
155. 393 U.S. at 229.
156. 1966 Trade Cas. ¶71,870 (S.D.N.Y. 1966).

ucts sold by Liquid Carbonic. Included in the list were the dollar sales by each supplier to General Dynamics. General Dynamics executives then contacted "target companies" to persuade them to purchase from Liquid Carbonic, using the "leverage" of General Dynamics enormous purchasing power.

The court held that agreements between General Dynamics and six named companies "were predicated on reciprocity considerations" and therefore illegal under Section 1 of the Sherman Act. As to two of the companies—Standard Oil of California and Shell Oil— the court found that purchases from Liquid Carbonic were obtained by the defendants' use of reciprocity, and further found that total sales of those two companies attributable to the use of reciprocity amounted to $177,225. The court described the agreement with Standard Oil of California as a mutual patronage arrangement, i.e., General Dynamics and Standard Oil agreed to buy from each other in return for increased sales. The court found that Section 1 of the Sherman Act was violated on the theory that the reciprocal arrangement was like a tie-in arrangement:

> The legality of the use of reciprocity under Sherman 1 is a question of first impression. . . .
>
> While the general areas of inquiry are unique, the court is not without guidelines. Those who have had occasion to consider the use of reciprocity as an anti-competitive practice have invariably analogized it to "tying-in" agreements. . . . The court finds, for reasons to be discussed shortly, that the analogy is sound. It therefore adopts, for purposes of this case, the standards of decision delineated by the Supreme Court in those cases.[157]

38. Exclusive dealing agreements

Another type of business arrangement that has been subjected to antitrust scrutiny is the exclusive dealing arrangement. Akin to the tie-in arrangement, the exclusive dealing arrangement normally requires the buyer to purchase exclusively from one supplier for a significant period of time. As a result, the supplier's competitors are foreclosed from selling to the buyer for the period of time involved. Such agreements may also forbid the buyer from purchasing from the seller's competitors.

157. *Ibid.*

Exclusive dealing arrangements have fared better under the antitrust laws than tying arrangements because, in certain circumstances, they may be procompetitive in effect rather than motivated by anticompetitive desires on the part of the seller. The standard of illegality has been the "rule of reason" rather than the *per se* rule; thus, some analysis of the anticompetitive effects of the exclusive dealing arrangement is required.

In *Standard Oil Co. of California* v. *United States,*[158] the Supreme Court affirmed a lower court decree enjoining Standard Oil from entering exclusive supply contracts with independent station operators requiring the latter to purchase all their supplies of gasoline and automobile accessories from Standard Oil. In finding a violation of Section 3 of the Clayton Act,[159] the Court assumed that the exclusive dealing agreements did not improve Standard Oil's competitive position, that their duration was not excessive, and that Standard Oil did not dominate the market. The Court found, however, that Standard Oil was a major competitor when the requirements contract system was adopted and that its position might have deteriorated but for adoption of the system. The Court refused to engage in an economic investigation of the impact the system had on the market:

> To insist upon such an investigation would be to stultify the force of Congress' declaration that requirements contracts are to be prohibited wherever their effect "may be" to substantially lessen competition. If in fact it is economically desirable for service stations to confine themselves to the sale of the petroleum products of a single supplier, they will continue to do so though not bound by contract, and if in fact it is important to retail dealers to assure the supply of their requirements by obtaining the commitment of a single supplier to fulfill them, competition for their patronage should enable them to insist upon such an arrangement without binding them to refrain from looking elsewhere.[160]

---

158. 337 U.S 293 (1949).

159. In view of the fact that the Court found Standard Oil to be in violation of Section 3 of the Clayton Act it did not decide if there was also a violation of Section 1 of the Sherman Act, which also had been charged.

160. 337 U.S. at 313–14. The dissent argued that the effect of the majority opinion was to place exclusive dealing contracts in the *per se* category. The dissent argued that "[i]t does not seem to me inherently to lessen this real competition when an oil company tries to establish superior service by providing the consumer with a responsible dealer from which the public can purchase adequate and timely supplies of oil, gasoline, and car accessories of some known and reliable standard of quality." *Id.* at 323.

A second case of some note, *Federal Trade Commission* v. *Brown Shoe Co.,*[161] although decided under Section 5 of the Federal Trade Commission Act, sheds further light on that which is and is not permissible conduct with relation to exclusive sales arrangements. In that case the defendant Brown Shoe initiated a Brown Franchise Stores' Program pursuant to which it sold shoes to some 650 retail stores. The plan provided that store operators who restricted their purchases of shoes for resale to the Brown Shoe lines were to be given special treatment and valuable benefits not provided to customers declining to enter the plan. Such special treatment and valuable benefits included architectural store plans, costly merchandising records, services of a Brown Shoe field representative, and a right to participate in group insurance at lower rates than otherwise available. In finding such a plan illegal the Supreme Court stated that the program, which used additional services and benefits to induce purchasers to handle the Brown Shoe line exclusively, conflicted "with the central policy of both §1 of the Sherman Act and §3 of the Clayton Act against contracts which take away freedom of purchasers to buy in the open market."[162] Thus, the exclusive dealing arrangement was found to be illegal.

The Rule of Reason

39. The rule of reason

In addition to the *per se* violation of Section 1 of the Sherman Act outlined above, consideration must be given to violations to which the "rule of reason" has been applied. If a case involves conduct that does not fit into one of the four *per se* categories,[163] then a violation of Section 1 of the Sherman Act can occur only if the restraint is unreasonable. This requires some market analysis and permits defendants to offer evidence that the conduct was procompetitive rather than anticompetitive, an analysis not permitted in the *per se* categories.

---

161. 384 U.S. 316 (1966).

162. *Id.* at 321.

163. The four *per se* categories of illegality are: price fixing, territorial allocation (horizontal), group boycotts, and tie-in arrangements.

To understand how the rule of reason standard is applied, consideration must be given to several of the earlier cases. In *Board of Trade of the City of Chicago* v. *United States,*[164] the Chicago Board of Trade, which is the leading commodity exchange for the trading of grain, promulgated a rule that members were forbidden to purchase grain after the close of business at any price other than the closing bid at the end of the business day. This price then remained in effect until the commencement of business the next day. The purpose of this rule was allegedly salutary in that it limited hours of trading, reduced the market power of the few warehousemen who gained an advantage by trading at night, and rendered the daytime market more perfect.

The Supreme Court, in holding that the rule was not an unreasonable restraint of trade, first noted that the restriction imposed by the rule was upon the *period* of price making rather than prices. It did not restrict business during the after-hours. Second, the rule applied only to a small part of the grain shipped to Chicago each day, called "to arrive" grain, which was grain already in shipment. The bulk of the grain sold was sold during business hours at any price. The Court set forth the rule of reason test as follows:

> [T]he legality of an agreement or regulation cannot be determined by so simple a test, as whether it restrains competition. Every agreement concerning trade, every regulation of trade, restrains. To bind, to restrain, is of their very essence. The true test of legality is whether the restraint imposed is such as merely regulates and perhaps thereby promotes competition or whether it is such as may suppress or even destroy competition. To determine that question the court must ordinarily consider the facts peculiar to the business to which the restraint is applied; its condition before and after the restraint was imposed; the nature of the restraint and its effect, actual or probable. The history of the restraint, the evil believed to exist, the reason for adopting the particular remedy, the purpose or end sought to be attained, are all relevant facts. This is not because a good intention will save an otherwise objectionable regulation or the reverse; but because knowledge of intent may help the court to interpret facts and predict consequences.[165]

164. 246 U.S. 231 (1918).
165. 246 U.S. at 238.

A second case, *Appalachian Coals, Inc.* v. *United States*,[166] further illustrates a rule of reason application to an alleged anticompetitive restraint. In the late 1920s and early 1930s excess capacity was chronic in the bituminous coal mining industry. Earnings were low or nonexistent, bankruptcy was common, and the industry faced serious competition from other sources of fuel energy. Faced with these conditions, 137 coal producers, accounting for 12 percent of national production and between 54 percent and 75 percent of regional production (depending on how the region was defined), joined together and organized an exclusive selling agent, Appalachian Coals. The selling agent was directed to sell the members' coal at "the best prices attainable and, if all cannot be sold, to apportion orders upon a stated basis...." The government challenged the arrangement on the ground that it eliminated competition among the members of the group and gave the selling agency power to affect or substantially control market prices.

The Supreme Court found the arrangement reasonable in light of the "deplorable economic conditions in the industry." The Court stated that in the application of the standard of reasonableness "[r]ealities must dominate the judgment. The mere fact that parties to an agreement eliminate competition among themselves is not enough to condemn it." While implying that if either purpose or effect was to fix market prices, the arrangement would be illegal, the Court accepted defendants' statements that their intent was not to do this. In any event the Court noted that a selling agent controlling only 12 percent of the market nationally would have little impact on prices, and therefore the defendants were not in a position to fix prices. The Court further stated:

> A cooperative enterprise, otherwise free from objection, which carries with it no monopolistic menace, is not to be condemned as an undue restraint merely because it may effect a change in market conditions, where the change would be in mitigation of recognized evils and would not impair, but rather foster, fair competitive opportunities.... The fact that the correction of abuses may tend to stabilize a business, or to produce fairer price levels, does not mean that the abuses should go uncorrected or that cooperative endeavor to correct them necessarily constitutes an unreasonable restraint of trade.[167]

166. 288 U.S. 344 (1933).
167. *Id.* at 373–374.

The rule of reason analysis has been applied in numerous cases, too many to analyze or even categorize. In many of the cases the primary task of the court was to determine whether the conduct in question came within a *per se* category or whether the rule of reason applied. For example, in *Broadcast Music, Inc.* v. *Columbia Broadcasting Systems, Inc.,*[168] CBS sued the American Society of Composers, Authors and Publishers (ASCAP) and Broadcast Music, Inc. (BMI), charging that the blanket licenses those two organizations issued, which permitted a licensee to perform any musical composition of any member of the respective organizations, constituted, among other things, price fixing, a *per se* violation. ASCAP was organized in 1914 by Victor Herbert and a handful of other composers to negotiate with all the persons desiring to perform their music for profit because they were unable to do so and to police unauthorized uses. ASCAP developed a blanket license whereby a performer could take a license covering the copyrighted works of all members for a fee, which was a percentage of total revenues or a flat dollar amount. BMI was organized in 1939 and had the same type of blanket license.[169]

After an eight-week trial, the district court ruled in favor of ASCAP and BMI and dismissed the complaint. The court of appeals reversed, holding that the pooling of copyrighted works by the members of the two organizations and the granting of blanket licenses at a fixed fee constituted price fixing, a *per se* violation. The Supreme Court reversed, holding that the pooling of copyrighted works and the granting of blanket license fees was not price fixing as such. To determine whether a practice came within the *per se* rule, it was necessary, the Court stated, to see "whether the practice facially appears to be one that would always or almost always tend to restrict competition and decrease output, and in what portion of the market, or instead one designed to 'increase economic efficiency and render markets more rather than less competitive.'"[170]

In applying the above test, the Court concluded that having a middleman (ASCAP and BMI) with blanket licensing capabilities was

168. 99 S.Ct. 1551 (1979).

169. In the late 1970s ASCAP had 22,000 members and BMI had 10,000 publishing companies as well as 20,000 authors and composers.

170. 99 S.Ct. at 1562.

an absolute necessity for the composers because thousands of individual negotiations were a virtual impossibility. The costs inherent in establishing individual fees, executing separate licenses and policing individual works would have been prohibitive if not impossible. Thus, the blanket license approach "reduces costs absolutely" because they are sold "only a few, instead of thousands, of times." Having determined that the case did not come within the *per se* test, the Court sent the case back to the court of appeals to determine if this was an illegal restraint of trade under the rule of reason.

Gough v. *Rossmoor Corp.*[171] also illustrates the problem courts have in determining whether a particular course of conduct fits within the *per se* category. There, a parent corporation, a builder and developer of a cooperative housing development, and its wholly owned subsidiary, a carpet and drapery concern, were alleged to have conspired to foreclose the plaintiff, a furniture and carpet store, from advertising in a community newspaper, which was controlled by the defendants and which was sold in the cooperative housing development. Plaintiff alleged that the conspiracy constituted a concerted refusal to deal, a *per se* violation of the Sherman Act, the intent and purpose of which was to eliminate plaintiff as a competitor of the subsidiary corporation.

The court analyzed the question of whether the restraint in question fit a *per se* category and concluded that it did not. First, it noted that the conspiracy was a vertical arrangement between a parent corporation and its subsidiary rather than a horizontal arrangement between competitors. Next, it concluded that only horizontal refusals to deal fell within the *per se* category, and because plaintiff failed to offer proof required in a rule of reason case, the complaint was ordered dismissed.

A third case, brought by the Federal Trade Commission, *In the Matter of The Coca-Cola Co.,*[172] illustrates a case in which the commission, after ruling that a *per se* violation did not exist, tried the case pursuant to the rule of reason standard and found a violation. In that case, Coca-Cola licensed various bottlers throughout the United States to produce Coca-Cola and other trademarked soft drinks, giv-

171. 585 F.2d 381 (9th Cir. 1978), *cert. denied*, 99 S. Ct. 1280 (1979).
172. Docket No. 8855, Federal Trade Commission, April 7, 1978, Trade Reg. Rep. (CCH) ¶21,509 (FTC, 1978).

ing each an exclusive territory in which to sell. In addition to licensing, Coca-Cola also sold the secret formula syrup to these bottlers. Subsequently, Coca-Cola bought out some of the bottlers and began operating itself as a bottler in potential competition with the other Coca-Cola bottlers.

The commission first determined that because the original allocation of the market was vertical, there was no *per se* violation of Section 1 of the Sherman Act.[173] However, in applying the rule of reason test the commission found that the allocation was illegal because it foreclosed geographical market expansion and eliminated potential competitors. It also deprived retailers and consumers of the opportunity to purchase soft drinks and allied products in bottles and cans in unrestricted markets at openly competitive prices. Thus, the restrictions in question were unreasonable, in violation of Section 1 of the Sherman Act.

The businessman as well as the lawyer may have great difficulty identifying a rule of reason violation. To prove a rule of reason case can be a massive undertaking because of the many complicated factors involved. For this reason, the total emphasis of this chapter has been on *per se* violations, which can readily be identified by the businessman, rather than rule of reason violations. It is safe to say that it is unlikely that the government will ever seek an indictment for a rule of reason violation, and the success factor in civil litigation brought by both the government and private individuals (treble damage actions) has been rather modest.

---

173. As noted *supra,* only territorial allocations that are horizontal in nature, that is, those entered into between competitors are *per se* violations of the law. This includes both purely horizontal allocations at the manufacturing or primary level as well as dual distributing allocations at the distributor or secondary level when the manufacturer is also acting as a distributor.

Chapter Four

Violations of Section 2
of the Sherman Act

Unlike *per se* violations of Section 1 of the Sherman Act, Section 2 is a highly complex area of the law, requiring complicated analyses of economic data and market considerations. For this reason the layman can accomplish far less in acquainting himself with this area of the Sherman Act in an effort to avoid potential violations. Thus, this chapter has been limited to a general evaluation of what constitutes monopolization, attempts to monopolize, and conspiracies to monopolize, Section 2 violations, with less emphasis on how such violations can be avoided.

While Section 1 prohibits contracts, combinations, or conspiracies in restraint of trade, Section 2 prohibits monopolization or attempts to monopolize and combinations or conspiracies to monopolize any part of the trade or commerce among the several states or with foreign nations.[1] The government has brought proportionately fewer criminal actions under Section 2 as compared to Section 1 of the Sherman Act, relying instead on civil or injunctive relief rather than

---

1. Section 2 of the Sherman Act, 15 U.S.C. §2 provides: "Every person who shall monopolize, or attempt to monopolize, or combine or conspire with any other person or persons, to monopolize any part of the trade or commerce among the several States, or with foreign nations, shall be deemed guilty of a felony."

fines and imprisonment to punish violators. This difference is probably due to the fact that fining a corporation that is guilty of monopolizing an industry does little to remove the monopoly, whereas an injunction or divestiture can have a rather conclusive correctional impact. Most of the criminal cases brought under Section 2 have also included a Section 1 charge.

Sections 1 and 2 of the Sherman Act are intended to complement each other in eliminating anticompetitive behavior in the market. Whereas Section 1 is directed at conspiratorial behavior, that is, concerted action between two or more persons or business entities, Section 2, additionally, covers the conduct of a *single* person or concern dominating a particular market. There can be, however, an overlap in the two sections so that conspiratorial behavior of two or more defendants may violate both sections. For example, a conspiracy to monopolize may have been accomplished through price-fixing agreements or territorial or customer allocations of the market, thus resulting in an indictment and conviction under both sections.

A major distinction between the two sections lies in the degree of proof required to establish the anticompetitive practices that each section prohibits. Because actual or potential monopoly power must be established in order to prove an actual monopoly or attempt to monopolize under Section 2, the quantum of proof required is greater than that required by a *per se* violation under Section 1. Section 1, on the other hand, requires that there be *concerted* activity of two or more parties to establish a violation, whereas Section 2 may cover the conduct of a single entity.

40. Monopolization

The offense of actual monopolization under Section 2 of the Sherman Act requires the existence of two elements. The person or persons charged with a violation must possess both (1) monopoly power in the "relevant market," coupled with (2) the intent and purpose to exercise that power. To establish the first element, monopoly power in a relevant market, two issues arise: (1) what is the relevant "product market," and what is the relevant "geographic market" in which the defendant asserts its power, and (2) does the defendant possess, in that market, the requisite percentage of power or control to constitute a monopoly.

Identifying the relevant product market raises a number of complex questions, which, for our purposes, can only be discussed in general terms. The leading case considering this question is *United States* v. *E. I. duPont DeNemours & Co.,*[2] in which duPont was charged with monopolizing, attempting to monopolize, and conspiring to monopolize the sale of cellophane, in violation of Section 2 of the Sherman Act. During the relevant period, duPont produced 75 percent of the cellophane sold in the United States. However, cellophane constituted only 20 percent of all flexible packaging material sold in the United States. The trial court, in entering judgment for duPont, found that the relevant *product* market was not just cellophane, but rather included all flexible packaging materials such as Saran, Pliofilm, foil, glassine, and polyethylene, which were used interchangeably with cellophane.

The Supreme Court affirmed the judgment for duPont, concluding that cellophane was just one of several products that were used interchangeably in the flexible packaging material market. Embarking upon an inquiry into whether the existence of substitutes for cellophane was such as to deprive duPont of the power to control prices and to exclude competition, the Court stated:

> When a product is controlled by one interest, without substitutes available in the market, there is monopoly power. Because most products have possible substitutes, we cannot ... give "that infinite range" to the definition of substitutes.[3] Nor is it a proper interpretation of the Sherman Act to require that products be fungible to be considered in the relevant market. ...
>
> But where there are market alternatives that buyers may readily use for their purposes, illegal monopoly does not exist merely because the product said to be monopolized differs from others.[4]

Although it recognized that cellophane differs in several respects from the other flexible packaging materials, the Court found that "despite cellophane's advantages, it has to meet competition from other materials in every one of its uses" and "a very considerable

2. 351 U.S. 377 (1956).

3. For example, while building materials could conceivably be considered substitutes for one another in the broad sense, differences in quality, characteristics, and prices make brick a product distinct from steel, wood, cement, or stone.

4. 351 U.S. at 394.

degree of functional interchangeability exists between these products.[5]

The Court next discussed what it considered to be cross-elasticity of demand, namely, "the responsiveness of the sales of one product to price changes of the other." In other words, "[i]f a slight decrease in the price of cellophane causes a considerable number of customers of other flexible wrappings to switch to cellophane, it would be an indication that a high cross-elasticity of demand exists between them; that the products compete in the same market."[6] Finding that the record supported such a conclusion, the Court stated:

> The "market" which one must study to determine when a producer has monopoly power will vary with the part of commerce under consideration. The tests are constant. That market is composed of products that have reasonable interchangeability for the purposes for which they are produced—price, use and qualities considered.[7]

In *International Boxing Club, Inc.* v. *United States,*[8] the Supreme Court found that there was lack of interchangeability between championship boxing matches and nonchampionship matches. Therefore, the relevant product market was limited to championship boxing matches, concerning which the defendants Norris and Wirtz, through their ownership and control of the Chicago Stadium, the Detroit Olympia Arena, the St. Louis Arena, as well as an interest in Madison Square Garden, had a monopoly. The facts of that case established that when Joe Lewis, then heavyweight boxing champion of the world, was ready to retire in January 1949, he entered an agreement with Norris and Wirtz to give up his title in exchange for exclusive promotion rights, including rights to radio, television, and movie revenues from each of the four leading contenders—Ezzard Charles, Joe Walcott, Lee Savold, and Gus Lesnevich. Upon receiving these exclusive contracts, Lewis assigned them to the defendant International Boxing Club, Illinois, which was organized by Norris and Wirtz for the purpose of promoting championship boxing. Louis

---

5. *Id.* at 399.
6. *Id.* at 400.
7. *Id.* at 404. See also *ABA Antitrust Law Developments,* p.49–50 (1975).
8. 358 U.S. 242 (1959).

was paid $150,000 cash plus an employment contract and a 20 percent stock interest in International Boxing Club.

The defendants then bought out other individuals and organizations having an interest in championship boxing, including the rights to Sugar Ray Robinson, the welterweight champion. Once the defendants had gained control of the key arenas, they gave a contender the choice of either signing with the defendants for exclusive handling or not fighting. Through this control, the defendants promoted thirty-six of forty-four championship fights (or 84 percent) during the period June 1949 to May 1953.

The Supreme Court had little difficulty concluding that championship boxing, over which the defendants obtained monopoly power, was a separate product from all other professional boxing, and thus a Section 2 violation had been established. The Court stated that "championship boxing is the 'cream' of the boxing business, and, as has been shown above, is a sufficiently separate part of the trade or commerce to constitute the relevant market for Sherman Act purposes."[9]

In addition to establishing the *product* market, the plaintiff must also establish the geographic market in which the alleged monopoly power is exercised. This may be the entire United States, some region thereof, or even a smaller area such as a single metropolitan area.[10] In *United States* v. *Grinnell Corporation,*[11] Grinnell owned three corporations engaged in the burglary and fire protection service industry. Each subsidiary offered a central station service whereby hazard-detecting devices installed on the protected premises automatically transmitted an electric signal to a central station. The central station then dispatched guards to the protected premises and directly notified the police or fire department. In the aggregate, the three subsidiaries controlled 87 percent of the protection service business in the United States. Defendants argued that the relevant market was local rather than the entire United States because an individual station

9. *Id.* at 252.
10. In United States v. Philadelphia Nat'l. Bank, 374 U.S. 321 (1963), the Court, in applying the same geographic market test in a Section 7 Clayton Act merger case, found that the relevant market for "commercial banking" was the Philadelphia metropolitan area, consisting of the City of Philadelphia and its three contiguous counties.
11. 384 U.S. 563 (1966).

provided services only within a radius of twenty-five miles. However, the Supreme Court disagreed, concluding that defendants' business operated on a national level and therefore an illegal monopoly was shown. The Court stated:

> But the record amply supports the conclusion that the business of providing such a service is operated on a national level. There is national planning. The agreements we have discussed covered activities in many States. The inspection, certification and rate-making is largely by national insurers. . . .
>
> As the District Court found, the relevant market for determining whether the defendants have monopoly power is not the several local areas which the individual stations serve, but the broader national market that reflects the reality of the way in which they built and conduct their business.[12]

A contrary result was reached in *Case-Swayne Co.* v. *Sunkist Growers, Inc.,*[13] where the court of appeals found the Southern California-Arizona area to be the relevant geographic market rather than the entire United States. In that case, the defendant Sunkist Growers was an association of citrus producers and had as its base 12,000 citrus growers in southern California and Arizona. Sunkist controlled 70 percent of the oranges grown in that area and 67 percent of the "product oranges" used for the production of orange juices. On a national basis Sunkist controlled only 6 to 7 percent of the total production of oranges, the primary competition coming from Florida. The plaintiff was engaged in the manufacture of canned orange juice and blends of orange juice with other fruit juices and purchased the oranges from the southern California-Arizona region. Plaintiff claimed that because of Sunkist's monopoly control over oranges used in the production of orange juice, it could not purchase oranges in the southern California-Arizona area at a low enough price to compete with producers of orange juice in Florida.

Defendant argued, and the trial court agreed, that the geographic market was the entire United States because the orange juice sold by plaintiff in California was in direct competition with Florida orange juice sold throughout the nation. The court of appeals reversed, holding that the *product* market was the oranges that plaintiffs and other

---

12. *Id.* at 575–76.
13. 369 F.2d 449 (9th Cir. 1966), *rev'd on other grounds,* 389 U.S. 384 (1967).

processors purchased and not the orange juice they produced and sold. Therefore, because Florida oranges were not shipped to California and sold to processors to make orange juice, the relevant geographic market for raw oranges was the southern California-Arizona area and not the entire United States. In that market, the court held, Sunkist was in a monopoly position because it was able to control prices.

Once a court has identified the relevant market, it must then be determined whether the defendant has a monopoly position in that market. Whether 70-percent or 75-percent control of the market is required is unclear, for the Supreme Court has been deliberately vague on the question. In *United States* v. *Aluminum Co. of America*,[14] the Second Circuit Court of Appeals stated that 90 percent of the market "is enough to constitute a monopoly; it is doubtful whether sixty or sixty-four percent would be enough; and certainly thirty-three percent is not." The Supreme Court, however, has qualified the above by stating the following, in *United States* v. *Columbia Steel Co.*:

> We do not undertake to prescribe any set of percentage figures by which to measure the reasonableness of a corporation's enlargement of its activities by the purchase of the assets of a competitor. The relative effect of percentage command of a market varies with the setting in which that factor is placed.[15]

One author, in analyzing the cases, suggests that if a firm controls 80 percent of the market, "there is a strong possibility that the court will hold that this percentage by itself constitutes the requisite degree of monopoly power for purposes of Section 2," but that if that control is less than 50 percent of the relevant market, monopoly power does not exist.[16]

In *International Boxing Club, Inc.* v. *United States*,[17] previously discussed, the Supreme Court had little difficulty in deciding that defendants' control of 81 percent of all championship fights constituted a monopoly, and in *United States* v. *Grinnell Corp.*,[18] also dis-

14. 148 F.2d 416 (2d Cir. 1945).
15. 334 U.S. 495, 527–28 (1948).
16. Von Kalinowski, *Antitrust Laws and Trade Regulation,* Vol. 1, §802 [3], p. 8–34.
17. 358 U.S. 242 (1959).
18. 384 U.S. 563 (1966).

cussed, that 87-percent control over all accredited central station alarm systems likewise demonstrated monopoly power. However, the mere existence of a monopoly or monopoly power does not mean that the defendant is guilty of the crime of monopolization under Section 2 of the Sherman Act. It is well settled that a monopoly is not in itself prohibited by the Sherman Act. The law has not reached the point that bigness is a crime.

Under Section 2, the crime of monopolizing is established only when monopoly power to control prices or to exclude competition is coupled with "the purpose or intent to exercise that power" for anticompetitive or exclusionary purposes.[19] The element of intent can be inferred from the general conduct of the defendant and does not have to be proven specifically. For example, intent can be where the defendant has obtained its monopoly position through unlawful or predatory means, or where the defendant, having obtained its monopoly position legally, has maintained that position or expanded it through unlawful, coercive, or unfair practices.

A leading example of the kinds of conduct that will render the acquisition of a monopoly unlawful is *United States* v. *Aluminum Co. of America.*[20] Alcoa is a corporation that was organized under the laws of Pennsylvania in 1888 under the name Pittsburgh Reduction Company. In 1889, Alcoa, through the acquisition of patents, secured a legal monopoly in the manufacture of pure aluminum which ran until the expiration of the last of these patents in 1909. Beginning in 1895, Alcoa secured an agreement from several power companies to provide power only to Alcoa and not to any other manufacturers of aluminum. It also entered cartel arrangements with foreign manufacturers of aluminum, which vastly limited their sales of aluminum in the United States. In some instances, Alcoa was involved in outright price fixing. In 1912, Alcoa entered a consent decree with the Department of Justice to cease the illegal conduct described above. From 1912 to 1938, Alcoa continued to expand and maintained its market share of over 80 percent for all years but 1921 and 1922, when its share dropped to 68 percent and 72 percent, respectively.

19. United States v. Griffith, 334 U.S. 100, 107 (1948).
20. 148 F.2d 416 (2d Cir. 1945).

The court recognized that the mere size of Alcoa was not in itself a violation of Section 2 of the Sherman Act, when it stated:

> Mere size . . . is not an offense against the Sherman Act unless magnified to the point at which it amounts to a monopoly. . . but size carries with it an opportunity for abuse that is not to be ignored when the opportunity is proved to have been utilized in the past. "Alcoa's" size was "magnified" to make it a "monopoly"; indeed, it has never been anything else; and its size, not only offered it an "opportunity for abuse," but it "utilized" its size for "abuse," as can be easily shown.[21]

The court then found that Alcoa's continued monopoly position during the period 1912 to 1938, when the government filed its complaint, was maintained through overly aggressive conduct designed to foreclose new competition. Although under no compulsion, Alcoa had continued to double and redouble its capacity in anticipation of new demands before others could enter the field. The court specifically recognized that this conduct did not involve "moral dereliction," yet it could "think of no more effective exclusion than progressively to embrace each new opportunity as it opened, and to face every newcomer with new capacity already geared into a great organization, having the advantage of experience, trade connections and the elite personnel."[22] The court thus found that Alcoa was in violation of Section 2 of the Sherman Act.[23]

In another case, *United States* v. *United States Steel Corporation*,[24] the Supreme Court found that U.S. Steel was not in violation

21. *Id.* at 430.

22. *Id.* at 431.

23. The decision of the court of appeals was handed down in 1945, five years after the case was tried, and the case returned to the trial court to determine whether Alcoa should be broken up. The trial court, which finally made its decision as to the appropriate form of relief in 1950, declined to order Alcoa to divest itself of any of its business, on the ground that the industry had vastly changed by 1950 as a result of World War II. With the aid of a loan from the Reconstruction Finance Corporation, Reynolds Metals Company entered the field in 1941. To meet wartime needs the government had also financed the construction of two large aluminum plants and a number of aluminum smelters, which were leased to Alcoa. After the war the leases were terminated and the plants sold to Reynolds and Kaiser Aluminum and Chemical Corporation. Thus by 1950, Alcoa had two integrated domestic competitors. Although Alcoa's percent of the domestically produced primary aluminum sold to nonintegrated producers was 87 percent, as compared to 15 percent for Reynolds and 3 percent for Kaiser, its percentage of total aluminum production, which included use of scrap aluminum, amounted to 51 percent, as compared to 31 percent for Reynolds and 18 percent for Kaiser.

24. 251 U.S. 417 (1920).

of Section 2 of the Sherman Act. In that case the government, seeking its dissolution, sued U.S. Steel, which was a holding company controlling twelve manufacturing concerns in the iron and steel industry. U.S. Steel had been organized in 1901 for the purpose of combining competing concerns, which altogether represented a combination of 180 independent concerns controlling 80 percent to 90 percent of the total production of iron and steel in the country. At the time the lawsuit was brought the combination had less than 50 percent of the market. The Supreme Court agreed with the trial court that there was no monopoly and that

> the Corporation . . . did not at any time abuse the power or ascendency it possessed. It resorted to none of the brutalities or tyrannies that the cases illustrate of other combinations. It did not secure freight rebates; it did not increase its profits by reducing the wages of its employees— whatever it did was not at the expense of labor; it did not increase its profits by lowering the quality of its products, nor create an artificial scarcity of them; it did not oppress or coerce its competitors—its competition, though vigorous, was fair; it did not undersell its competitors in some localities by reducing its prices there below those maintained elsewhere, or require its customers to enter into contracts limiting their purchases or restricting them in resale prices; it did not obtain customers by secret rebates or departures from its published prices; there was no evidence that it attempted to crush its competitors or drive them out of the market, nor did it take customers from its competitors by unfair means, and in its competition it seemed to make no difference between large and small competitors.[25]

Interestingly, evidence that U.S. Steel could not alone control the market, but rather had to persuade its competitors through "pools, associations, trade meetings, and through the social form of dinners" to illegally restrain competition was treated as persuasive evidence that there was no Section 2 violation. The Court noted that there may have been Section 1 violations, but because such conduct had ceased nine months before the suit was filed there was no reason to believe it would reoccur in the future. Thus, no Sherman Act violation was found for which dissolution of U.S. Steel was required.

In *United States* v. *United Shoe Machinery Co.,*[26] defendant

25. *Id.* at 440–41.
26. 110 F.Supp. 295 (D.Mass. 1953), *aff'd per curiam* 347 U.S. 521 (1954).

United Shoe Machinery Co. was held to have monopolized the shoe machinery industry and shoe factory supplies, in violation of Section 2 of the Sherman Act. It was found to have over 75 percent and probably 85 percent of the American shoe machinery market. The primary patents on its machines had terminated; however, some 3,915 secondary patents as well as the complexity of the machines made entry into the market very difficult. All of United Shoe's machines were leased, and through these leases United Shoe blocked the entry of competition. The leases were for ten years and required the lessee to use the machines to full capacity at all times when work was available. The lease also required the lessee to pay a substantial deferred payment or return charge if a machine was not kept for the full period of the lease. Finally, the leases included free repair services, a practice that the court found had prevented the development of an independent shoe machinery business. United Shoe also maintained discriminatory pricing by charging high rates for machines where there was little competition and a lower rate where competition was of major significance.

The trial court concluded that the lease arrangements were such that they discouraged competition that might otherwise exist, and thus they fostered United Shoe's monopoly position in an illegal manner. The court, to correct the illegal conduct, ordered the term of the lease shortened, the full-capacity clauses eliminated, the discriminatory return charge removed, and the separation of charges for repair services from the machines charges. On the theory that sold machines would ultimately enter the secondhand market and create additional competition, it also ordered that United Shoe make available its machines for sale as well as lease.[27]

In monopolization cases there is the defense that the monopoly was "thrust upon" the defendant. In the *Alcoa* case,[28] the court stated that monopoly power might be innocently acquired when demand is so limited that only a single large plant can economically supply it, when a change in cost or taste has driven out all but one supplier, or when one company out of several has survived by virtue

27. The trial court's decree also directed that the lease terms be set at a level which would not make it more advantageous to lease rather than buy the machines. It also provided for the compulsory licensing of patents at a reasonable royalty.

28. United States v. Aluminum Co. of America, 148 F.2d 416 (2d Cir. 1945).

of superior skill, foresight, and industry. In the *United Shoe* case, the trial court stated:

> [T]he defendant may escape statutory liability if it bears the burden of proving that it owes its monopoly solely to superior skill, superior products, natural advantages (including accessibility to raw materials or markets), economic or technological efficiency (including scientific research), low margins of profit maintained permanently and without discrimination, or license conferred by, and used within, the limits of law (including patents on one's own inventions, or franchises granted directly to the enterprise by a public authority).[29]

In *United Shoe,* the defendant failed to satisfy the above "thrust upon" test, the court stating:

> But United's control does not rest solely on its original constitution, its ability, its research, or its economies of scale. There are other barriers to competition, and these barriers were erected by United's own business policies. Much of United's market power is traceable to the magnetic ties inherent in its system of leasing, and not selling, its more important machines. The lease-only system of distributing complicated machines has many "partnership" aspects, and it has exclusionary features such as the 10-year term, the full-capacity clause, the return charges, and the failure to segregate service charges from machine charges. Moreover, the leasing system has aided United in maintaining a pricing system which discriminates between machine types.[30]

41. Combination or conspiracy to monopolize

The classical case of conspiracy to monopolize is *Standard Oil Co. of New Jersey* v. *United States,*[31] wherein the government, in an early Sherman Act test case (1911), sued Standard Oil Company of New Jersey, California, Indiana, Iowa, Kansas, Kentucky, Nebraska, New York, Ohio, and sixty-two other corporations and partnerships, as well as seven individuals, including John D. Rockefeller. The conspiracy was alleged to have been formed in 1870 by three of the individual defendants—Rockefeller, William Rockefeller, and

29. United States v. United Shoe Machinery Corp., 110 F.Supp. 295, 342 (D.Mass. 1953), *aff'd per curiam,* 347 U.S. 521 (1954).
30. 110 F.Supp. at 344.
31. 221 U.S. 1 (1911).

Henry M. Flager—who transferred their interests in three previously separate partnerships to the newly organized Standard Oil of Ohio. By 1872, this corporation had acquired all but three or four of the forty-five refineries in Cleveland. The combination then obtained preferential rates and rebates from the railroads, and by means of this advantage, competitors were either forced to join the combination or be driven out of business. The combination also acquired control over a large number of refineries in New York, Pennsylvania, Ohio, and elsewhere, as well as control of the oil pipelines from the Eastern oil fields to the refineries. With control of 90 percent of the oil industry, the combination was able to fix the price of crude and refined petroleum.

In 1882, a trust agreement was executed pursuant to which the stock of forty corporations, including Standard Oil of Ohio, and other properties held by members of the combination were transferred to nine trustees, chiefly individual defendants, in exchange for trust certificates. Such property was to be held and managed in the joint interests of all the parties. The trustees then organized Standard Oil Company of New Jersey and Standard Oil Company of New York, transferring certain assets to those corporations. In 1899, the individual defendants amended the charter of Standard Oil of New Jersey and transferred all the stock of the original trust to that corporation. Thereafter, the defendants obtained rebates, preferences, and other discriminatory treatment from the railroads, controlled pipelines, and engaged in unfair practices against competing pipelines. The government contended that the defendants had committed such unfair practices as cutting local prices to destroy competition, engaging in espionage activities, creating bogus independents, granting illegal rebates, and allocating territories. This conduct resulted in the defendants making inordinately large profits.

The Supreme Court affirmed the lower court's ruling that the trust was in violation of Sections 1 and 2 of the Sherman Act and mandated a dissolution of the trust combination. The Court gave as one of its reasons:

> Because the unification of power and control over petroleum and its products which was the inevitable result of the combining in the New Jersey corporation by the increase of its stock and transfer to it of the stocks of so many other corporations, aggregating so vast a capital,

gives rise, in and of itself, in the absence of countervailing circumstances, to say the least, to the *prima facie* presumption of intent and purpose to maintain the dominancy over the oil industry, not as a result of normal methods of industrial development, but by new means of combination which were resorted to in order that greater power might be added than would otherwise have arisen had normal methods been followed, the whole with the purpose of excluding others from the trade, and thus centralizing in the combination of a perpetual control of the movements of petroleum and its products in the channels of interstate commerce.[32]

A second case of importance is *American Tobacco Co. v. United States,*[33] in which the defendants American Tobacco Company, R. J. Reynolds Tobacco Company, Liggett and Myers Tobacco Company, and certain officials of those companies were charged with criminal conspiracy to restrain trade in violation of Section 1 and monopolizing, conspiring to monopolize, and attempting to monopolize in violation of Section 2. During the period 1931 through 1939, American, Liggett, and Reynolds accounted for 68 to 90.7 percent of the national domestic cigarette market. Although no written agreements were offered into evidence by the government, there was sufficient evidence to sustain a jury verdict of guilty that the three companies had conspired to fix and control prices and to foreclose any potential competition attempting to intrude into the market.

The government's evidence established that each defendant purchased in a particular market only if all three were represented. Without the presence of the three defendants, a market could not operate. Thus, the defendants by unanimous consent after consultation determined new markets and their locations. Defendants placed limitations upon their buyers and restrictions on the prices to be paid for tobacco, which at all times were uniform among the three defendants. When manufacturers of lower-priced cigarettes began taking a larger share of the market, all three defendants made larger purchases of the cheaper tobacco leaves in order to remove the product from the market and push up the price.

Defendants maintained, with several exceptions, from 1923 to 1939, the same prices and profits for their jobbers. In 1931, all three

32. *Id.* at 75.
33. 328 U.S. 781 (1946).

defendants increased their list prices to the same price. As a result, however, they lost a substantial share of the market to cheaper brands, which prior to the price increase had 0.28 percent of the market as compared to 22.98 percent afterward. Two years later, to meet this inroad, the defendants substantially cut their prices, which resulted in a decrease in the sale of cheaper brands from 22.78 to 6.43 percent of the market. Having accomplished this result, the defendants again raised their prices. At all times the defendants' prices, price cuts, and price increases were identical. The defendants also acted in concert to impose upon retailers the requirement that they sell the defendants' cigarettes at a differential of no more than 3 cents above the cheaper brands' prices.

The Supreme Court affirmed the convictions based upon this concerted action to monopolize:

> Where the conspiracy is proved, as here, from the evidence of the action taken in concert by all parties to it, it is all the more convincing proof of an intent to exercise the power of exclusion acquired through the conspiracy. The essential combination or conspiracy in violation of the Sherman Act may be found in a course of dealings or other circumstances as well as in any exchange of words.
>
> • • •
>
> The authorities support the view that the material consideration in determining whether a monopoly exists is not that prices are raised and that competition actually is excluded but that power exists to raise prices or to exclude competition when it is desired to do so.[34]

A third case of great interest in this regard is *United States* v. *New York Great Atlantic and Pacific Tea Co.*,[35] in which A&P, a number of its subsidiaries, officers, and employees were indicted for a conspiracy to restrain trade and to monopolize in violation of Sections 1 and 2 of the Sherman Act. The A&P system in the 1940s was comprised of fourteen integrated companies that engaged in the food industry as buyer, manufacturer, processor, broker, and retailer. It operated 5,800 retail stores in forty states and the District of Columbia.[36] The buying policy of A&P was to use its power to obtain lower prices on merchandise purchased from suppliers than that charged

34. *Id.* at 809–10, 811.

35. 173 F.2d 79 (7th Cir. 1949).

36. A&P itself was a holding company, 99 percent of the stock of which was owned by the George H. Hartford Trust.

competitors. Suppliers were coerced into selling at lower prices by the threat that they would be placed on A&P's blacklist if they did not conform to its program or that A&P would go into the manufacturing business in direct competition with recalcitrant suppliers. A&P kept secret all predatory discounts it received, which accounted for 22.15 percent of A&P's total profits in 1939, 22.47 percent in 1940, and 24.59 percent in 1941.

A&P also used its power to force suppliers to discontinue practices that were detrimental to A&P. For instance, some A&P suppliers made store-door deliveries to A&P's competitors. Since A&P delivered to its own stores from its warehouses, it was unable to obtain the full benefit of its warehousing policy as long as its competitors received such a service. A&P therefore forced some manufacturers to "widen the spread" between store deliveries and warehouse deliveries—to A&P's decided advantage. A&P also forced other suppliers to discontinue their practice of merchandising through giving premiums to customers. A&P neither wanted to give premiums nor wanted its competitors to gain the advantage of their use.

A&P also set up a wholly owned subsidiary that acted as a broker for sellers of fruits, vegetables, and other produce. On sales made to A&P, the brokerage fee went to A&P, thus further lowering its costs. On sales made to A&P competitors, the subsidiary still received its brokerage fee, which was passed on to A&P. Furthermore, as a broker, the subsidiary was able to purchase the best-quality products at the lowest prices for A&P before serving its other buyers.

The Seventh Circuit Court of Appeals found that this exercise of monopoly power created both a boycott and an illegal monopoly in violation of Sections 1 and 2 of the Sherman Act.

> No court has yet said that the accumulation and use of great power is unlawful *per se*. Bigness is no crime, although "size is itself an earmark of monopoly power. For size carries with it an opportunity for abuse.". . . That there was an accumulation of great power by A&P cannot be denied. How it used that power is the question. When A&P did not get the preferential discount or allowance it demanded, it did not simply exercise its right to refuse to contract with the supplier. It went further and served notice on the supplier that if the supplier did not meet the price dictated by A&P, not only would the supplier lose the business at the moment under negotiation, but it would be put upon the unsatisfactory list or blacklist of A&P and could expect no

more business from the latter. This was a boycott and in and of itself is a violation of the Sherman Act. . . .

While it is not necessary to constitute a violation of Sections 1 and 2 of the Sherman that a showing be made that competitors were excluded by the use of monopoly power . . . there is evidence in this record of how some local grocers were quickly eliminated under the lethal competition put upon them by A&P when armed with its monopoly power. As the evidence showed in this case, A&P received quantity discounts that bore no relation to any cost savings to the supplier. While A&P tried to rig up various contracts with its suppliers that would give the supplier a semblance of compliance with the Robinson-Patman Act, by colorably relating the discriminatory preferences allowed to cost savings, the primary consideration with A&P seemed to be to get the discounts, lawfully, if possible, but to get them at all events. The conclusion is inescapable on this record that A&P was encouraging its suppliers to violate the Robinson-Patman Act. . . .[T]o obtain these preferences, pressure was put on suppliers not by the use but by the abuse of A&P's tremendous buying power.[37]

42. Attempt to monopolize

In addition to monopolization and conspiracy to monopolize, attempts to monopolize are covered by Section 2 of the Sherman Act. Few judicial decisions have discussed attempts to monopolize, as distinguished from consummated monopolization. In most attempt cases, the allegations of attempt to monopolize have been coupled with charges of conspiracy to monopolize, monopolization, or conspiracy to restrain trade under Section 1, and the issue of attempt has received only incidental treatment.

Attempts to monopolize may involve a single firm or a combination of firms. In either situation, the power exerted may fall short of a monopoly and yet, if exercised with exclusionary or predatory conduct, may constitute an unlawful attempt to monopolize. In order to prove a violation two elements must be established: first, it must be shown that the firm or firms in question had a specific intent to monopolize and, second, that there was a "dangerous probability" that the attempt would be successful in achieving the monopoly in the relevant market.

37. 173 F.2d at 87–88.

In *Lessig* v. *Tidewater Oil Company,*[38] plaintiff Lessig leased a gasoline station from Tidewater Oil Company, but three years later the lease was terminated. Plaintiff sued, claiming that Tidewater was guilty of fixing the prices at which its dealers, including plaintiff, resold gasoline (vertical price fixing); that Tidewater illegally imposed a system of exclusive dealing and tying arrangements in the purchase of petroleum products, tires, batteries, and automobile accessories upon dealers (exclusive dealing and tie-in arrangements); and that Tidewater, through the above illegal conduct, was attempting to monopolize the market in the sale of petroleum, tires, batteries, and accessories. A jury found for Tidewater. The court of appeals reversed, holding that the trial court had made certain reversible errors in the course of the trial.

On the issue of attempt to monopolize, which the trial court had dismissed before trial, the court of appeals found that there was evidence of a violation, which should have gone to the jury. The court of appeals stated that if the jury found that Tidewater intended to fix the price at which 2,700 independent service station operators resold gasoline, to exclude other suppliers of petroleum products and such items as tires, batteries, and car accessories, and took steps to accomplish those purposes, the jury "could properly conclude that Tidewater attempted to monopolize a part of interstate commerce in violation of Section 2 of the Sherman Act."

In *Kansas City Star Company* v. *United States,*[39] the defendants Kansas City Star Company, its president and chairman of the Board of Directors, and its director of advertising, who was also the treasurer and a director, were indicted for attempting to monopolize and monopolizing news and advertising in violation of Section 2 of the Sherman Act. The evidence showed that Kansas City Star owned three newspapers—the *Kansas City Times,* a daily morning paper, the *Kansas City Star,* a daily evening paper, and the *Sunday Star,* a Sunday paper—which were sold in the Kansas City, Missouri, metropolitan area. It also owned WDAF, a radio station, and WDAF-TV, a television station. In order to strengthen its position in advertising, the defendant refused to take advertising from advertisers if they advertised in a competitive publication. For example, the man-

38. 327 F.2d 459 (9th Cir.), *cert. denied,* 377 U.S. 993 (1964).
39. 240 F. 2d 643 (8th Cir. 1957).

ager of three movie theaters in Kansas City, Missouri, was told to take his ad out of a competing newspaper or his advertising would be left out of the *Kansas City Star* and *Times.*

The local advertising manager for Sears, Roebuck was told by a solicitor for the defendant that its newspapers did not like to see ads running in a competing newspaper and, "If you don't desist, you will either injure your position in the *Kansas City Star* or if we have additional newsprint to allocate you may not get your share." A *Star* solicitor informed one of the partners of a florist shop that was owned jointly with a major league baseball player (Gleeson) that the *Star* would discontinue publicizing the baseball player if the florist shop continued using a competitive newspaper for advertising. The solicitor was instructed by the defendant to tell the manager of the florist shop that if Gleeson "knocked 100 home runs in the year his name would never appear in the paper outside the box score." Advertisers were also informed that they could not buy advertising time on the defendant's television station unless they also advertised in defendant's papers.

The court of appeals affirmed the conviction. In discussing the crime of attempt to monopolize, the court noted a proper definition of the crime:

> The phrase "attempt to monopolize" means the employment of methods, means and practices which would, if successful, accomplish monopolization, and which, though falling short nevertheless approach so close as to create a dangerous probability of it.[40]

Finally, in *Times-Picayune Pub. Co.* v. *United States,*[41] the Court found that the government had failed to prove an attempt-to-monopolize charge because there was no evidence of specific intent. In that case the defendant owned morning and afternoon newspapers, which were distributed in the New Orleans metropolitan area. Defendant's afternoon publication competed against another afternoon newspaper. In order to increase advertising revenues defendant required any advertiser to purchase advertising in both of its papers through a unit plan. As a result, since 1950, advertisers could not buy space in either of defendant's newspapers unless they agreed to insert identical copy

---

40. *Id.* at 663.
41. 345 U.S. 594 (1953).

in both. This unit plan adversely affected the other afternoon daily, inasmuch as an advertiser might only have sufficient revenues to advertise in two papers rather than all three New Orleans dailies. In ruling for the defendant the Court expressed concern for the difficulties newspapers were encountering in their efforts to economically survive. The Court noted that in 1951, there were 1,773 papers serving 1,443 American cities while in 1909 there were 2,600 dailies in 1,207 cities.

On the Section 2, attempt-to-monopolize charge, the Court held there was no evidence of a "specific intent" to monopolize. This was not a case where a monopolist in one segment of the market sought "to nose into a second market" through illegal or unfair means. Thus, the Court was able to distinguish *Lorain Journal* v. *United States*,[42] where a single newspaper had refused to sell space to advertisers unless they would forego advertising over a competing local radio station. The conduct in *Lorain Journal,* the Court stated, manifested "bold, relentless, and predatory commercial behavior" not present in the instant case.

42. 342 U.S. 143 (1951).

Chapter Five

The Robinson-Patman Act

43. History of the Robinson-Patman Act

On June 19, 1936, President Roosevelt signed into law the Robinson-Patman Act. Few statutes have created as much confusion and dissention from inception to the present time as the Robinson-Patman Act. It has been praised by some as the "Magna Carta" of small independent business enterprises and condemned by others for its basic inconsistencies with the goals and philosophies of the Sherman and Clayton Acts.

The Robinson-Patman Act is actually an amendment to the much older Clayton Act, which was passed by Congress in 1914. Section 2 of the latter act sought to foreclose trusts and the other vast business combinations created in the late 1800s and early 1900s from further entrenching their monopolistic positions by such means as price cutting and discriminatory pricing. The history books are replete with instances wherein the Standard Oil Trust and the other large trusts eliminated much smaller competitors by cutting prices below cost in a local or regional area for a sustained period of time and financing those prices with higher prices in other areas of the country.

In the 1920s another form of discriminatory pricing emerged that was just as damaging to small business. The large grocery chain stores and other mass merchandisers began to utilize their large-volume purchasing power to secure discriminatory price concessions and other special allowances from their suppliers, who were frequently considerably smaller than the chain store and thus vulnerable to such pressures. Such practices, which resulted in the partial demise of the independent retail trade, became the target of widespread public animosity. There existed a deep-seated feeling that discriminatory pricing practices were inconsistent with the concepts of equality of economic opportunity and the preservation of a competitive economy. Public antipathy was heightened by the increasing control exerted by chain stores over the channels of distribution and the increased demise of small independent stores, which was augmented by the Great Depression of 1929.

Section 2 of the Clayton Act, which had somewhat checked the large trusts in their predatory practices, proved inadequate to prevent chain store buyers from obtaining price concessions not accorded their smaller independent competitors. The Federal Trade Commission, which had primary responsibility to enforce the Clayton Act, brought few actions, and those that were brought were lost.

The Robinson-Patman Act was enacted in response to this public concern. The statute is very technical and difficult to enforce. In essence, it prohibits any seller engaged in commerce from directly or indirectly discriminating in the price charged purchasers in the sale of commodities of like grade and quality, where the effect may be substantially to lessen, injure, destroy, or prevent competition with any person who grants or knowingly receives a discrimination, or the customer of either.[1] There are related provisions dealing with brokerage, promotional, and advertising allowances and services as well as a provision for buyer liability. Statutory defenses as well as criminal sanctions are also set out in the act.[2]

Before discussing the various elements of the act, it should be observed that businessmen frequently express greater concern over discriminatory pricing than potential price fixing. As noted earlier, it has not been uncommon for competitors to contact each other in bidding situations to confirm competitive pricing in an effort to

1. 15 U.S.C. §13(a)–(f). Section 2(a) of the Clayton Act is also referred to, at times, as Section 2(a) of the Robinson-Patman Act.
2. 15 U.S.C. §13a.

invoke the "meeting competition" defense available under the Robinson-Patman Act. Thus, when a manufacturer has been forced to lower his price to a single customer in order to meet the equally low price of a competitor, confirmation of that competitive price has frequently been made through direct communications with the competitor. Although originally thought to be legal under the meeting competition defense of the act, recent Supreme Court decisions have made it clear that such conduct may constitute price fixing under Section 1 of the Sherman Act and lead to criminal indictments and subsequent convictions.[3]

When confronted with the decision of either discriminating in price or potentially fixing prices by contacting a competitor to confirm a price under the "meeting competition" defense of the Robinson-Patman Act, the choice should not be difficult to make. "Inadvertent" price fixing can lead to fines of $100,000 and three years in jail for the individual perpetrator for each offense and $1,000,000 for the corporation for each offense. On the other hand, discriminatory pricing will most likely go unpunished for the following reasons: first, as hereinafter discussed, recent court decisions have made proof of violations of the Robinson-Patman Act more difficult; second, private enforcement faces severe problems of proof because of the technical nature of the statute itself, particularly in proving injury to competition; third, criminal prosecutions by the government have been few and almost uniformly unsuccessful, thus negating the possibility of future criminal proceedings being commenced;[4] and fourth, the Federal Trade Commission has enforced the act sparingly in recent

3. United States v. Container Corp. of America, 393 U.S. 333 (1969); United States v. United States Gypsum Company, 438 U.S. 422 (1978).

4. Section 3 of the Robinson-Patman Act, which provides for a fine of $5,000 and/or imprisonment of not more than one year, has been seldom utilized, primarily because the government in the past has had very limited success in prosecuting offenders. For example, in United States v. Borden Co., 48 Cr. 362 (N.D.Ill. 1949) and United States v. American Petroleum Inst., Civ. No. 8524 (D.D.C. 1940), the cases were voluntarily dismissed. United States v. Bowman Dairy Co., 48 Cr. 361 (N.D.Ill. 1949), resulted in a directed verdict of acquittal. In United States v. Maryland & Virginia Milk Producers Ass'n., Cr. 991–55 (D.D.C. 1956), the indictment was dismissed by the court just before trial. Section 3 proscribes three broad types of trade practices: (a) general price discriminations, (b) geographic price discriminations, and (c) selling "at unreasonably low prices for the purpose of destroying competition or eliminating a competitor." The constitutionality of this statute has been questioned, and the U.S. Supreme Court, in United States v. National Dairy Prods. Corp., 384 U.S. 883 (1966), upheld the third clause—selling at unreasonably low prices for predatory purposes—but only as it applied in that particular case. A primary obstacle to successfully prosecuting offenders has been the requirement that the government prove "knowledge" and "predatory intent."

years, and when successful the only penalty levied for a first violation has been a cease and desist order.

44. Elements of a Section 2(a) violation

To establish a violation of Section 2(a) of the Clayton Act, as amended by the Robinson-Patman Act, six elements must be established: first, it must be shown that there was a price discrimination, that is, that the seller sold at two different prices; second, that at least one of the sales was made in interstate commerce, that is, across state lines; third, that two actual sales were made; fourth, that the products sold were commodities, that is, tangible, physical, movable articles of commerce; fifth, that the products sold were of like grade and quality; and sixth, that there was competitive injury.

Before discussing each element of the violation, it is important to keep in mind the distinction between "primary-line" competition and "secondary-line" competition, because each requires different proof. A primary-line case arises when a seller drops its price in a particular market with the intent of driving out its competition, as the Standard Oil Trust did in the late 1800s and early 1900s. The complaining or injured party is the competitor of the seller, that is, a party on the same level of competition with the person discriminating in price. A secondary-line case occurs when a seller sells to two or more buyers in the same market at different prices, thereby favoring one buyer over the other. In this instance, the complaining or injured party is the disfavored buyer who, standing in a vertical relationship with the seller, is injured by the lower price being charged his competitor.

In any given set of circumstances, there may be both primary-line and secondary-line ramifications. Take, for example, the auto glass replacement industry made up of several manufacturers of auto glass, including Libby-Owens-Ford (LOF) and Pittsburgh Plate Glass (PPG). If LOF decided to lower its price in the Chicago metropolitan market to the largest auto glass replacement dealer, Globe Glass & Trim Company, but keep its price up to all other glass replacement dealers in that market, a potential primary-line and secondary-line case may arise. PPG, as well as other competitors of LOF, may have been injured by the loss of Globe Glass' business, thus giving rise to a potential primary-line case. Also, the competitors of Globe Glass may also have been injured because they were required to pay a higher price for auto glass and therefore could not compete as effectively against Globe Glass, a potential secondary-line case.

45. A price discrimination or price difference

The first element of a Section 2(a) violation requires the seller to sell to two customers at different prices. In other words, he must discriminate in price. Proof of this element of the violation will depend on whether a primary or secondary-line case is being tried. In a primary-line case, where the complainant or injured party is a competitor of the seller, it does not matter where in the United States the two sales at different prices arc made. Thus, if the seller, a beer manufacturer, sells its beer to taverns and beer distributors in Milwaukee at a higher price than that at which it sells the same beer in St. Louis, a price discrimination or price difference has been established in a primary-line case. Beer manufacturers competing against the defendant in St. Louis, who are injured by a loss of sales, can satisfy this first element of a Section 2(a) violation.

However, if this is a secondary-line case, that is the complaining party is not a competitor of the defendant, but a customer, such as a tavern or beer distributor in Milwaukee paying the higher price, a price discrimination cannot be shown, because all taverns and beer distributors in Milwaukee, against whom the complaining party competes, also pay this same higher price. Only if it could be shown that a tavern or beer distributor in Milwaukee is competing against taverns or distributors in St. Louis, which receive the lower price, can it be said that a price difference exists. In other words, in a secondary-line case, the injured customer paying the higher price must be in *competition* with the favored customers paying the lower price.

The leading primary-line competition case establishing price discrimination is *Federal Trade Commission* v. *Anheuser-Busch, Inc.*[5] In that case, most of the national breweries in 1953, including Anheuser-Busch, granted employees higher wages, and in doing so, put a general price increase into effect. Although many regional and local breweries throughout the country followed suit, Falstaff, Griesedieck Western, and Griesedieck Brothers in St. Louis, Missouri, did not. Sales of Anheuser-Busch declined nationally; however, in the

5. 363 U.S. 536 (1960).

St. Louis market, where the above-named companies were strong, its sales remained the same. In 1954, in the St. Louis market, Anheuser-Busch lowered its price of Budweiser, a premium beer that traditionally commanded a substantially higher price than local beers, to the same price as the local beers sold by Falstaff, Griesedieck Western, and Griesedieck Brothers. During the subsequent fifteen months, Anheuser-Busch sales increased from 26.8 to 39.3 percent of the market, while Falstaff's sales dropped slightly, Griesedieck Western's sales dropped from 38.9 to 23.1 percent of the market, and Griesedieck Brothers' sales dropped from 14.4 to 4.8 percent of the market.

During the same period of time, Anheuser-Busch maintained its higher premium price for Budweiser in other parts of the United States, including Chicago, Illinois, Cincinnati, Ohio, etc. Based on this price "difference" the Court concluded that a price discrimination, the first element of a Section 2(a) violation, had been established in this primary-line case.[6]

The underlying rationale of a primary-line price discrimination case is that a seller will use the higher prices charged in other areas to offset the lower prices charged in the target area; and that if the seller is big enough, he can sustain "losses" in the target area until he has driven out his competition. In *Moore* v. *Mead's Fine Bread Co.,*[7] the plaintiff was engaged in the bakery business in Santa Rosa, New Mexico. The defendant operated bakery plants in Lubbock and Bic Spring, Texas, and at Hobbs, Roswell, and Clovis, New Mexico, and sold its products under the name "Mead's Fine Bread." Out of its Clovis, New Mexico, plant, defendant sold bread across state lines in Farwell, Texas. Plaintiff and defendant got into a price war in Santa Rosa, with the latter cutting its price on bread from 14 cents to 7 cents for a pound loaf. Ultimately plaintiff was driven out of business and brought a lawsuit under Section 2(a) of the Clayton Act, alleging a primary-line price discrimination case. The Supreme Court found the defendant in violation of the Robinson-Patman Act:

> We think that the practices in the present case are also included within the scope of the antitrust laws. We have here an interstate

---

6. The ultimate resolution of the lawsuit exonerated Anheuser-Busch of any wrongdoing on the basis that the requisite injury to competition had not been demonstrated. Anheuser-Busch, Inc. v. Federal Trade Commission, 289 F.2d 835 (7th Cir. 1961).

7. 348 U.S. 115 (1954).

industry increasing its domain through outlawed competitive practices. The victim, to be sure, is only a local merchant; and no interstate transactions are used to destroy him. But the beneficiary is an interstate business; the treasury used to finance the warfare is drawn from interstate, as well as local, sources which include not only respondent [defendant] but also a group of interlocked companies engaged in the same line of business; and the prices on the interstate sales ... are kept high while the local prices are lowered. If this method of competition were approved, the pattern for growth of monopoly would be simple. As long as the price warfare was strictly intrastate, interstate business could grow and expand with impunity at the expense of local merchants. The competitive advantage would then be with the interstate combines, not by reason of their skills or efficiency but because of their strength and ability to wage price wars. The profit made in interstate activities would underwrite the losses of local price-cutting campaigns.[8]

46. A sale in interstate commerce

The second element of a Section 2(a) violation requires at least one of the sales in question to have been made in interstate commerce. As hereinafter shown, this is one of the more difficult elements to prove, and failure of proof has resulted in a large number of Robinson-Patman Act cases being dismissed.

In proving this element of the violation, it is not enough that the defendant is an interstate corporation or that it is engaged in interstate commerce. Proof must be made that the product in question has been sold *across state lines*. In *Gulf Oil Corp.* v. *Copp Paving Co.*,[9] the plaintiff, a firm that manufactured and sold asphaltic concrete for highway construction in the southern half of Los Angeles County, brought an action against Union Oil, Gulf Oil, Edgington Oil, and their subsidiaries engaged in the asphalt business in southern California, charging violations of, *inter alia,* Section 2(a) of the Robinson-Patman Act. The defendants were alleged to have discriminated in price by selling asphaltic concrete at higher prices in those areas where plaintiff was not competing, as compared to those areas where

8. *Id.* at 119.
9. 419 U.S. 186 (1974).

plaintiff was competing. It also alleged that the defendants sold their solid liquid asphalt at discriminatory prices.

Because all of the asphaltic concrete manufactured by the defendants had to be 275° F when laid in highway construction, defendants restricted the sale of their product to a radius of thirty-five miles from their plant. Thus, the record established that none of defendants' sales crossed state lines. Plaintiff argued that interstate sales requirement of Section 2(a) was satisfied in that large amounts of the asphaltic concrete were used in the construction of interstate highways. The Court rejected this argument, holding that unlike the Sherman Act, the Robinson-Patman Act required proof that at least one sale of the product in question was made across state lines. This portion of the case, therefore, was dismissed.

Another example of the stringency of the "sale across state lines" requirement of the Robinson-Patman Act is *Hampton* v. *Graff Vending Company*.[10] In that case, the defendant Graff was the world's largest bulk vending distributor with warehouses and outlets in many states, including Texas. The source of most of Graff's gum was W. R. Grace Company in Chicago, Illinois, which manufactured Leaf gum. Plaintiff was a wholesaler competing against Graff in the San Antonio and Houston areas. Plaintiff obtained a favorable contract with a gum manufacturer and was thereby able to compete effectively against Graff. Graff then approached W. R. Grace Company seeking further discounts on the gum purchased for the San Antonio–Houston market so that it could lower its price there. This price concession was granted, and Graff dropped its price to retailers to that at which plaintiff was purchasing its gum.

Plaintiff sued under Section 2(a), claiming that defendant supported the lower San Antonio-Houston prices with higher prices in other markets, such as Oakland, California, where defendant sold its Leaf gum at the regularly listed price. The court of appeals ruled that plaintiff's case was insufficient in that there was no evidence of a sale by Graff of Leaf gum across state lines. Admittedly, the gum was "purchased" in interstate commerce from W. R. Grace Company in Chicago, Illinois. But upon reaching defendant's warehouse in Texas, the "sale" of the gum was wholly within Texas. Similarly, defendant made no sales across state lines out of its other ware-

10. 478 F.2d 527 (5th Cir. 1973).

houses. Thus, there was no violation of Section 2(a) of the Robinson-Patman Act.

The stringency of the "sale across state lines" requirement has been avoided in a number of cases. If a product travels across state lines and is temporarily stored before being sold locally, courts have held, in certain situations, that the interstate character of the product has not been broken. Under this "flow of commerce" theory, the Supreme Court has held that there was a sale in interstate commerce.

Standard Oil Co. of Indiana v. *Federal Trade Commission*[11] illustrates the application of this "flow of commerce" theory. Standard Oil is an Indiana corporation with its principal office in Chicago, Illinois. Its gasoline, at the time of the suit late in the 1940s, was obtained from oil fields in Kansas, Oklahoma, Texas, and Wyoming. The actual refining of the gasoline was done at its plant in Whiting, Indiana. Gasoline sold in the Detroit, Michigan, area was carried on tankers from Indiana via the Great Lakes to its marine terminal at River Rouge, Michigan. Enough gasoline was accumulated there during each navigation season to meet winter needs when the Great Lakes could not be navigated. In the Detroit area, Standard Oil sold the gasoline at a lower price to certain jobbers selling at retail than to independent retailers operating Standard Oil gas stations. The Federal Trade Commission brought an action under Section 2(a), claiming that such pricing was discriminatory and a violation of the act. Standard Oil argued that all sales made in the Detroit area were local or intrastate and none crossed state lines. Thus, it argued, there were no sales in interstate commerce.

The Supreme Court ruled that the gasoline in question was shipped in interstate commerce from Whiting, Indiana, to Detroit, Michigan, and that its temporary storage in tanks, an accommodation to the northern winters when the Great Lakes freeze over, was only a temporary interruption, which was insufficient to deprive the gasoline of its interstate character. The Court added:

> Any other conclusion would fall short of the recognized purpose of the Robinson-Patman Act to reach the operations of large interstate businesses in competition with small local concerns. Such temporary storage of the gasoline as occurs within the Detroit area does not deprive the gasoline of its interstate character.[12]

11. 340 U.S. 231 (1951).
12. *Id.* at 237–38.

In *Foremost Dairies, Inc.* v. *Federal Trade Commission,*[13] Foremost, which in 1959 owned and operated fifty-nine milk processing plants in twenty-four states and maintained 182 distribution facilities in twenty-nine states, was charged with discriminatory pricing practices in Albuquerque, New Mexico. Foremost granted Barber, a retail establishment with eight stores in Albuquerque, a 5 percent discount above that granted to any other retail store in the city. Barber had insisted that Foremost was not being competitive and, without checking on what the competition was offering, Foremost granted Barber a 5 percent cash rebate to retain its business. The rebates were discontinued two years later when Foremost fortuitously learned that its competition had long since eliminated any such price concessions.

Foremost attacked the Federal Trade Commission's finding that there had been sales in interstate commerce. It argued that all sales were made locally in Albuquerque and that none had crossed state lines. However, the court noted that 20 percent of the milk processed by Foremost in its Santa Fe, New Mexico, plant was produced in Colorado. Normally, Foremost's milk entered and left its Santa Fe plant on the same day and was trucked to Albuquerque for distribution from its branch located there. The Federal Trade Commission found that there had been a "constant flow" of milk that originated outside of New Mexico and that had remained in interstate commerce from its point of origin with delivery to Foremost's customers in Albuquerque. The court concluded that the "flow of commerce" theory applied:

> In the case before us, the fluid milk undergoes a rather negligible processing, in general moving in a constant flow from the Colorado dairy farms to meet the fairly predictable demand of the retail grocers in Albuquerque. This processing no more interrupts the flow of commerce than the temporary storage of the gasoline in the *Standard Oil* case.[14]

The "flow of commerce" theory has been applied in a number of other situations. For example, if a wholesaler such as Graff Vending Company, in Houston, purchased Leaf gum in Chicago pursuant to an actual order of a retail outlet in Houston, Texas, the movement

13. 348 F.2d 674 (5th Cir. 1965).
14. *Id.* at 678.

of the gum from Chicago through Graff Vending Company to the retailer would be treated as a sale in interstate commerce under the flow of commerce theory. Similarly, where the goods are purchased from outside the state and brought into the state pursuant to an understanding with a retailer that the goods would be delivered on a regular basis, an interstate sale has been demonstrated.

47. The requirement of two sales

Section 2(a) of the Robinson-Patman Act applies only when goods have been sold to "two" or more "purchasers" at different prices. Thus, a sale at one price and a refusal or an offer to sell does not satisfy the requirements of the act. Likewise, the act does not apply to transactions that are not strictly sales, such as leases to real estate, licensing of movie films, and agency or consignment arrangements.

In *Klein* v. *Lionel Corporation*[15] the plaintiff, a retailer of toy electric trains and accessories located in Wilmington, Delaware, sued Lionel for its alleged discriminatory pricing practices, which had resulted in the plaintiff paying higher prices than other competing retailers selling Lionel's products. Plaintiff purchased its products from jobbers and middlemen and not directly from Lionel. Lionel did sell directly to some retailers, giving them a greater discount than what plaintiff was getting from its suppliers. Summary judgment was granted to Lionel on the ground that plaintiff could not assert a cause of action under Section 2(a) against Lionel because he was not a "purchaser" of any products from the defendant.

In *Gaylord Shops, Inc.* v. *Pittsburgh Miracle Mile Town and Country Shopping Center, Inc.,*[16] the defendant owned and operated the Pittsburgh Miracle Mile shopping center located in Western Pennsylvania, leasing a large portion to J. C. Penney Co. and a much smaller portion to plaintiff. Because J. C. Penney was the largest tenant, there allegedly existed an agreement between it and the defendant giving the former a "veto" power over any changes or increases in the amount of space leased to smaller tenants of Miracle Mile, including the plaintiff. Pursuant to the agreement a number of discriminatory benefits were granted J. C. Penney not afforded the

15. 237 F.2d 13 (3d Cir. 1956).
16. 219 F.Supp. 400 (W.D.Pa. 1963).

plaintiff and others. When plaintiff sought to obtain additional warehouse space, J. C. Penney vetoed this and plaintiff was ultimately forced out of business.

Although defendant's executive offices were located in Columbus, Ohio, defendant argued there was no sale in interstate commerce into Pennsylvania as required by Section 2(a) of the Robinson-Patman Act. It is also argued that there were no sales of any products or commodities, but rather the leasing of store and warehouse facilities; thus, a second requirement of the act had not been satisfied. The court agreed with the defendant and held that there was no sale in interstate commerce and that "leases, as distinguished from sales, were beyond the scope of §2 of the Clayton Act."[17] The court further stated:

> Without belaboring the point, it seems clear from a reading of the Act that where the agreement is not for the transfer of chattels, or the sale of personal property, the defendants cannot be guilty of violation of the Robinson-Patman Act.[18]

The plaintiffs in *Baum* v. *Investors Diversified Services, Inc.*[19] brought suit against Investors Diversified Services, Inc. (IDS) because of its practice of granting discounts on the commissions charged based on the cumulative quantity of shares owned by an investor. The criteria for determining whether a purchaser was entitled to a lower commission rate was not based on the size of the block of shares purchased by an investor at any one time, but rather on the size of the block of shares he had accumulated. For example, a purchaser of a $500,000 block was charged the same commission rate as a purchaser of a $1,000 block who had already purchased an aggregate of $499,000 shares of the Investors Group funds. Plaintiffs purchased an aggregate of $4000 in shares and were charged the maximum commission. The alleged price discrimination was based on the cumulative discount schedule that was geared to the amount of accumulated shares owned by the investor. The court dismissed the action on the ground that the sale of mutual fund shares was a service and not the sale of a commodity:

> A mutual fund share represents a fractional ownership in a large investment account. It is, in essence, a service contract between the

17. *Id.* at 404.
18. *Id.* at 403.
19. 409 F.2d 872 (7th Cir. 1969).

investor and the investment company whereby the investor places his money in the hands of the investment company in expectation of realizing a financial gain.[20]

Finally, in *Lubbock Glass & Mirror Co.* v. *Pittsburgh Plate Glass Co.,*[21] plaintiff charged its competitor PPG with selling glass, aluminum doors, frames, windows, and related items for use in commercial buildings at a lower price in Lubbock, Texas, than that charged in other areas of the United States. Defendant argued that the installation of such items was essentially a service provided pursuant to installation contracts and not the sale of commodities. Moreover, defendants contended that those contracts varied from job to job with any seeming difference in price attributable to intangibles inherent in the bidding business. The court agreed that each installment contract was unique:

> Under these circumstances, the Court is of the opinion that commercial installation contracts are not of "like grade and quality" as required by the Robinson-Patman Act. These requirements of "like grade and quality" mean that commodities must have similar characteristics before a charge of price discrimination under the Act can be maintained. Actual and genuine difference between products generally remove differential pricing of the two from the reach of the Robinson-Patman Act.[22]

48. Commodities of like grade and quality

In selling commodities or products at different prices, a plaintiff must show that those commodities or products were essentially the same, that is of "like grade and quality." If the product is in some way physically different, then a discriminatory sale has not been established.

In *Federal Trade Commission* v. *Borden Co.*[23] Borden produced and sold evaporated milk under the Borden name, which it advertised nationally. At the same time, Borden packaged and marketed evaporated milk under various private labels for large chain stores, which it sold to those stores at prices regularly below its Borden labeled

20. *Id.* at 874.
21. 313 F.Supp. 1184 (N.D.Tex. 1970).
22. *Id.* at 1187.
23. 383 U.S. 637 (1966).

evaporated milk. Physically and chemically the milk sold under the Borden name was identical to that sold under the private labels. Borden argued that a determination of "like grade and quality" should not be limited to physical properties, but should consider such additional factors as relative public acceptance evidenced by the higher price paid for the Borden product. The Supreme Court rejected this argument, holding that the act was intended to deal with the "characteristics of the product itself," and not consumer preference based on what the consumer thinks of the product or is willing to pay for it.

In *Universal-Rundle Corp.*,[24] the Federal Trade Commission found that Rundle had sold bathtubs to Sears at prices lower than those charged to its other customers who competed against Sears. However, the commission found that the bathtub sold to Sears was not of a like grade and quality to the bathtub sold to others. Although both tubs were made of the same material by the same process, the bathtub sold to Sears' competitors generally was one inch higher than the Sears tub, 2¾ inches wider, two square feet larger, had a ¾-inch higher water level, and had a wide front apron forming a 6½ inch seat with two built-in soap dishes, which were missing in the Sears product. The commission concluded that there had been "a showing of physical variations between [the] two products of such a nature as to create a consumer preference for one over the other." Thus, no violation was found as to the bathtubs.

49. Injury to competition—primary-line

The final element of a Section 2(a) Robinson-Patman Act violation is a showing of competitive injury. The act does not proscribe all price discriminations—only those having the prescribed adverse effect on competition. The statutory test of illegality is whether the effect of a price discrimination "may be substantially to lessen competition or tend to create a monopoly in any line of commerce" or to "injure, destroy, or prevent competition with any person who either grants or knowingly receives the benefits of such discrimination, or with customers of either of them." Many plaintiffs' cases are lost because the

24. 65 FTC 924 (1964).

plaintiff is unable to show injury to competition as distinguished from his own injury.

The distinction between primary-line and secondary-line cases becomes extremely important on the issue of injury to competition. A primary-line case requires a showing of predatory intent, which is not required in a secondary-line case; that is, in a primary-line case, the plaintiff must prove that the defendant discriminated in price not only to gain more business for itself, but actually to drive its competition out of business.

Lowering of prices is the essence of competition and the cornerstone of Section 1 of the Sherman Act. Lower prices, even on a discriminatory basis, normally stimulates competition to the benefit of the consumer. Therefore, for discriminatory pricing to be declared illegal there must be a showing that "competition" has been or may be destroyed and not simply stimulated as would normally be expected. The line between stimulation and destruction (predatory intent) of the market structure is not always clear and has caused great difficulties in the courts.

The clearest examples of predatory intent involve cases where the defendant has sold its product at below cost for a sustained period of time to drive out competition, conduct attributed to such famous entities as the Standard Oil Trust, the Tobacco Trust, the Sugar Trust. Where predatory intent has not been clearly demonstrated, courts have leaned heavily toward finding no violation lest they infringe on the very basic of all Sherman Act tenets, price competition.

In *Anheuser-Busch, Inc.* v. *Federal Trade Commission,*[25] discussed previously, the Seventh Circuit Court of Appeals considered whether Anheuser-Busch, by reducing its premium-priced Budweiser to that of the local beers in St. Louis, had acted with a predatory intent. The court concluded that there was no evidence of predatory intent and that, indeed, Anheuser-Busch had acted with restraint:

> Turning now to the situation at bar, we find that, there being no showing that AB [Anheuser-Busch] had aid from its other markets and despite a decrease in its national sales, AB forthrightly met its robust competition in the St. Louis market by a multiple-pronged program, which included but was not limited to a two-step reduction in its price

25. 289 F.2d 835 (7th Cir. 1961).

to exactly meet that of its competitors. The record affirmatively shows that AB used restraint in its competitive efforts. Its conduct was in conformity with the principle that competition is the decisive force in the market place. That conduct is the antithesis of the predatory misconduct condemned in the above territorial pricing cases relied upon by the Commission. In each of those cases the motive for the price cut was vindictive and the effect was punitive. There was not even a pretense that the price change was incident to a general intensification of the sales effort, as in the case at bar. It was a single lethal weapon aimed at a victim for a predatory purpose.[26]

The most important case to date in which predatory intent was found is *Utah Pie Co.* v. *Continental Baking Co.*[27] Plaintiff, a frozen pie company selling in Utah and surrounding states, brought suit against the Pet Milk Company, the Continental Baking Company, and the Carnation Company for discriminatory pricing in the Salt Lake City, Utah, frozen pie market. Although long in the pie business, plaintiff entered the frozen pie—apple, cherry, boysenberry, peach, pumpkin, and mince—business in 1957 and was immediately successful. Because it operated from a new plant in Salt Lake City, its prices were initially lower than the defendants who sold from plants located in other states. To meet plaintiff's pricing, Pet Milk entered an agreement with Safeway to sell pies at a substantially lower price, below plaintiff's price, than the price it charged others in the same Salt Lake City market and in California. It also sold two other brands of pies in the Salt Lake City market at a lower price than that charged elsewhere.

The Supreme Court found that predatory intent had been established. The Court reasoned that Pet Milk's lower prices were aimed at plaintiff because it was, in Pet Milk's words, an "unfavorable factor" in the market, one which had "d[u]g holes in our operation" and posed a constant "check" on Pet Milk's performance in the Salt Lake City market. Furthermore, Pet Milk admitted that during the period when it was establishing its relationship with Safeway, it had sent an

26. *Id.* at 841–42. The court discussed a number of cases that had found predatory intent. *See* Moore v. Mead's Fine Bread Co., 348 U.S. 115 (1954); Maryland Baking Co. v. Federal Trade Commission, 243 F.2d 716 (4th Cir. 1957); E.B. Muller & Co. v. Federal Trade Commission, 142 F.2d 511 (6th Cir. 1944); Porto Rican Tobacco Co. v. American Tobacco Co., 30 F.2d 234 (2d Cir. 1929).

27. 386 U.S. 685 (1967).

industrial spy into Utah Pie's plant to seek information that Pet Milk could use to convince Safeway not to do business with plaintiff.

The second defendant, Continental Baking, was unable to penetrate the Salt Lake City pie market because of its substantially higher costs and corresponding prices. Thus, in June 1961, it slashed its prices substantially in that market to the point that its pie prices were below "its direct costs plus an allocation for overhead." Pie sales increased from 1.8 to 8.3 percent of the market, and plaintiff was forced to slash its prices to a new low in order to salvage its business. The Court concluded that Continental Baking's sales below cost established the requisite predatory intent.

Like Continental Baking, Carnation also slashed its prices to below cost in order to spur further growth. In analyzing the conduct of all three defendants the Court stated:

> In this case there was some evidence of predatory intent with respect to each of these respondents [defendants]. . . . We believe that the Act reaches price discrimination that erodes competition as much as it does price discrimination that is intended to have immediate destructive impact. In this case, the evidence shows a drastically declining price structure which the jury could rationally attribute to continued or sporadic price discrimination.[28]

In a similar case, *International Air Industries, Inc.* v. *American Excelsior Company,*[29] the court concluded that predatory intent had not been shown. Plaintiff was a New Mexico corporation engaged in the business of manufacturing handmade evaporative cooler pads, which it sold in Arizona, New Mexico, and western Texas. The defendant was a subsidiary of Texstar Company and also manufactured evaporative cooler pads, which it sold throughout the southwestern and far western parts of the United States. Because of intense competition, plaintiff dropped its prices 5 percent below existing prices to a 14.5 percent discount below list price. Reacting to this, defendant decided to drop its price 25 percent below list price in plaintiff's market, which plaintiff learned of and met before it went into effect. Because defendant picked up no new business nor recaptured business lost when plaintiff went to the 15.5 percent discount, it dropped its price to 32.5 percent below list price, which plaintiff

28. *Id.* at 702–03.
29. 517 F.2d 714 (5th Cir. 1975), *cert. denied,* 424 U.S. 943 (1976).

immediately met. Plaintiff could not sustain this price and quickly returned to the 25 percent discount. At this point defendant gained new customers from plaintiff. During the entire period of the price war plaintiff did not lose sales, but did suffer a decline in profits.

The court determined that defendant had charged a lower price in plaintiff's marketing area than it did in other areas of the country. However, the court held that the mere fact that plaintiff had lost profits was not enough to establish the requisite injury to competition; predatory intent also had to be demonstrated. Discussing "predatory intent" the court stated:

> [P]redatory intent has never been clearly defined. Its appearance has been characterized by phrases such as "putting a crimp" into one's competitors, punitively or destructively attacking other firms, and acting vindictively with punitive effect. . . .
>
> By "predatory" we mean AMXCO [defendant] must have at least sacrificed present revenues for the purpose of driving Vebco [plaintiff] out of the market with the hope of recouping the losses through subsequent higher prices.[30]

The court went on to determine that no predatory intent had been demonstrated because defendant had sold at a profit and not below costs and because only plaintiff's profits and not its sales had decreased.

50. Injury to competition—secondary-line

The degree of evidence required to establish injury in a secondary-line case, that is, a case where a manufacturer discriminates in price between two or more buyers competing in the same market, is considerably less than that required in a primary-line case. Here, predatory intent need not be shown. To establish the requisite injury, it is sufficient that the price differential was a sustained one or influenced resale prices, or that the favored buyers enjoyed increased profit margins, or were able to offer more attractive services to their customers as a result of the differential.

In *National Dairy Products Corp.* v. *Federal Trade Commission,*[31] National Dairy, in 1958, granted thirteen customers in the Toledo

---

30. *Id.* at 722–23.
31. 395 F.2d 517 (7th Cir. 1968), *cert. denied,* 393 U.S. 977 (1969).

(Ohio)-Monroe (Michigan) market a fluid milk discount of 12 percent, eight customers 10 percent, and one customer 7 percent. These twenty-two discounts were in excess of those received by National Dairy's other retail store customers in that market. The court found that competitive injury had been shown, stating that "any substantial, sustained differential between competing" buyers establishes injury.[32] Besides this injury, the evidence also established that National Dairy's discounts resulted "in price differentials between competing purchasers, sufficient in amount to influence their resale prices of milk."[33] Finally, the court noted:

> Since all these factors were present here, the Commission's finding of probable competitive injury must stand. This is true even if there had been direct testimony by non-favored customers that the price discriminations had not injured their businesses. [As pointed out in] *Foremost Dairies, Inc.* v. *Federal Trade Commission* ... injury may be inferred even if the favored customer did not undersell his rivals, for a substantial price advantage can enlarge the favored buyer's profit margin or enable him to offer attractive services to his customers.[34]

The defendant in *United Biscuit Co.* v. *Federal Trade Commission*[35] was charged with violating Section 2(a) of the Robinson-Patman Act because it allegedly sold to chain stores at a lower price than that charged small independents. United Biscuit manufactured and sold cookies and crackers and sold them in a number of areas throughout the United States, including the Midwest. In selling to the large chain stores, including The Great Atlantic & Pacific Tea Company, The Kroger Company, and National Food Stores, defendant used graduated monthly discount schedules. This meant that if a purchaser owned several stores, its discount was based on the aggregate purchases of all its stores. As a result independents, which might purchase more than the individual stores owned by a chain, often could not take advantage of the largest discount available, whereas the chain stores on an aggregate basis always purchased enough to enable each store to receive the maximum discount.

32. *Id.* at 521.
33. *Id.* at 522.
34. *Id.* at 522.
35. 350 F.2d 615 (7th Cir. 1965), *cert. denied,* 383 U.S. 926 (1966).

United Biscuit argued that the alleged discrimination amounted to only a few dollars per month difference in costs on a minor sales item and therefore had little or no effect on competition between stores. The court rejected this argument, and in finding a violation stated:

> [E]ven though price discriminations covering a single item in a grocery store may appear to be relatively insignificant when considered alone, they may assume the stature of substantiality when considered in the context of the store's total operation and as an incipient harm which could grow into reality if extended to all of the items handled by the grocer.[36]

51. Granting quantity discounts

In the course of selling to customers, the manufacturer or seller has the right to provide discounts based on the volume of goods purchased. However, the seller cannot provide a discount schedule that only the very largest customers can use. *Federal Trade Commission v. Morton Salt Co.*[37] is an example of where a manufacturer established a discount schedule pursuant to which only its five largest customers in the United States were big enough to utilize the largest discount. A question arose as to whether this was discriminatory pricing under Section 2(a) of the Robinson-Patman Act.

Morton Salt manufactured several different brands of table salt, which it sold at a delivered price. The discount schedule provided for $1.60 per case for less than a carload purchase, $1.50 per case for a carload purchase, $1.40 per case for 5,000 case purchases in any consecutive twelve months, and $1.35 per case for 50,000 case purchases in any consecutive twelve months. Only National Tea Company, Kroger Grocery Company, Great Atlantic & Pacific Tea Company, Safeway Stores, Inc., and American Stores Company were big enough to purchase in 50,000-case quantities to obtain the $1.35 price. Morton Salt argued that its discount schedule was equally available to all purchasers of its salt and that there were no hidden or special rebates, allowances, prices, or discounts. However, the Supreme Court found that the discounts created discriminatory pric-

---

36. *Id.* at 622.
37. 334 U.S. 37 (1948).

ing, inasmuch as the largest discounts were "functionally" unavailable to its customers except for the five largest. The Court stated:

> Theoretically, these discounts are equally available to all, but functionally they are not. For as the record indicates ... no single independent retail grocery store, and probably no single wholesaler, bought as many as 50,000 cases or as much as $50,000 worth of table salt in one year. Furthermore, the record shows that, while certain purchasers were enjoying one or more of [Morton Salt's] standard quantity discounts, some of their competitors made purchases in such small quantities that they could not qualify for any of [Morton Salt's] discounts, even those based on carload shipments. The legislative history of the Robinson-Patman Act makes it abundantly clear that Congress considered it to be an evil that a large buyer could secure a competitive advantage over a smaller buyer solely because of the larger buyer's quantity purchasing ability. The Robinson-Patman Act was passed to deprive a large buyer of such advantages except to the extent that a lower price could be justified by reason of a seller's diminished cost due to quantity manufacture, delivery or sale, or by reason of the seller's good faith effort to meet a competitor's equally low price.[38]

On the issue of injury to secondary-line competition, the Supreme Court noted that the Robinson-Patman Act barred "discriminatory prices upon the 'reasonable possibility' that different prices for like goods to competing purchasers may have the defined effect." It then held that Morton Salt's quantity discounts "did result in price differentials between competing purchasers sufficient in amount to influence their resale prices of salt."[39]

A more difficult question arises when a large retailer performs its own wholesale function, thereby demanding the wholesale discount, or when a group of retailers join together and establish a wholesale organization in order to obtain wholesale prices. In these instances the manufacturer or seller is faced with the problem of whether it can charge the wholesale price, thereby in effect giving the retailers operating the wholesale organization a price that is lower than competing retailers paying the regular retail price. *General Auto Supplies, Inc.* v. *Federal Trade Commission*[40] is an example of this latter situation.

38. *Id.* at 42–43.
39. *Id.* at 47.
40. 346 F.2d 311 (7th Cir.), *cert. dismissed,* 382 U.S. 923 (1965).

In *General Auto,* some fifty auto parts jobbers organized National Parts Warehouse, a limited partnership, for the purpose of acting as a buying and wholesale distribution organization for the jobbers. There was no question that National Parts performed many of the functions of a wholesaler, such as purchasing for its own account, warehousing merchandise, billing its jobber customers and settling its account with suppliers on a monthly basis, and receiving discounts and allowances from suppliers in accordance with its arrangements with them. The savings through wholesale discounts, which National Parts accrued, were then distributed at year-end to the jobbers owning an interest in National Parts. The court of appeals concluded that this wholesale arrangement was discriminatory and a violation of the Robinson-Patman Act since jobbers who had an interest in National Parts received rebates annually in proportion to the amount of their purchases. This rebate gave them a price advantage over competing jobbers not participating in the National Parts setup.

52. Defenses to a Section 2(a) Robinson-Patman Act violation

There are two primary defenses to a Section 2(a) Robinson-Patman Act violation: cost justification and good faith meeting of competition. A third defense, which should be noted in passing, is set forth in the concluding paragraph of Section 2(a) and extends protection to "price changes from time to time in response to changing conditions affecting the market for or the marketability of the goods concerned, such as but not limited to actual or imminent deterioration of perishable goods, obsolescense of seasonal goods, distress sales under court process, or sales in good faith in discontinuance of business in the goods concerned." This proviso is intended to protect perishable food interests and seasonal food producers experiencing the price fluctuations characteristic of their industries.

53. The "cost justification" defense

Price differentials that are otherwise unlawful under Section 2(a) of the Robinson-Patman Act are expressly permitted if such differentials "make only due allowance for difference in cost of manufacture, sale or delivery" and if such cost differences are those "resulting from the differing methods or quantities in which the goods are "sold or delivered" to the two or more customers paying the different prices being questioned. The cost justification defense is simply stated, but its application has proven highly complex, costly, and for the most part unsuccessful.

In simplest terms the cost justification defense permits a seller to grant price preferences not exceeding his savings in the cost of serving favored buyers as compared with his cost of serving other buyers. Such savings do not include marginal costs. For example, a seller with idle capacity can profitably supply a new customer for very much less than the full cost of supplying his usual customers for whom he maintains his plant and establishment. Nevertheless, the new customer does benefit from the permanent facilities. To measure permitted price differences by incremental costs would "justify" any rational price preference to a customer, which the seller could plausibly characterize as "incremental." However, the act does not recognize such cost savings since they are not attributable to differing methods or quantities of sale or delivery.

The defense does recognize actual savings accrued in the manufacturing process, such as those resulting from early ordering, which permits smoother scheduling, avoidance of overtime, and more efficient production during the slack season. Where production for particular customers requires special equipment, tooling, or plant arrangements, the cost of such special arrangements can be allocated to the relevant order, thereby resulting in lower unit production costs for large orders as compared to small ones. Although such savings in manufacturing costs can be passed on to a particular customer pursuant to the terms of the cost justification defense, few manufacturers have attempted to prove cost savings in this manner in a Section 2(a) case.

A more viable method of proving differences in costs is in the area of sales and delivery. For example, a manufacturer selling an advertised brand through one distribution channel and unbranded goods through another may allocate all advertising costs to the former, thereby charging the latter a lower price. Similarly, if a manufacturer is required to maintain a warehouse for servicing some customers while others take direct delivery from the plant, such cost savings can be passed on to the latter. Savings in the cost of transportation may be passed on to a customer. For example, savings

incurred in shipping in truckloads or railroad-car quantities as compared to shipping in single crates or boxes may be passed on to the
buyer.

It is clear that when a manufacturer deals directly with a large
buyer and therefore bypasses a commission agent, the savings in brokerage fees cannot be passed on to the buyer. Similarly, if a large
buyer takes over the delivery function, thereby saving the manufacturer money, but incurs additional expenses itself, the only savings
that can be passed on are what the manufacturer actually saves and
not the additional expenses incurred by the buyer.

54. "Meeting competition" defense

The primary defense utilized by sellers against a Robinson-Patman
Act charge is that the discriminatory price charged was made in good
faith to meet an equally low price of a competitor. In asserting the
"meeting competition" defense under Section 2(b) of the Robinson-
Patman Act, the defendant has the burden of proving that his price
met, but did not beat, an equally low price of a competitor selling or
offering to sell to the same customer. The standard of compliance is
"good faith"; thus, the seller must in good faith establish what his
competitor's price was that he was seeking to meet.

"Good faith" meeting of competition can be established in a number of ways. A copy of a competitor's invoice given to the customer
is perhaps the best evidence. If such a document is unavailable, a
written statement of the customer as to the price or prices offered by
the competitor is the next best evidence. Because buyers normally
express a reluctance to provide such a document, a satisfactory alternative is for the manufacturer or seller to prepare a document setting
forth in writing the prices offered by a competitor as stated by the
customer. Some firms use a standard form, which their salesmen fill
out in the ordinary course of business, setting forth a competitor's
price as orally disclosed by the customer. A copy of this document
may or may not be sent to the customer for its records.

In *Federal Trade Commission* v. *A. E. Staley Mfg. Co.,*[41] the discriminatory prices in question were made in response to "verbal"
information that a competitor had granted an equally low price.

41. 324 U.S. 746 (1945).

However, defendant made no effort to investigate or verify the alleged competitive price, and there was no evidence as to the reliability of the informants upon whom defendant relied. The Supreme Court denied the meeting competition defense, stating:

> Section 2(b) does not require the seller to justify price discriminations by showing that in fact they met a competitive price. But it does place on the seller the burden of showing that the price was made in good faith to meet a competitor's. The good faith of the discrimination must be shown in the face of the fact that the seller is aware that his discrimination is unlawful, unless good faith is shown, and in circumstances which are peculiarly favorable to price discrimination abuses. We agree with the Commission that the statute at least requires the seller, who has knowingly discriminated in price, to show the existence of facts which would lead a reasonable and prudent person to believe that the granting of a lower price would in fact meet the equally low price of a competitor. Nor was the Commission wrong in holding that [A. E. Staley Co.] failed to meet this burden.[42]

In view of this admonition, manufacturers or sellers have been tempted to verify a competitor's price by simply calling the competitor, when all other means of price verification have failed. Yet more recent cases have demonstrated that such pricing contacts with competitors could lead to a more serious charge of price fixing under Section 1 of the Sherman Act. Certainly the risk of a cease and desist order of the Federal Trade Commission resulting from the failure to verify a competitor's price is in no way comparable to a felony conviction under Section 1 of the Sherman Act, which could result if verification is made directly through the competitor.[43]

Another problem arises as to whether a seller can lower its price to one customer in an effort to assist it in competing with that customer's competitor. In *Federal Trade Commission* v. *Sun Oil Co.*,[44] a Sunoco gas station operated by McLean was located diagonally across the street from a station operated by Super Test Oil Company. Super Test commenced a "sporadic" series of price cuts, each of which occasioned a substantial decline in McLean's sales. McLean complained to Sun Oil, requesting price assistance, which was

42. *Id.* at 759–60.

43. *See* United States v. United States Gypsum Co., 438 U.S. 422 (1978); United States v. Container Corp. of America, 393 U.S. 333 (1969).

44. 371 U.S. 505 (1963).

granted by Sun Oil lowering its price to McLean. No corresponding price reduction was given by Sun Oil to any of its other dealers in the area. During the period when McLean was the only Sunoco dealer receiving a price concession, the sales of other Sunoco dealers in the vicinity deteriorated substantially. Some customers who formerly went to other Sunoco dealers began buying gasoline from McLean. When the other Sunoco dealers sought the same concessions given McLean, they were refused even though a price war had subsequently broken out.

Sun Oil asserted the meeting competition defense on the theory that Super Test was not merely a competitor of McLean, but also Sun Oil's competitor, because in the last analysis all competition was directed to the sales of the final product—gasoline—to the motoring consumer. Anything that threatens to reduce the sales of a branded gasoline at the retailer's pump, Sun Oil contended, was a threat to the supplier whose business was a direct function of its station's marketing success or failure. Sun Oil further argued that the individual station was but a "conduit" for the supplier, and therefore Sun Oil was in competition with Super Test. The Supreme Court rejected this argument, stating:

> In a very real sense, however, every retailer is but a "conduit" for the goods which it sells and every supplier could, in the same sense, be considered a competitor of retailers selling competing goods. We are sure Congress had no such broad conception of competition in mind when it established the §2(b) defense [meeting competition] and, certainly, it intended no special exception for the petroleum industry. . . . Only differences of degree distinguish the situation of the gasoline station operator from that of many other retail outlets, and in numerous instances the distinction, if any, is slight. The "conduit" theory contains no inherent limitations and its acceptance would so expand the §2(b) defense as to effect a return to the broader "meeting competition" provision of the Clayton Act, which the Robinson-Patman Act amendments superseded.[45]

55. Brokerage payments and allowances

Section 2(c) of the Robinson-Patman Act prohibits the parties to a sales transaction from granting or receiving a "commission, broker-

45. *Id.* at 524–25.

age . . . or any allowance or discount in lieu thereof, except for services rendered in connection with the sale or purchase of goods." The purpose of this section of the act was to eliminate the practice of granting "dummy" or "fictitious" brokerage fees.

Before the Robinson-Patman Act was passed, large buyers, who maintained their own elaborate purchasing departments and therefore did not need the services of a seller's broker because they bought their merchandise directly from the seller, demanded and received allowances reflecting these savings in the cost of distribution. In many cases they required that "brokerage" fees be paid to their own purchasing agents. After the act was passed they discarded the facade of brokerage fees and merely received a price reduction equivalent to the seller's ordinary brokerage expenses in sales to other customers. They argued that because no brokerage services were needed by them because of their large size, they were entitled to a price differential reflecting this cost saving. In other words, under the cost justification defense the seller, not having to pay the normal brokerage fee, could pass this on to the buyer pursuant to Section 2(a). However, at an early date the courts, as well as the Federal Trade Commission, rejected the argument that such a price reduction was lawful because the buyer's purchasing organization had saved the seller the amount of his ordinary brokerage expense.

Federal Trade Commission v. *Henry Broch & Co.*[46] involved a broker or sales representative for a number of principals, including Canada Foods, who sold food products. J. M. Smucker Co., a buyer, sought to purchase apple concentrate from Canada Foods for $1.25 per gallon. Canada Foods at first refused, stating that its price was $1.30 per gallon. It then agreed to sell at $1.25 per gallon if the broker, Henry Broch, would agree to reduce its commission from 5 percent to 3 percent. Broch agreed, and the arrangement was consummated, although Broch continued to receive the 5 percent brokerage commission on all Canada Foods' sales made to other customers. Broch argued that the seller had the right to pass on to the buyer, in the form of a price reduction, any differential between his ordinary brokerage expense and the brokerage commission that he paid on a particular sale, because the cost justification defense of Section 2(a) allows any cost savings in the selling of a product to be passed on to

46. 363 U.S. 166 (1960).

the buyer. Thus, it was argued, the broker should not be held liable under Section 2(c) for having done that which was lawful under 2(a).

The Court concluded that Section 2(c) was independent of Section 2(a) and was enacted to foreclose certain abuses not covered by Section 2(a). The Court, in finding a violation, stated:

> Congress enacted the Robinson-Patman Act to prevent sellers and sellers' brokers from yielding to the economic pressures of a large buying organization by granting unfair preferences in connection with the sale of goods. The form in which the buyer pressure is exerted is immaterial and proof of its existence is not required. It is rare that the notice in yielding to a buyer's demands is not the "necessity" for making the sale. An "independent" broker is not likely to be independent of the buyer's coercive bargaining power. He, like the seller, is constrained to favor the buyers with the most purchasing power. If [Broch] merely paid over part of his commission to the buyer, he clearly would have violated the Act. We see no distinction of substance between the two transactions. In each case the seller and his broker make a concession to the buyer as a consequence of his economic power. In both cases the result is that the buyer has received a discriminatory price. In both cases the seller's broker reduces his usual brokerage fee to get a particular contract. There is no difference in economic effect between the seller's broker splitting his brokerage commission with the buyer and his yielding part of the brokerage to the seller to be passed on to the buyer in the form of a lower price.[47]

56. Allowances and services provisions

Sections 2(d) and 2(e) of the Robinson-Patman Act prohibit a seller from granting advertising and promotional allowances or services to customers unless they are available to all competing customers on proportionally equal terms. The Supreme Court in *Federal Trade Commission* v. *Simplicity Pattern Co.*[48] held that the proscriptions set forth in Sections 2(d) and 2(e) are absolute and require no showing of competitive injury, thus foreclosing the defense of cost justification. In that case the defendant Simplicity Pattern manfactured and sold tissue patterns, which were used in the home for making women's and children's wearing apparel. The patterns were sold to

47. *Id.* at 174–75.
48. 360 U.S. 55 (1959).

some 12,300 retailers with 17,200 outlets. Eighteen percent of these customers were department and variety stores which accounted for 70 percent of the sales made, while the remaining 82 percent of its customers were small stores whose primary business was the sale of yard-good fabrics.

Simplicity Pattern charged a uniform price to all customers; however, it did not grant uniform services and facilities to all customers. To variety stores it furnished patterns on a consignment basis, requiring payment only as the patterns were sold—thus affording them an investment-free inventory. The fabric stores had to pay cash for their patterns. Additionally, cabinets and catalogs were furnished free to variety stores, while the fabric stores were charged $2 to $3 for each catalog. Finally, all transportation costs in connection with business done with variety stores were absorbed by Simplicity Pattern, while none of such costs were absorbed concerning business done with fabric stores.

The defendant argued that there was no competition between the variety and fabric stores, that the differential treatment only reflected the differences in costs in dealing with the two types of customers, and that there was no injury to competition. The Court found that the variety and fabric stores, which stood side by side, were in competition. It further stated:

> Subsections (c), (d) and (e) . . . unqualifiedly make unlawful certain business practices other than price discriminations. Subsection (c) applies to the payment or receipt of commissions or brokerage allowances "except for services rendered." Subsection (d) prohibits the payment by a seller to a customer for any services or facilities furnished by the latter, unless "such payment . . . is available on proportionally equal terms to all other [competing] customers. Subsection (e), which as noted is the provision applicable in this case, makes it unlawful for a seller "to discriminate in favor of one purchaser against another purchaser or purchasers of a commodity bought for resale . . . by . . . furnishing . . . any services or facilities connected with the processing, handling, sale, or offering for sale of such commodity so purchased upon terms not accorded to all purchasers on proportionally equal terms."
>
> In terms, the proscription of these three sections are absolute. Unlike §2(a), none of them requires, as proof of a prima facie violation, a showing that the illicit practice has had an injurious or destruc-

tive effect on competition. Similarly, none has any built-in defensive matter, as does §2(a).[49]

The Court concluded that the cost justification defense was unavailable for violation of Sections 2(c), (d), and (e).

The defendant, The Great Atlantic and Pacific Tea Company, which operated some 200 A&P stores in the Chicago metropolitan area, was charged in *State Wholesale Grocers* v. *The Great Atlantic & Pacific Tea Co.*[50] with selling advertising space in its *Woman's Day* magazine to the defendants General Foods Corporation, Morton Salt Company, and Hunt Foods, Inc. *Woman's Day* was a magazine published by Woman's Day, Inc., a wholly owned subsidiary of A&P. The magazine originally had been given away at the A&P checkout counter, but since 1951 was sold for 7 cents per copy. Unlike its competition—*Good Housekeeping, Ladies' Home Journal, McCall's* and *Woman's Home Companion*—*Woman's Day* could be obtained only at the A&P checkout counter. The magazine was primarily an advertising device for A&P stores. The annual cost of producing the magazine in 1954 and 1955 was $9,000,000, only one third of which was recovered through sales, with the remainder being recovered through the sale of advertising space. Advertising charges were comparable to any other like magazine.

The court found that there was a violation of Section 2(d) because the defendant suppliers paid *Woman's Day,* a subsidiary of A&P, for advertising services in a magazine furnished by A&P in connection with the sale of products manufactured, sold, or offered for sale by those suppliers. Section 2(d) made the transaction unlawful, "unless such payment or consideration was available on proportionally equal terms to all other customers competing in the distribution of such products."[51]

Another leading case in this area is *Federal Trade Commission* v. *Fred Meyer, Inc.*[52] In that case Fred Meyer operated a chain of thirteen supermarkets in the Portland, Oregon, area, which engaged in the retail grocery, drug variety items, and clothing business. In 1957 Meyer's sales exceeded $40 million which accounted for one fourth

49. *Id.* at 65.
50. 258 F.2d 831 (7th Cir. 1958), *cert. denied,* 358 U.S. 947 (1959).
51. *Id.* at 837.
52. 390 U.S. 341 (1968).

of the retail food sales in the area. Since 1936, Meyer had annually conducted a four-week promotional campaign based on the distribution of coupon books to consumers. The books contained seventy-two pages, each featuring a single product being sold by Meyer at a reduced price. The consumer bought the book for the nominal sum of 10 cents and surrendered the appropriate coupon when making his purchase of goods. A coupon represented a savings of one third or more in the price of a product. Meyer sold 138,700 books in 1957 and 121,270 books in 1958. To finance the books, Meyer charged the supplier of each featured product a fee of at least $350 for each coupon page advertising his product. Some participating suppliers further underwrote the promotion by giving Meyer price reductions on its purchases of featured items.

Defendants argued that there was no violation of Section 2(d) of the act because two of the suppliers in question participating in the program did not sell directly to retail stores competing against Meyer, but rather to wholesalers who in turn sold to retail stores. Failure to give these wholesalers the same allowances given Meyer, it was argued, could not violate the act because such wholesalers were not competing against Meyer. Likewise, defendants contended, the retailers who did compete against Meyer were outside the protection of Section 2(d) because they were not customers of the suppliers who sold to Meyer. The Supreme Court rejected this reasoning.

The Court premised its decision with the proposition that "[t]he Robinson-Patman Act was enacted in 1936 to curb and prohibit all devices by which large buyers gained discriminatory preferences over smaller ones by virtue of their greater purchasing power."[53] The Court next stated that it did not matter whether disfavored customers were sold to directly by the supplier as long as the supplier afforded a "direct" buyer the kind of competitive advantage which Section 2(d) prohibits. In reaching this conclusion, the Court held that

> when a supplier gives allowances to a direct-buying retailer, he must also make them available on comparable terms to those who buy his products through wholesalers and compete with the direct buyer in resales. Nothing we have said bars a supplier, consistently with other

---

53. *Id.* at 349, quoting Federal Trade Commission v. Henry Broch & Co., 363 U.S. 166, 168 (1960).

provisions of the antitrust laws, from utilizing his wholesalers to distribute payments or administer a promotional program, so long as the supplier takes responsibility, under rules and guides promulgated by the Commission for the regulation of such practices, for seeing that the allowances are made available to all who compete in the resale of his product.[54]

In response to the Court's decision, the Federal Trade Commission promulgated its 1969 Guides for Advertising Allowances and Other Merchandising Payments and Services.[55] These guides require the seller to treat all purchasers buying from wholesalers on the same terms as though they were buying directly from it, and to extend them all promotional allowances on comparable terms to those given direct buyers. The primary test of the seller's obligations under the *Fred Meyer* standards is a "good faith" effort to carry them out. In this regard the seller may enter an agreement with wholesalers or distributors which provides that such intermediaries will perform all or part of the seller's obligations under the rules.

57. The buyer's liability

Section 2(f) of the Robinson-Patman Act, the so-called "buyer provision," prohibits a buyer from knowingly inducing or receiving a discriminatory price that is unlawful under Section 2(a). Few cases have been brought under Section 2(f) for the simple reason that a seller is unlikely to complain about the illegal conduct of a buyer because such a complaint would undoubtedly cost the seller all future business. Thus, buyers not infrequently violate Section 2(f) in their attempts to induce sellers to lower their prices, but they do so with some comfort in the fact that sellers are not in a position to complain to the Federal Trade Commission or sue directly.

The leading decision in this area is *Automatic Canteen Co.* v. *Federal Trade Commission.*[56] In that case the defendant was a large buyer of candy and other confectionary products, which it resold through approximately 230,000 automatic vending machines operated in thirty-three states and the District of Columbia. Evidence was

---

54. *Id.* at 358.
55. 16 C.F.R. §240, 1–17.
56. 346 U.S. 61 (1953).

offered at trial that the defendant had solicited prices that were as much as 33 percent lower than the prices quoted other purchasers. A question arose as to whether the lower price received by the defendant was cost justified and who had the burden of proving whether it was or was not. The Supreme Court took the position that the plaintiff, or, in this case, the Federal Trade Commission, had the burden of coming forward with evidence showing the buyer's "knowledge" of the illegality of the price or, in other words, that it was not cost justified. However, to prove this knowledge, the Court said that the plaintiff could rely on "trade experience." The Court stated:

> By way of example, a buyer who knows that he buys in the same quantities as his competitor and is served by the seller in the same manner or with the same amount of exertion as the other buyer can fairly be charged with notice that a substantial price differential cannot be justified. The Commission need only to show, to establish its *prima facie* case, that the buyer knew that the methods by which he was served and quantities in and which he purchased were the same as in the case of his competitor. If the methods or quantities differ, the Commission must only show that such differences could not give rise to sufficient savings in the cost of manufacture, sale or delivery to justify the price differential, and that the buyer, knowing these were the only differences, should have known that they could not give rise to sufficient cost savings. The showing of knowledge, of course, will depend to some extent on the size of the discrepancy between cost differential and price differential, so that the two questions are not isolated. A showing that the cost differences are very small compared with the price differential and could not reasonably have been thought to justify the price difference should be sufficient.[57]

In *American Motors Specialties Co.* v. *Federal Trade Commission,*[58] action was brought against seventeen automotive replacement parts jobbers operating in the New York City metropolitan area and two corporate buying groups organized by the seventeen jobbers, Automotive Group Buyers, Inc. and its successor, Metropolitan Automotive Wholesalers Cooperative, Inc. The purpose of the two buying groups was to achieve certain economies and price advantages granted to large-scale buyers. The procedure followed was for manufacturers to submit price lists to the group's executive secretary and,

57. *Id.* at 80.
58. 278 F.2d 225 (2d Cir.), *cert. denied,* 364 U.S. 884 (1960).

if approved, the seventeen members would place their individual orders on written forms bearing the buying group's name. Shipment of goods was made directly to each member. The stated reason for the buying group was to take advantage of the annual rebates given by manufacturers based on the dollar volume purchased, the percentage of rebate increasing with the increase in volume. By receiving a larger percentage rebate, each individual member had a price advantage over its unorganized competitors. The court found that there was an unlawful inducement of discriminatory prices in violation of Section 2(f):

> [Defendants] of course knew that they, as individual firms, were receiving goods in the same quantities and were served by sellers in the same manner as their competitors and hence organized themselves into a buying group in order to obtain lower prices than their unorganized competitors. Hence, by the very fact of having combined into a group and having obtained thereby a favorable price differential, they each, under Automatic Canteen, were charged with notice that this price differential they each enjoyed could not be justified. And this knowledge of each of the seventeen individual firms is imputable to the organization of which they were all members.[59]

As one can see from this discussion there are many obstacles to proving a Robinson-Patman Act violation. However, it should be noted that government enforcement of the act in recent years has been less than enthusiastic. At one time, Robinson-Patman cases accounted for a major part of the Federal Trade Commission's antitrust enforcement effort. Today, the commission's complaints have declined in number to but a few per year. Angry congressmen have accused the commission of administrative repeal of the Robinson-Patman Act and have ominously suggested that those responsible are in contempt of Congress.

In 1975, the Antitrust Division, as part of the Ford Administration's deregulation program, proposed repeal or reform of the Robinson-Patman Act. Three alternative legislative proposals were made: outright repeal, with subsequent reliance on Section 2 of the Sherman Act to reach predatory price discriminations; or the enactment of a Predatory Practices Act to protect primary-line competition only; or, as a third alternative, the enactment of a Robinson-Patman

---

59. *Id.* at 228.

Reform Statute to protect both primary- and secondary-line competition.

Even before the legislative proposals were made, small business organizations and supporters of small business in Congress came to the defense of the act. The House Small Business Committee established an ad hoc subcomittee to hold hearings on the Robinson-Patman Act. Ultimately, efforts to repeal the act failed, but opposition to it from both governmental and business quarters remains strong, thus portending a decreasing importance for the act in antitrust enforcement.

Chapter Six

The Clayton Act

Section 2 of the Clayton Act, commonly known as the Robinson-Patman Act, has already been discussed in Chapter 5. The Clayton Act, in Sections 3, 7, and 8, proscribes other forms of business conduct that deserve some mention in passing. Section 3, which, like the Robinson-Patman Act, is of limited utility today, covers certain exclusionary buying and selling practices. Section 7 deals with horizontal, vertical, and, to a limited extent, conglomerate mergers. Section 8 proscribes interlocking directorates created by persons serving as directors of competing business corporations or as directors or employees of several banks. For the most part, this area of the law is complex and beyond what can be satisfactorily discussed in the space allotted. Thus, discussion of these sections will focus on fundamental considerations rather than the more intricate aspects of the law.

58. Section 3 of the Clayton Act

Section 3 of the Clayton Act prohibits three types of restrictive arrangements, which are also encompassed within the broader provisions of Section 1 of the Sherman Act.[1]

1. To the extent that an agreement between a seller and buyer requires the latter to use his "best efforts" in reselling a manufacturer's goods, there is no antitrust violation. *See* Matthew Conveyor Co. v. Palmer-Bee Co., 135 F.2d 73 (6th Cir. 1943).

1. Exclusive dealings arrangements
2. Requirements contracts
3. Tying arrangements

Because each of these violations has already been discussed in terms of the Sherman Act, repetition of the cases and discussion will be held to a minimum.

An exclusive dealings arrangement arises when a seller agrees to sell to a buyer on the condition that the buyer agrees not to deal in products of the seller's competitors. For example, an exclusive dealings contract between a manufacturer and a wholesaler would bar the latter from acting as a wholesaler for the goods of a competing manufacturer. Requirements contracts are essentially exclusive dealings contracts under which the buyer agrees to purchase all or substantially all of his needs of a particular product from the manufacturer or seller. A tying arrangement requires the buyer to agree to purchase a second or "tied" product from the seller as a condition of purchasing a desired or "tying" product. A tying arrangement requiring the purchaser to accept the seller's entire line of goods in order to obtain a desired product is commonly termed full-line enforcing.

Tie-in restrictions are viewed more critically than exclusive dealings or requirements contracts and are treated as *per se* illegal under Section 1 of the Sherman Act. The vice of a tie-in restriction is that it denies competitors free access to the market for the tied or second product, not because the party imposing the tie-in has a better product or a lower price, but because he has power or leverage created by the tying or desired product. For this reason they have been described by the Supreme Court as hardly serving any purpose other than the suppression of competition.[2]

Exclusive dealings and requirements contracts are treated less harshly by the courts. When used by new businesses to gain a foothold in the market or to obtain outlets for a marginal competitor, they have been held legal. Requirements contracts probably fare the best because, unlike exclusive dealings contracts, they may be advantageous to buyers as well as to sellers, particularly when a buyer

---

2. Because tie-in restrictions involve Section 1 Sherman Act violations as well as Section 3 Clayton Act violations, the tie-in cases discussed in Chapter 3 are equally applicable here. Indeed, most tie-in cases plead both Section 1 Sherman Act and Section 3 Clayton Act violations.

needs an assured source of supply. The legality of exclusive dealings and requirements contracts is normally determined by the reasonableness of the arrangement and whether the contract in fact forecloses competition from a substantial portion of the market.

A leading case in the requirements contracts area is *Tampa Electric Co.* v. *Nashville Coal Co.*[3] The plaintiff Tampa Electric, a public utility located in Tampa Bay, Florida, operated two electrical generating plants in 1954, which consumed oil as their fuel. In 1955, it expanded its facilities by constructing an additional generating plant known as the "Francis J. Gannon Station," which was to consume coal. To assure an adequate supply of coal, Tampa Electric entered a contract with the defendant Nashville Coal Company, which provided that the latter would supply Tampa Electric with all of its requirements of coal, and not less than 225,000 tons per year, for a twenty-year period. After Tampa Electric had expended some $3,000,000 more than the cost of constructing oil burning units, Nashville Coal Company repudiated the contract on the ground that it violated the antitrust laws including Section 3 of the Clayton Act.

The lower courts found that there was a violation of Section 3 of the Clayton Act because the contract excluded some 700 other coal producers, which could sell in the same market, from selling coal to Tampa Electric for a twenty-year period. The Supreme Court, however, noted that in the seven-state area serviced by the other 700 coal producers, Tampa Electric had contracted to consume only 1 percent of the total marketed production. The Court concluded that preemption of competition to the extent of the tonnage involved did not tend substantially to foreclose competition in the relevant coal market, and therefore the contract was legal. In reaching this conclusion the Court stated that a twenty-year contract assured Tampa Electric of a steady and ample supply of fuel, which was necessary "in the public interest." The Court further observed:

> It may well be that in the context of antitrust legislation protracted requirements contracts are suspect, but they have not been declared illegal *per se*. Even though a single contract between single traders may fall within the initial broad proscription of the section, it must also suffer the qualifying disability, tending to work a substantial—not remote—lessening of competition in the relevant competitive market. It is urged that the present contract preempts competition to the

3. 365 U.S. 320 (1961).

extent of purchases worth perhaps $128,000,000, and that this "is, of course, not insignificant or insubstantial." While $128,000,000 is a considerable sum of money, even in these days, the dollar volume, by itself, is not the test, as we have already pointed out.

The remaining determination, therefore, is whether the preemption of competition to the extent of the tonnage involved tends to substantially foreclose competition in the relevant coal market. We think not. That market sees an annual trade in excess of 250,000,000 tons of coal and over a billion dollars—multiplied by 20 years it runs into astronomical figures.[4]

A second case, *Standard Oil of California* v. *United States,*[5] further illustrates the applicability of Section 3 of the Clayton Act. Standard Oil Company of California owned petroleum-producing resources and refining plants in California and sold petroleum products in Arizona, California, Idaho, Nevada, Oregon, Utah, and Washington. It sold its products through its own service stations, as well as to independent service stations and industrial users. In this six-state area it was, in 1946, the largest seller of gasoline, accounting for 23 percent of the total taxable gallonage sold. Standard was charged with entering exclusive supply contracts with operators of 5,937 independent stations, which accounted for 16 percent of the retail market. There were two types of exclusive contracts: one involved an agreement that the station operator would purchase from Standard all his requirements of petroleum products as well as tires, tubes, and batteries; the other required the station operator to purchase only from Standard all his requirements of petroleum products. It was undisputed that all of Standard's major competitors employed similar exclusive dealing arrangements.

The United States Supreme Court first observed that requirements contracts may be of economic benefit to both the buyer and seller. The buyer is assured a constant supply with concomitant protection against rising prices, thereby facilitating long-term planning on the basis of known costs. Moreover, such contracts obviate the buyer's expense and risk of having to store sufficient quantities of the commodity to compensate for fluctuating demand. From the seller's point of view, requirements contracts may make possible a reduction in selling expenses, give protection against price fluctuations, and—

4. *Id.* at 333–34.
5. 337 U.S. 293 (1949).

of particular advantage to a newcomer in the field—offer the possibility of a predictable market.

Although Standard's competitive position did not improve during the period of the requirements contracts and the period of those contracts was not excessive, the Court still found a violation of Section 3:

> When it is remembered that all the other major suppliers have also been using requirements contracts, and when it is noted that the relative share of the business which fell to each remained about the same during the period of their use, it would not be far fetched to infer that their effect has been to enable the established suppliers individually to maintain their own standing and at the same time collectively, even though not collusively, to prevent a late arrival from wresting away more than an insignificant portion of the market.[6]

The Court concluded that sufficient competition was foreclosed to satisfy the "injury to competition" requirements of Section 3. The fact that a Standard dealer could not purchase the products from others in competition with Standard and that dealers of the other major oil companies were similarly bound created a "potential clog on competition as it was the purpose of §3 to remove."[7]

Unlike tying violations, exclusive dealings and requirements contracts have generated a minimal number of Section 3 cases, perhaps because of the difficulty of proving the requisite injury to competition.

59. Mergers and acquisitions—Section 7 of Clayton Act

Section 7 of the Clayton Act provides that no corporation engaged in interstate commerce shall acquire, directly or indirectly, in whole or in part, the stock or assets of another corporation also engaged in interstate commerce where the effect may substantially lessen competition or tend to create a monopoly.[8] Essentially, three types of

6. *Id.* at 309.

7. *Id.* at 314.

8. 15 U.S.C. §18. The statute further provides that it does not apply to corporations purchasing such stock solely for investment and not using the same by voting or otherwise to bring about a substantial lessening of competition. Also, the statute does not foreclose a corporation from forming subsidiary corporations for the carrying on of their lawful business or from holding all or part of the stock of such subsidiary corporations, when the effect is not to lessen substantially competition.

mergers are of concern to the courts—horizontal, vertical, and conglomerate mergers—and each will be considered in some depth.

The elimination of competition through mergers and acquisitions has been of such concern to the Department of Justice that it has established "Department of Justice's Merger Guidelines" setting forth its overall enforcement scheme with regard to Section 7 of the Clayton Act. Pursuant to these guidelines the primary role of Section 7 enforcement is to preserve and promote market structures conducive to competition. With respect to mergers between direct competitors—horizontal mergers—governmental enforcement of Section 7 has the following interrelated purposes: (1) preventing elimination as an independent business entity of any company likely to have been a substantial competitive influence in a market, (2) preventing any company or small group of companies from obtaining a position of dominance in a market, (3) preventing significant increases in concentration in the market, and (4) preserving significant possibilities for eventual deconcentration in a concentrated market. In a highly concentrated market, where the four largest firms account for 75 percent or more of the business, the government will ordinarily challenge mergers between firms accounting for approximately the following percentages:

Acquiring Firm	*Acquired Firm*
4% or more	4% or more
10% or more	2% or more
15% or more	1% or more

In less highly concentrated markets, that is, those where the four largest firms control less than 75 percent of the business, the government will ordinarily challenge mergers between firms accounting for approximately the following percentages:

Acquiring Firm	*Acquired Firm*
5%	5% or more
10%	4% or more
15%	3% or more
20%	2% or more
25% or more	1% or more

The government will apply stricter standards in challenging mergers in markets where there is a significant trend toward increased concentration. Such a trend is deemed to be present when the aggregate market share of any grouping of the largest firms in the market from the two largest to the eight largest has increased by approximately 7 percent or more over a five- to ten-year period prior to the merger up to the time of the merger. An increase of 2 percent of the market share of any such large firm acquiring another will be challenged.

With respect to vertical mergers, where a firm either integrates backward by acquiring its sources of supply or forward by acquiring its distribution channels, the government's enforcement policy is intended to prevent changes in the market structure likely to lead over the course of time to significant anticompetitive consequences. In general, such consequences exist whenever a particular vertical acquisition, or series of acquisitions by a firm in a supplying or purchasing market, significantly tends "to raise barriers to entry" in either market or to disadvantage existing nonintegrated or partly integrated firms in either market in ways unrelated to economic efficiency. Such barriers are the following:

1. Foreclosing equal access to potential customers, thus reducing the ability of nonintegrated firms to capture competitively the market share needed to achieve an efficient level of production, or imposing the burden of entry on an integrated basis (i.e. at both the supplying and purchasing levels) even though entry at a single level would permit efficient operation.
2. Foreclosing equal access to potential suppliers, thus either increasing the risk of a price or supply squeeze on the new entrant or imposing the additional burden of entry on an integrated firm.
3. Facilitating promotional product differentiation when the merger involves a manufacturing firm's acquisition of firms at the retail level.

In applying the above standards in the supplying firm's market, the government attaches primary significance to (1) the market share of the supplying firm, (2) the market share of the purchasing firm or firms, and (3) the conditions of entry in the purchasing firm's market.

Thus, the government will ordinarily challenge a merger or series of mergers between a supplying firm, accounting for approximately 10 percent or more of the sales in its market, and one or more purchasing firms, accounting *in toto* for approximately 6 percent or more of the total purchases in the market, unless it clearly appears that there are no significant barriers to entry into the business of the purchasing firm or firms. The same standard is applied when the adverse effect is felt in the purchasing firm's market.

Conceptually, conglomerate mergers are more difficult to deal with because they are neither horizontal nor vertical, but involve acquisitions in unrelated areas. The government's policy with respect to such mergers is to prevent changes in market structure that appear likely over the course of time either to cause a substantial lessening of competition that would otherwise exist or tend to create a monopoly. Two categories of conglomerate mergers have been targeted as having identifiable anticompetitive consequences sufficient to warrant government action: mergers involving potential entrants and mergers creating a danger of reciprocal buying. In the first category, the government will ordinarily challenge a merger between a firm that is a likely entrant into a market and any of the following firms:

1. Any firm with approximately 25 percent or more of the market.
2. One of the two largest firms in a market in which the shares of the two largest firms amount to approximately 50 percent or more.
3. One of the four largest firms in a market in which the shares of the eight largest firms amount to approximately 75 percent of the market or more, providing the merging firm's share of the market amounts to approximately 10 percent or more.
4. One of the eight largest firms in a market in which the shares of these firms amount to approximately 75 percent or more, provided either (a) the merging firm's share of the market is not insubstantial and there are no more than one or two likely entrants into the market, or (b) the merging firm is a rapidly growing firm.

Additionally, the government will challenge a merger between an existing competitor in the market and a firm that is likely to enter, when the merger is consummated for the purpose of preventing the competitive disturbance or disruption a new competitor in the market might create.

Similarly, the government will challenge any merger that creates a significant danger of reciprocal buying. Such danger will be found to exist if 15 percent or more of the purchases made in a particular market (in which one of the parties to the merger sells) are made by firms that make sales in markets where the other party to the merger is a substantial buyer—"a more substantial buyer than all or most of the competitors" of the first party to the merger. The government will also challenge (1) any merger undertaken for the purpose of facilitating the creation of reciprocal buying arrangements, and (2) any merger creating the possibility of substantial reciprocal buying where one (or both) of the merging firms has, within the recent past, actually engaged in reciprocal buying or done so after the consummation of the merger. Similarly, also subject to challenge are direct or indirect attempts to induce firms with which the merging or recently merged firms deal to engage in reciprocal buying in the product markets in which the possibility of reciprocal buying has been created.

Finally, the government may bring legal action where the acquisition of a leading firm in a relatively concentrated or rapidly concentrating market may serve to entrench or increase the market power of that firm or raise barriers to entry in that market. Examples of this type of merger include (1) a merger that produces a very large disparity in absolute size between the merged firms and the largest remaining firm, (2) a merger of firms producing related products which may induce purchasers, concerned about the merged firms possible use of leverage, to buy products of the merged firm rather than those of competitors, and (3) a merger that may enhance the ability of the merged firm to increase product differentiation in the relevant market.

60. Horizontal mergers

In *Brown Shoe Co.* v. *United States*,[9] the government filed an action under Section 7 of the Clayton Act to bar a merger between the G.

9. 370 U.S. 294 (1962).

R. Kinney Company, Inc. and the Brown Shoe Company, Inc., which was to be effectuated by an exchange of Kinney stock for Brown stock. At the time of the proposed exchange in late 1955, Brown was the third largest seller of shoes in terms of dollar volume in the United States, it was a leading manufacturer of men's, women's, and children's shoes, and it was a retailer with over 1,230 owned, operated, or controlled retail outlets. Kinney was, based on dollar volume, the eighth largest company in the sale of shoes. It was also a large manufacturer of shoes and a retailer with over 350 retail outlets. Brown argued that the proposed merger would have little or no effect on competition because Kinney manufactured less than 0.5 percent and retailed less than 2 percent of the nation's shoes.

Examining the record, the Court concluded that there were three relevant *product* markets—men's shoes, women's shoes, and children's shoes. These three categories of shoes were generally produced in separate factories and, in many instances, sold in separate stores. The Court stated that the acquisition of Kinney by Brown resulted in a horizontal combination at both the *manufacturing* and *retailing* levels of their businesses. However, the government dropped its argument that the acquisition by Brown of Kinney's manufacturing facilities violated the Clayton Act and concentrated instead on the illegal effect of the acquisition of Kinney's retail facilities.

The Court first noted that prior to the merger Brown and Kinney competed at the retail level in selling men's, women's and children's shoes. In analyzing the geographic market in which this competition took place, the Court stated that the geographic market selected must correspond to the commercial realities of the industry and be economically significant:

> Thus, although the geographic market in some instances may encompass the entire Nation, under other circumstances it may be as small as a single metropolitan area. . . . The fact that two merging firms have competed directly on the horizontal level in but a fraction of the geographic markets in which either has operated, does not, in itself, place their merger outside the scope of §7. That section speaks of "any . . . section of the country," and if anticompetitive effects of a merger are probable in "any" significant market, the merger—at least to that extent—is proscribed.[10]

10. *Id.* at 337.

The Court agreed with the trial court that the relevant geographic market for *manufacturing* was the entire nation, but for *retailing* it was limited to those cities with a population exceeding 10,000 and their environs in which both Brown and Kinney retailed shoes through their own outlets. "Such markets are large enough to include the downtown shops and suburban shopping centers in areas contiguous to the city."[11]

In finding that the merger violated Section 7 of the Clayton Act, the Court noted that during 1955 in thirty-two separate cities—ranging in size and location from Topeka, Kansas, to Batavia, New York, and Hobbs, New Mexico—the combined share of Brown and Kinney sales of women's shoes exceeded 20 percent. In thirty-one cities the combined share of children's shoe sales exceeded 20 percent; in six cities their share exceeded 40 percent. In Dodge City, Kansas, their combined share of the market for women's shoes was over 57 percent; their share of the children's shoe market in that city was 49 percent. In seven cities in which Brown and Kinney's combined shares of the market for women's shoes were greatest (ranging from 33 percent to 57 percent), each of the parties prior to the merger had individually captured substantial portions of those markets (ranging from 13 to 34 percent); the merger intensified this existing concentration. In 118 separate cities the combined shares of the market of Brown and Kinney in the sale of one of the relevant lines of commerce exceeded 5 percent. In forty-seven cities, their share exceeded 5 percent in all three lines.

The Court noted that although Brown, with the Kinney acquisition, controlled only 7.2 percent of the shoe store outlets, the merger further spurred the increasing trend toward concentration in the shoe industry:

> If a merger achieving 5% control were now approved, we might be required to approve future merger efforts by Brown's competitors seeking similar market shares. The oligopoly Congress sought to avoid would then be furthered and it would be difficult to dissolve the combinations previously approved. Furthermore, in this fragmented industry, even if the combination controls but a small share of a particular market, the fact that this share is held by a large national chain can adversely affect competition.[12]

11. *Id.* at 339.
12. *Id.* at 343–44.

United States v. *Philadelphia National Bank*[13] is another excellent example of the application of Section 7 of the Clayton Act. In that action the government brought a suit to enjoin a proposed merger of the Philadelphia National Bank and Girard Trust Corn Exchange Bank. The federal district court held that the merger did not violate Section 7 of the Clayton Act, but the Supreme Court found such a violation and ordered the merger enjoined. The Philadelphia National Bank was, at the time of the proposed merger, the second largest bank and the Girard the third largest of the forty-two commercial banks with head offices in the Philadelphia metropolitan area. The assets of the Philadelphia National Bank were over $1 billion and the Girard about $750 million. The proposed merger would have made the resulting bank the largest bank in the metropolitan area, with 36 percent of the area banks' total assets, 36 percent of deposits, and 34 percent of net loans.

Of importance to the Court's decision was the fact that both the Philadelphia National Bank and Girard had grown through prior mergers with other institutions and "the trend toward concentration is noticeable in the Philadelphia area generally."[14] Defendants took the position that although both banks were viable, the bank resulting from the merger, with its greater prestige and increased lending limit, would be better able to compete with large out-of-state (particularly New York) banks, would attract new business to Philadelphia, and in general would promote the economic development of the metropolitan area.

The Court held that the *product market* was "commercial banking," which included checking accounts, trust administration, and personal loans. The more difficult question was defining the "geographic market," which it concluded was the four-county Philadelphia metropolitan area. In reaching this conclusion the Court rejected the defendants' principal contention that the merger would more effectively permit competition with the New York banks. The Court stated that

> it is suggested that the increased lending limit of the resulting bank will enable it to compete with the large out-of-state bank, particularly the New York banks, for very large loans. . . . If anticompetitive

13. 374 U.S. 321 (1963).
14. *Id.* at 331.

effects in one market could be justified by procompetitive consequences in another, the logical upshot would be that every firm in an
industry could, without violating §7, embark on a series of mergers
that would make it in the end as large as the industry leader. For if
all the commercial banks in the Philadelphia area merged into one, it
would be smaller than the largest bank in New York City. This is not
a case, plainly, where two small firms in a market propose to merge
in order to be able to compete more successfully with the leading firms
in that market. Nor is it a case in which lack of adequate banking
facilities is causing hardships to individuals or businesses in the community. The present two largest banks in Philadelphia have lending
limits of $8,000,000 each. The only businesses located in the Phila-
delphia area which find such limits inadequate are large enough to
obtain bank credit in other cities.[15]

Where a major competitor in a *concentrated* industry has acquired
a minor competitor with only a small share of the market, the
Supreme Court has still found a violation of Section 7 of the Clayton
Act. In *United States* v. *Aluminum Co. of America,*[16] Alcoa, the leading producer in several lines of aluminum wire and cable, acquired
Rome Cable Corporation, a corporation manufacturing and selling
copper wire and cable line as well as some aluminum wire and cable.
In the year prior to the merger, both Rome and Alcoa were engaged
in the production of base aluminum wire cable, which was used for
overhead public utility lines. Rome produced 4.7 percent of the total
industry production and Alcoa 32.5 percent. However, copper wire
was also used in utility lines, and if both aluminum and copper wire
and cable were considered the relevant product market, as defendant
argued they should, then Alcoa's and Rome's respective percentages
of the market would have been considerably less.

The Supreme Court ruled that although they were used for the
same purpose, aluminum wire and cable was a separate *product market* from the copper wire and cable because aluminum prices were
50 to 65 percent less than copper prices and thus not responsive to
one another. The Court further concluded that there was a substantial lessening of competition, as required by Section 7 of the Clayton
Act, even though Rome added little to Alcoa's share of the market.

15. *Id.* at 370.
16. 377 U.S. 271 (1964).

This decision was based on the following considerations:

1. Alcoa was first in the market with 27.8 percent of production.
2. The market was highly concentrated with the top nine companies, including Rome, accounting for 95.7 percent of production.
3. Rome was an aggressive independent competitor that had been a pioneer in aluminum insulation and continued to have an active and efficient research and sales organization.
4. Rome had a broad line of quality copper wire and cable products and special aptitudes and skill in insulation. The Court concluded: "Preservation of Rome, rather than its absorption by one of the giants, will keep it as an 'important competitive factor.'. . . Rome seems to us the prototype of the small independent that Congress aimed to preserve by §7."[17]

61. Vertical mergers

Vertical mergers, of course, do not involve the elimination of direct competition between competitors, but instead involve the elimination of competition at a different level from that of the acquiring or merged firm. For example, in *United States* v. *E. I. duPont deNemours & Co.,*[18] duPont, during the period 1917–1919, purchased 23 percent of the stock in General Motors Corporation. By 1949, when the government brought suit to enjoin such ownership, duPont was General Motors' major supplier of automotive finishes (paints) and fabrics. The defendants argued that duPont's finish and fabric sales constituted only a negligible percentage of the total market for these materials, thereby negating any showing of restraint on trade or a monopoly in the products in question. DuPont's finish sales to General Motors constituted 3.5 percent of all sales of finishes to industrial users, and its fabric sales to General Motors comprised 1.6 percent of the total market for the type of fabric used by the automobile industry.

The Court, however, determined that the relevant *product markets* were finishes and fabrics sold to the automobile industry.

17. *Id.* at 281.
18. 353 U.S. 586 (1957).

Because General Motors accounted for 50 percent of the automobiles manufactured in the United States, duPont's sales to General Motors of finishes and fabrics, which accounted for 68 percent and 52.3 percent respectively of the latter's purchases, constituted a "substantial share of the relevant market."

Defendants further argued that thirty years lapsed before this action was commenced, thereby demonstrating that the requisite effect on competition had not been established. However, the Court rejected this argument, noting first that at the time of the initial acquisition of General Motors stock in 1917, General Motors' position in the automobile market was far less commanding, accounting for only 11 percent; therefore, its requirements of finishes and fabrics "were far short of the proportions they assumed as it forged ahead to its present place in the industry."[19] Second, duPont's purchases of stock were hardly for the purpose of investment: "[t]he inference is overwhelming that duPont's commanding position was promoted by its stock interest and was not gained solely on competitive merit."[20] Finally the Court stated:

> The statutory policy of fostering free competition is obviously furthered when no supplier has an advantage over his competitors from an acquisition of his customer's stock likely to have the effects condemned by the statute. We repeat, that the best test of a violation of §7 is whether at the time of suit there is a reasonable probability that the acquisition is likely to result in the condemned restraints. The conclusion upon this record is inescapable that such likelihood was proved as to this acquisition. The fire that was kindled in 1917 continues to smolder. It burned briskly to forge the ties that bind the General Motors market to duPont, and if it has quieted down, it remains hot, and, from past performance, is likely at any time to blaze and make the fusion complete.[21]

Similarly, the court in *Reynolds Metals Co.* v. *Federal Trade Commission*,[22] found that the Reynolds Metals Company's acquisition of Arrow Brands, Inc. violated Section 7 of the Clayton Act. Reynolds, in 1956, was the largest producer of aluminum foil in the world, which it sold to companies converting the aluminum foil into

19. *Id.* at 599.
20. *Id.* at 605.
21. *Id.* at 607.
22. 309 F.2d 223 (D.C. Cir. 1962).

decorative foil used in the florist trade. Arrow was such a converter company and enjoyed approximately 33 percent of the florist decorative foil business. The court first held that the florist foil converting industry was a separate *product market* from the considerably larger decorative foil industry for two reasons: (1) pricing for florist decorative foil was considerably different than for decorative foil, generally, and (2) the industry and consumer recognized this segment of the industry as a separate economic entity.

The requisite adverse effect on competition was demonstrated by the fact that Arrow, with 33 percent of the business, was eliminated as a buyer for any other aluminum foil except for that sold by Reynolds, thereby injuring other manufacturers competing against Reynolds. However, the court did not rely on this injury, but instead noted that Arrow's assimilation into Reynolds, with the latter's enormous capital structure and resources, gave Arrow an immediate advantage over its competitors who were contending for a share of the florist foil market:

> The power of the "deep pocket" or "rich parent" for one of the florist foil suppliers in a competitive group where previously no company was very large and all were relatively small opened the possibility and power to sell at prices approximating cost or below and thus to undercut and ravage the less affluent competition. The [Federal Trade Commission] is not required to establish that the Reynolds' acquisition of Arrow did in fact have anticompetitive consequences. It is sufficient if the Commission shows the acquisition had the capacity or potentiality to lessen competition. That such a potential emerged from the combination of Reynolds and Arrow was enough to bring it within Sec. 7.[23]

The court went on to find that actual competition had been injured because, as an apparent consequence of retroactive price reductions for Arrow foil after the acquisition, florist sales for five of Arrow's seven competitors dropped 14 percent to 47 percent below the prior year's sales. Over the same period Arrow's sales increased 18.9 percent.

In any number of cases, there have been both vertical and horizontal considerations under Section 7. Already discussed were the

23. *Id.* at 229–30.

horizontal aspects of the merger of Brown Shoe and Kinney in *Brown Shoe Co.* v. *United States*.[24] That merger, however, also raised vertical problems. Brown Shoe, as a shoe manufacturer, acquired Kinney, including its retail shoe stores, thereby enabling Brown Shoe to sell shoes to those stores as a captured market.

The Court noted here that the *geographic market* was the entire United States and the *product markets* were men's, women's, and children's shoes. The Court then examined various economic and historical factors in order to determine whether the merger had the requisite effect on competition. To answer this, the Court first noted that Brown Shoe was one of the leading manufacturers of men's, women's and children's shoes and that Kinney, with over 350 retail stores, owned and operated the largest independent chain of family shoe stores in the nation. "Thus, in this industry, no merger between a manufacturer and an independent retailer could involve a larger potential market foreclosure."[25] The Court further noted that Brown Shoe "would use its ownership of Kinney to force Brown shoes into Kinney stores,"[26] such action, the Court stated, being analogous to a "tying" arrangement.[27]

Finally, the Court was convinced that the industry trend toward concentration demonstrated the requisite effect on competition:

> The existence of a trend toward vertical integration, which the District Court found, is well substantiated by the record. Moreover, the court found a tendency of the acquiring manufacturers to become increasingly important sources of supply for their acquired outlets. The necessary corollary of these trends is the foreclosure of independent manufacturers from markets otherwise open to them. And because these trends are not the product of accident but are rather the result of deliberate policies of Brown and other leading shoe manufacturers, account must be taken of these facts in order to predict the probable future consequences of this merger. It is against this background of continuing concentration that the present merger must be viewed.[28]

24. 370 U.S. 294 (1962).

25. *Id.* at 331–32.

26. *Id.* at 332.

27. A tying arrangement, which requires a buyer to purchase a second or tied product as a condition to purchasing a desired or tying product, has faired rather poorly in the law, inasmuch as it is treated as a *per se* violation under Section 1 of the Sherman Act.

28. 370 U.S. at 332–33.

Unquestionably, growing concentration in an industry will have the greatest impact on a court's determination of illegal effect. In the *Brown Shoe* case, Brown Shoe manufactured only 5.5 percent of children's shoes and Kinney sold a little over 2 percent of those children's shoes, yet the Court found that such a vertical merger would tend substantially to lessen competition. Except for the growing concentration in the shoe industry, it is questionable whether the Court would have found the requisite injury.

62. Conglomerate mergers

Conglomerate mergers present far more difficult and complex problems than either horizontal or vertical mergers since conglomerate acquisitions do not have any direct or immediate effect on market concentration. Essentially, there are three types of conglomerate mergers: (1) "pure conglomerate" merger, in which there is no discernible relationship between the business of the acquiring and the acquired firms, (2) "product extension" merger, in which the acquired firm sells related or complementary products to that sold by the acquiring firm, and (3) "market extension" merger, in which the acquired firm sells the same product as acquiring firm but in a different geographical area. Thus far, the Supreme Court has primarily condemned those conglomerate mergers that have threatened competition through raising barriers to entry into the market, eliminating potential competition in the market, or creating opportunities for reciprocity.

When a strong conglomerate enterprise acquires a stagnant or inefficient firm in an industry dominated by a few powerful firms, competition in the marketplace may be increased rather than eliminated. However, if the same conglomerate acquires an already dominant company in a highly concentrated market, the adverse effects condemned by Section 7 of the Clayton Act may be present. Such was the case in *Federal Trade Commission* v. *Procter & Gamble Co.*[29] In that case the government attacked Procter & Gamble's acquisition of the assets of Clorox Chemical Co., which was the dominant firm in the household liquid bleach industry with 48 percent of the national sales and substantially higher percentages in various

29. 386 U.S. 568 (1967).

local markets. For five years Clorox sales, through heavy advertising, had increased to nearly $40 million per year, while Procter & Gamble's sales were in excess of $1.1 billion in 1967. Although Procter & Gamble was not in the liquid bleach industry, it was heavily engaged in the related detergent-soap-cleanser business. In 1957, its large advertising and promotional expenditures of $127 million enabled it to obtain substantial discounts in media advertising, and its status as a multiproduct producer facilitated substantial savings through its ability to advertise several products at one time.

The U.S. Supreme Court had little difficulty in finding a Section 7 violation. The Court found that it was reasonable "to assume that the smaller firms" competing against Clorox "would become more cautious in competing due to their fear of retaliation by Procter," and that "a new entrant would be much more reluctant to face the giant Procter than it would have been to face the smaller Clorox."[30] The Court concluded that "the substitution of the powerful acquiring firm for the smaller but already dominant firm may substantially reduce the competitive structure of the industry by raising entry barriers and by dissuading the smaller firms from aggressively competing. . . ."[31] The Court also noted that the acquisition would also eliminate Procter & Gamble as a potential entrant into the market, which would further enhance competition. This, the Court held, was clearly possible because of Procter & Gamble's already aggressive promotion and sales of closely related products.[32]

In a similar case, *General Foods Corp.* v. *Federal Trade Commission,*[33] the court found that General Foods' acquisition of S.O.S., which was engaged in the household steel wool pads industry, violated Section 7 of the Clayton Act. General Foods, in the 1960s, was one of the largest producers and distributors of packaged foods in the United States, with sales in 1967 of $1.3 billion and net assets of $436 million. General Foods spent the largest part of its advertising budget on television and ranked third overall in advertising in the United States.

S.O.S. nationally had 51 percent of the steel wool industry with sales of $18.6 million; in comparison, its largest competitor, Brillo,

30. *Id*. at 578–79.
31. *Id*. at 578.
32. *Id*. at 580.
33. 386 F.2d 936 (3d Cir. 1967).

enjoyed 47.6 percent of the market or $13.6 million in sales. After the merger, S.O.S.' sales increased to $19.2 million in 1962 or 56 percent of the market, while Brillo's sales decreased. Brillo, in December 1963, ceased operations as an independent company and merged with Purex Corporation, Ltd.

General Foods took the position that the relevant product market was scouring devices generally and not household steel wool alone. However, the court found that there was a definite industry recognition of household steel wool as a separate economic entity. Other nonsteel wool pads, which possessed different characteristics and stated uses, offered only indirect competition to household steel wool.

In finding a Section 7 violation, the court noted that the merger eliminated the competitive balance between S.O.S. and Brillo, the two dominant members of the industry, and left S.O.S. with "decisive competitive advantages over Brillo."[34] It further noted that substitution of General Foods for S.O.S. in the already concentrated steel wool soap pad market would confront "the existing competitors and such potential competitors as existed [with] an even more formidable opponent," thereby substantially raising the "factual and psychological barriers to entry" and tending to make the market "an even more rigid oligopoly."[35]

One last conglomerate merger case should be considered—*United States* v. *Falstaff Brewing Corp.*[36]—because it introduces the "potential competitor" doctrine, which the government had asserted to demonstrate the requisite injury to competition. In that case the government charged that the 1965 acquisition of Narragansett Brewing Co. by Falstaff violated Section 7. The relevant *geographic market* was the New England states where Narragansett was sold. Falstaff did not sell in this market, and although it was the fourth largest beer company in the United States, its eastern distribution extended only as far as western Ohio and Washington, D. C. For some time prior to the acquisition, Falstaff had been interested in entering the New England market, had made public statements to that effect, and had comissioned studies on the subject. It was noted that national brewers "possess competitive advantages since they are able to advertise on

34. *Id.* at 945.
35. *Id.* at 945–46.
36. 410 U.S. 526 (1973).

a nationwide basis, their beers have greater prestige than regional or local beers, and they are less affected by the weather or labor problems in a particular region."[37]

Although a study indicated that entry into New England with Falstaff beer rather than through acquisition was preferable, Falstaff went ahead with the acquisition because profits would be higher and because it would inherit an existing distributor organization, which Falstaff considered essential to successful market entry. Competition at the time of the merger was vigorous, and the merger in no way diminished it. Indeed, Narragansett's market share dropped from 21.5 percent in 1964 to 15.5 percent in 1969, while the shares of the two leading national brewers increased from 16.5 to 35.8 percent.

The trial court found there was no violation and dismissed the government's complaint. However, the Supreme Court reversed, holding that if Falstaff, apart from the merger, would have entered the market directly, thereby increasing competition, the merger violated Section 7. The Supreme Court therefore sent the case back to the trial court with directions to determine if Falstaff would have been a direct potential competitor if the merger had not been consummated. The trial court was directed to appraise the economic facts about Falstaff and the New England market in order to determine whether in any realistic sense, Falstaff could be said to be a potential competitor on the fringe of the market with likely influence on existing competition. The trial court was further admonished that testimony of Falstaff officers about actual intention was relevant; however, this testimony was not necessarily determinative of whether Falstaff should be considered as a potential entrant into the New England market.

It would seem clear from the review of the cases that the standards of illegality, particularly in the conglomerate merger cases, are inordinately vague and difficult to decipher. If the businessman is confused, he may have less comfort in the fact that lawyers are just as uncertain as to where the Supreme Court is going in this vital area.

63. Failing company doctrine

The Supreme Court has stated that the acquisition of a failing company might withstand a Section 7 Clayton Act attack where (1) the

37. *Id.* at 529.

resources of the acquired company are so depleted and the prospects of rehabilitation so remote that it faces the distinct likelihood of bankruptcy from which it cannot be viably reconstituted, and (2) the acquiring company is the only available purchaser and the acquired firm made bona fide efforts to seek alternate purchasers.

The theory behind this defense is that it is more desirable to have a failing company merge into another firm, thereby remaining a viable factor in the market, rather than withdrawing from the marketplace as a competitive factor through bankruptcy. However, since the merger will affect competition, the courts have mandated strict compliance with the doctrine's requirements.

Thus, in *Citizens Publishing Co.* v. *United States,*[38] the *Star* and *Citizen* were the only two daily newspapers of general circulation in Tucson, Arizona. Prior to 1940, they competed vigorously, and although their circulations were about equal, the *Star* sold 50 percent more advertising space. Over a several-year period the *Star* operated at a slight profit and the *Citizen* sustained losses. In 1940 a joint operating agreement was entered into providing for a 50–50 joint venture. All departments of the newspapers, except news and editorial policy, were operated jointly. Subscription and advertising rates were set jointly, profits were pooled and distributed to the *Star* and *Citizen* pursuant to an agreed ratio, and it was further agreed that neither the *Star* nor *Citizen* nor their stockholders, officers, or executives would engage in any other business in Tucson in conflict with the agreement.

The government challenged the joint venture agreement, alleging that it involved price fixing and territorial allocation of the market under Sections 1 and 2 of the Sherman Act and that it constituted an illegal acquisition under Section 7 of the Clayton Act. The defendants, in answer to the Section 7 charges, argued that *Citizen* was a failing company and therefore there was no violation.

The Supreme Court rejected the "failing company" defense on the ground that there was no evidence that "the joint operating agreement was the last straw" nor that the acquiring company was the "only available purchaser."[39] The Court further noted: " . . . no effort was made to sell the *Citizen;* its properties and franchise were not

38. 394 U.S. 131 (1969).
39. *Id.* at 137.

put in the hands of a broker; and the record is silent on what the market, if any, for *Citizen* might have been."[40] The burden of proof of establishing a failing company defense was placed on defendants, and the Court concluded that they had not satisfied their burden.

64. Interlocking directorates

Section 8 of the Clayton Act prohibits a person from serving as a director of several corporations when one of the corporations is engaged in interstate commerce and it has capital, surplus, and undivided profits aggregating more than $1 million, and the corporations are or were competitors, "so that the elimination of competition by agreement between them would constitute a violation of any of the provisions of any of the antitrust laws."[41] Few actions have been litigated under this statute primarily because once a complaint is filed, the offending director will normally resign, thereby correcting the violations charged without litigation.[42]

In *United States* v. *Sears, Roebuck & Co.,*[43] one of the few Section 8 cases actually litigated, the government brought an action seeking the resignation of Sidney J. Weinberg as a director of either Sears or the B. F. Goodrich Company. The defendants admitted that both corporations exceeded the $1 million-required size, that Weinberg was a director of both corporations, that each corporation was involved in interstate commerce, and that the two corporations competed in the sale of seven categories of goods at retail in ninety-seven communities in thirty-one states. In the sale of the goods in question, Sears' sales exceeded $65 million and Goodrich's exceeded $16 million.

Defendant argued that Section 8 was not applicable unless the

---

40. *Id.* at 138.

41. 15 U.S.C. §19.

42. In United States v. W. T. Grant Co., 345 U.S. 629 (1953), the Court noted, in passing, that Section 8 has not been systematically enforced and held that the director's resignation from the board of one of the competing corporations rendered injunctive relief unnecessary.

43. 111 F.Supp. 614 (S.D.N.Y.) (opinion and summary judgment) 1952–1953 Trade Cas. ¶ 67,561 (S.D.N.Y. 1953) (injunction). In a subsequent action, United States v. Sears, Roebuck & Co., 165 F.Supp. 356 (S.D.N.Y. 1958), the court held that the decree barred Weinberg from serving as a trustee of the Sears Savings and Profit Sharing Pension Fund, which held 26 percent of the total Sears shares outstanding while he continued as a director of Goodrich.

government demonstrated that the effect of an "assumed" consolidation of Sears and Goodrich would violate Section 7 of the Clayton Act. The court rejected this argument, stating that whether Weinberg's directorships with the two corporations violated Section 8 of the Clayton Act did not depend on whether a consolidation of the two entities would violate Section 7, but whether joint action of the two corporations would violate "any of the provisions of the antitrust laws." "Since Sears and Goodrich are competitors, since a price fixing or division of territory agreement would eliminate competition between them, and since such an agreement would per se violate at least one of the provisions of . . . the antitrust laws, namely §1 of the Sherman Act, it follows that §8 forbids defendant Weinberg to be a director of both corporations."[44]

Paramount Pictures Corp. v. *Baldwin-Montrose Chemical Co., Inc.*[45] involved a power play for control of Paramount Pictures in 1966. Herbert J. Siegel, principal stockholder and chairman of the board of directors of Baldwin-Montrose Chemical, was elected to the board of directors of Paramount Pictures. Because of serious friction that immediately ensued, Paramount Pictures sought to have him removed; in furtherance of that end Paramount sued under Section 8 of the Clayton Act, claiming that Siegel's position as a director of both Baldwin-Montrose and Paramount Pictures would result in a continuing elimination of competition between their respective subsidiaries, which were in competition. Baldwin-Montrose was engaged in the plastics and chemical business, and its subsidiary, General Artists Corporation (GAC), was engaged in the business of representing actors, writers, and musical composers. Paramount Pictures was a major producer and distributor of motion picture films, and several of its subsidiaries were arguably in competition with GAC.

The trial court found there was no violation of Section 8 of the Clayton Act for several reasons: first, because Baldwin-Montrose and Paramount Pictures, the two corporations of which Siegel was a director, were not in competition, there could be no Section 8 violation. The mere fact that subsidiary corporations might have been in competition did not alter this fact because Siegel was not a director of those subsidiaries. Second, the competition which existed between

44. *Id.* at 621.
45. 1966 Trade Cas. ¶ 71,678 (S.D.N.Y. 1966).

the subsidiaries was very minor or, as the court characterized it, *de minimis,* which is not covered by Section 8. Finally, at the time the order was entered Baldwin-Montrose had given up all interest in GAC and, therefore, any competition between the corporations in question no longer existed, and there was no present ability to resume such competition.

Chapter Seven

Private Civil Actions
Under the Clayton Act

One of the truly potent weapons in the antitrust arsenal is the private treble damage action brought by those persons actually injured by illegal conduct. An injured party may recover not only the actual losses to his business or property but three times that amount plus the cost of suit and reasonable attorney's fees. Section 4 of the Clayton Act provides that "any person who shall be injured in his business or property by reason of anything forbidden in the antitrust laws may sue therefor in any district court of the United States in the district in which the defendant resides or is found or has an agent, without respect to the amount in controversy, and shall recover threefold the damages by him sustained, and the cost of suit, including a reasonable attorney's fee."[1]

Since the Electrical Equipment cases[2] of the 1960s, there has been a dramatic increase in both the number of private treble damage

1. 15 U.S.C. §15.

2. *E.g.* Brigham City Corp. v. General Elec. Co., 210 F.Supp. 574 (D.Utah 1962), *rev'd sub nom.* Public Service Co. v. General Elec. Co., 315 F.2d 306 (10th Cir.), *cert. denied,* 374 U.S. 809 (1963); Atlantic City Elec. Co. v. General Elec. Co., 207 F.Supp. 613 (S.D.N.Y.), *aff'd,* 312 F.2d 236 (2d Cir. 1962), *cert. denied,* 373 U.S. 909 (1963).

actions filed and the amount of damages recovered.[3] Additionally, greater use has been made of Section 16 of the Clayton Act, which enables private parties to obtain injunctive relief to enjoin, for example, attempted takeovers of corporations, compel competitors' divestitures of acquisitions made in violation of Section 7 of the Clayton Act, or achieve other management objectives.[4]

65. Violations not subject to private antitrust actions

Private civil actions commenced under Sections 4 and 16 of the Clayton Act may be brought for violations of four statutes—the Sherman Act, parts of the Wilson Tariff Act, an act amending the Wilson Tariff Act, and the Clayton Act itself. Thus, Section 2 of the Robinson-Patman Act, which amends the Clayton Act, is a source of treble damages as well as injunctive relief for discriminatory pricing practices. However, Section 3 of the Robinson-Patman Act, which provides criminal penalties for certain *predatory* pricing practices, is not a statute pursuant to which private actions may be commenced.[5] Similarly, Section 5 of the Federal Trade Commission Act,[6] which declares that unfair methods of competition in interstate commerce as well as unfair or deceptive acts or practices are declared unlawful, is not a source of private antitrust litigation.[7]

66. Who may sue under the Clayton Act

Not every person injured in their business or property because of a price-fixing conspiracy, for example, can sue for treble damages or injunctive relief. The plaintiff must be one who is "directly," rather than "remotely," injured, and thus within the target area of the statute. In other words, the injured plaintiff must have "standing" to sue. For example, employees of a corporation who have lost their jobs

3. *See, e.g.,* West Virginia v. Chas. Pfizer & Co., 440 F.2d 1079 (2d Cir.), *cert. denied,* 404 U.S. 871 (1971) (settlement fund of $82,000,000); Trans World Airlines, Inc. v. Hughes, 308 F.Supp. 679 (S.D.N.Y. 1969), *modified on other grounds,* 449 F.2d 51 (2d Cir. 1971), *rev'd on other grounds,* 409 U.S. 363 (1973) ($137,611,435.95 damage award after trebling and attorney's fees of $7,500,000).

4. *E.g.,* International Tel. & Tel. Corp. v. Gen. Tel. & Electronics Corp., 351 F.Supp. 1153 (D.Hawaii 1972).

5. *See* Nashville Milk Co. v. Carnation Co., 355 U.S. 373 (1958).

6. 38 Stat. 719 (1914), codified at 15 U.S.C. §45 (1976).

7. *See* Atlantic Brick Co. v. O'Neal, 44 F.Supp. 39 (E.D.Tex. 1942); Holloway v. Bristol Myers Corp., 327 F.Supp. 17 (D.D.C. 1971), *aff'd,* 485 F.2d 986 (D.C.Cir. 1973).

because the defendants' illegal conspiracy bankrupted their employer are said to be too remote from the injury to recover under Section 4 of the Clayton Act. Similarly, lessors, or landlords, suppliers, franchisers, stockholders, creditors, and patentees of an injured corporation have been held to be outside the target area of the statute and therefore may not seek treble damages under the Clayton Act.[8]

In *Karseal Corp.* v. *Richfield Oil Corp.,*[9] the district court granted a motion to dismiss the complaint on the ground that the plaintiff, a manufacturer of car wax, was too far removed from a conspiracy directed against independent service stations, which purchased car accessories and parts as well as such products as car wax. Plaintiff charged that Richfield Oil required its independently owned service stations to purchase tires, batteries, and other accessories, including car wax, from suppliers designated by Richfield. Richfield argued that the "target area" of the alleged conspiracy was its independent stations, which allegedly had paid more for the products in question than what they would have paid had there been competition.

The court of appeals reversed, holding that the plaintiff Karseal was within the target area of the conspiracy and thus, as a supplier, had standing to sue. The court stated:

> Primarily the operation and effect of the illegal practices was on the products (including Karseal's wax) which were competitive to Richfield sponsored products. The impact was on the market. The gist of the violation was the prevention or impeding of the sale of these competitive products. Logically, . . . the illegal acts were directed against the manufacturers and distributors of the competing products, includ-

8. *See,* Calderone Enterprises Corp. v. United Artists Theatre Circuit, Inc., 454 F.2d 1292 (2d Cir. 1971), *cert. denied,* 406 U.S. 930 (1972) (theater landlord); Kauffman v. Dreyfus Fund, Inc., 434 F.2d 727 (3d Cir. 1970), *cert.denied,* 401 U.S. 974 (1971) (stockholder); Billy Baxter, Inc. v. Coca-Cola Co., 431 F.2d 183 (2d Cir. 1970), *cert. denied,* 401 U.S. 923 (1971) (franchisor); SCM Corp. v. Radio Corp. of America, Inc., 407 F.2d 166 (2d Cir.), *cert. denied,* 395 U.S. 943 (1969) (patentee claiming royalty losses attributable to injuries to licensees); Volasco Prods. Co. v. Lloyd A. Fry Roofing Co., 308 F.2d 383 (6th Cir. 1962), *cert. denied,* 372 U.S. 907 (1963) (suppliers); Martens v. Barrett, 245 F.2d 844 (5th Cir. 1957) (stockholders); Productive Inventions, Inc. v. Trico Prods. Corp., 224 F.2d 678 (2d Cir. 1955), *cert. denied,* 350 U.S. 936 (1956) (patentee); Coast v. Hunt Oil Co., 195 F.2d 870 (5th Cir.), *cert. denied,* 344 U.S. 836 (1952) (partner in injured business partnership); Loeb v. Eastman Kodak Co., 183 F.2d 704 (3d Cir. 1910) (stockholder-creditor); Contreras v. Grower Shipper Vegetable Ass'n., 1971 Trade Cas. ¶ 73,592 (N.D. Cal. 1971) (lettuce workers injured by conspiracy to raise price of lettuce); Brewer Sewing Supplies Co. v. Fritz Gegaut, Ltd., 1970 Trade Cas. ¶ 73,139 (N.D. Ill. 1970) (creditor); Miley v. John Hancock Mut. Life Ins. Co., 148 F. Supp. 299 (D. Mass.) *aff'd mem.,* 242 F.2d 758 (1st Cir.), *cert. denied,* 355 U.S. 828 (1957) (insurance agent representing an injured underwriter).

9. 221 F.2d 358 (9th Cir. 1955).

ing Karseal's wax. Such persons and such products were the "target" of the illegal practices.[10]

A somewhat different question was presented in *Illinois Brick Co.* v. *Illinois.*[11] In that case, the state of Illinois and a large number of local governmental entities in the Chicago area sued certain manufacturers of concrete blocks for injuries sustained as a result of an alleged price-fixing conspiracy. The defendants manufactured and sold bricks to masonry contractors, who then submitted bids to general contractors for the masonry portions of construction projects; the general contractors, in turn, submitted bids for these projects to customers such as the state of Illinois and the other plaintiffs. Because defendants fixed the price of concrete blocks sold to the masonry contractors, who passed on the higher prices to the general contractors, who, in turn, passed on the higher prices to Illinois and the other plaintiffs, the plaintiffs were "indirect" rather than "direct" purchasers. The legal question presented was whether an indirect purchaser to whom an overcharge was passed had standing to bring a treble damage action under Section 4 of the Clayton Act.

The Supreme Court ruled that the indirect purchaser, who actually bore the brunt of the price-fixing conspiracy, could not sue. The Court reasoned that allowing such suit would subject defendants to double liability—once by the direct purchaser, who has a right to sue even though he may have passed on the higher prices to his customers, and the indirect purchaser, who actually bears the burden of the higher prices.[12]

A person, in order to sue under Section 4 of the Clayton Act, must also demonstrate that the illegal conduct in question inflicted injury upon his "business or property." This right extends to a person whose property is diminished by a payment of money wrongfully exacted.[13] Interference with a valid contract constitutes an actionable injury to "property." If a contract has not been consummated because the par-

10. *Id.* at 364.

11. 431 U.S. 720 (1977).

12. Proponents of the multiple-damage theory argue "that it is better for the defendant to pay sixfold or more damages than for an injured party to go uncompensated . . . ('a little slopover on the shoulders of the wrongdoers . . . is acceptable')." However, the Supreme Court rejected this position, stating "[w]e do not find this risk acceptable." 431 U.S. at 731 n.11.

13. Chattanooga Foundry Pipe Works v. City of Atlanta, 203 U.S. 390, 396 (1906).

ties are still at the negotiating stage, the requisite injury is lacking.[14] The term "business" extends not only to commercial or industrial activities but to employment or occupation by which a person enjoys a living. Injury to an enterprise, even in the planning stage, if sufficiently advanced, may be actionable.[15]

Although a plaintiff is not required to show with precision the amount of the damages he has sustained by the illegal conduct, he is required to show the fact of damage, that is, that he was in fact injured by the defendant's conduct. Having established the fact of damage or casual connection with the illegal activity charged, a certain amount of speculation is permitted as to the amount of damages sustained. In *Story Parchment Co.* v. *Paterson Parchment Paper Co.,*[16] the Supreme Court reversed a court of appeals holding that plaintiff had not sustained the burden of proving that it suffered recoverable damages. The Court stressed the contrast between proving the fact of damage and proving the extent of damage:

> Nor can we accept the view of that court that the verdict of the jury, insofar as it included damages for the first item, cannot stand because it is based upon mere speculation and conjecture. . . . It is true that there was uncertainty as to the extent of damage, but there was none as to the fact of damage; and there is a clear distinction between the measure of proof necessary to establish the fact that [plaintiff] has sustained some damage and the measure of proof necessary to enable the jury to fix the amount. The rule which precludes recovery of uncertain damages applies to such as are not the certain result of the wrong, not to those damages which are definitely attributable to the wrong and only uncertain in respect to their amount.[17]

67. The length of time to bring a lawsuit

Under Section 4(b) of the Clayton Act, a party has four years from the date that he was wronged to commence a lawsuit.[18] If, prior to

14. Peller v. International Boxing Club, 227 F.2d 593, 596 (7th Cir. 1955).

15. *See* Woods Exploration & Producing Co. v. Aluminum Co. of America, 438 F.2d 1286 (5th Cir. 1971), *cert. denied,* 404 U.S. 1047 (1972).

16. 282 U.S. 555 (1931).

17. *Id.* at 562.

18. Section 4(b) of the Clayton Act provides: "Any action to enforce any cause of action under sections 15 or 15a of this title shall be forever barred unless commenced within four years after the cause of action accrued. . . ."

the end of the four-year period, the government commences a civil or criminal action,[19] the running of the four-year period (statute of limitations) stops. After the government action is completed, the injured party has an additional year to initiate his lawsuit even if the government action was instituted on the last day of the four-year period. Generally, the subject matter of the private action must be "based in whole or in part on any matter complained of" in the government proceeding. Significantly, such tolling has been permitted when there has been a "substantial identity" of issues and parties at the time a comparison is made between the private and government actions.[20] The four-year limitation provision of Section 4(b) is suspended not only by Department of Justice actions, but also by Federal Trade Commission antitrust enforcement proceedings.[21]

If the defendants have actively concealed the conspiracy, the four-year period will not commence until the conspiracy is discovered or becomes known to the party suing. In *Atlantic City Electric Co.* v. *General Electric Co.,*[22] the defendants not only conspired to fix the prices of heavy electrical equipment sold to public utilities throughout the United States, but they concealed the conspiracy by rigging price quotations and bids. In this manner the defendant selected to receive a job would bid low and the remaining defendants would bid high in order to create the semblance of competitive bidding and pricing. Defendants argued that the doctrine of fraudulent concealment, that is, concealing the illegal conduct in question, did not apply to Section 4(b) of the Clayton Act. The court disagreed and held that any time defendants conceal their illegal conduct, the four-year statute of limitations is tolled until the conspiracy is discovered by the injured party or should have been discovered by him.

68. Use of prior government proceedings as evidence in private civil litigation

Whenever the government indicts under the Sherman Act, numerous private treble damage actions are invariably brought by private citi-

19. Commencement by the government of a single damage action will not toll the four-year statute of limitations.

20. Leh v. General Petroleum Corp., 382 U.S. 54 (1965).

21. Minnesota Mining & Mfg. Co. v. New Jersey Wood Finishing Co., 381 U.S. 311 (1965).

22. 207 F.Supp. 613 (S.D.N.Y.), *aff'd,* 312 F. 2d 236 (2d Cir. 1962), *cert. denied,* 373 U.S. 909 (1963).

zens allegedly injured by the illegal conduct charged. Should the defendants be convicted in the criminal action or plead guilty to the charges, the judgment entered may be used as *prima facie*[23] evidence against the defendants in the private action. Section 5(a) of the Clayton Act provides:

> A final judgment or decree heretofore or hereafter rendered in any civil or criminal proceeding brought by or on behalf of the United States under the antitrust laws to the effect that a defendant has violated said laws shall be *prima facie* evidence against such defendant in any action or proceeding brought by any other party against such defendant under said laws or by the United States under section 15a of this title, as to all matters respecting which said judgment or decree would be an estoppel as between the parties thereto: *Provided,* that this section shall not apply to consent judgments or decrees entered before any testimony has been taken or to judgments or decrees entered in actions under section 15a of this title.[24]

A judgment entered on a plea of guilty comes within the terms of Section 5(a) and, like a criminal trial and conviction, constitutes *prima facie* evidence in any subsequent treble damage action brought by private parties. However, a plea of nolo contendere, or "no contest," is treated as a consent judgment within the meaning of the last clause of Section 5(a) and may not be used in a subsequent private treble damage or injunctive action. This is, of course, the reason that defendants seek to plead nolo contendere rather than plead guilty to criminal antitrust charges. Whether the plea of nolo contendere will be accepted is a discretionary matter left up to the court; however, such pleas are often opposed by the government. The government likes to use its support of a nolo contendere plea as leverage to obtain willing witnesses to testify against those who choose to stand trial.

69. In pari delicto and unclean hands

A question arises as to whether a party who voluntarily participates in conspiratorial conduct can withdraw from the conspiracy and then sue to recover damages under Section 4 of the Clayton Act. Defendants have argued that a plaintiff's willing participation should bar

---

23. "Prima facie" means nothing more than that plaintiff has met his burden of proof in presenting his case, and the defendant is then required to offer evidence in rebuttal or he will lose.

24. 38 Stat. 731 (1914), codified at 15 U.S.C. § 16(a) (1970).

him from later suing his coconspirators; this argument is based on the doctrine of *in pari delicto,* that is, the plaintiff is "of equal fault." In *Perma Life Mufflers, Inc.* v. *International Parts Corp.,*[25] the Supreme Court of the United States ruled that a plaintiff's willing participation in a conspiracy will not foreclose it from later suing under the antitrust laws.

The plaintiffs in the *Perma Life* case were dealers who operated Midas Muffler Shops under franchise agreements granted by Midas, Inc. The complaint charged that Midas had entered into a conspiracy with its parent corporation—International Parts Corp.—two other subsidiaries, and six individual defendants who were officers or agents of the corporations to restrain trade and commerce in violation of Section 1 of the Sherman Act and Section 3 of the Clayton Act. Pursuant to this conspiracy, Midas franchisees were required, under the franchise agreement, to purchase all their mufflers from Midas, to honor the Midas guarantee on mufflers sold by any dealer, and to sell the mufflers at resale prices fixed by Midas and at locations specified in the agreements. The Midas dealers were also obligated to purchase all their exhaust system parts from Midas, to carry the complete line of Midas products, and in general to refrain from dealing with any of Midas' competitors. In return Midas promised to underwrite the cost of the muffler guarantee and gave the dealer permission to use the registered trademark "Midas" and the service mark "Midas Muffler Shops." The dealer was also granted the exclusive right to sell "Midas" products within his defined territory. Plaintiffs argued that the restrictions in the franchise agreements constituted price fixing, territorial allocations, tie-ins, and exclusive dealings. One of the plaintiffs was terminated when he purchased exhaust parts from a Midas competitor.

The case was dismissed in the trial court, which was affirmed by the court of appeals on the ground that the plaintiffs voluntarily participated in the plan and benefited substantially from it. The Supreme Court reversed, stating:

> Although [plaintiffs] may be subject to some criticism for having taken any part in [defendants'] allegedly illegal scheme and for eagerly seeking more franchises and more profits, their participation was not voluntary in any meaningful sense. They sought the franchises

25. 392 U.S. 134 (1968).

enthusiastically and they did not actively seek each and every clause of the agreement. Rather, many of the clauses were quite clearly detrimental to their interests, and they alleged that they continually objected to them. [Plaintiffs] apparently accepted many of these restraints solely because their acquiescence was necessary to obtain an otherwise attractive business opportunity.... Moreover, even if [plaintiffs] actually favored and supported some of the other restrictions, they cannot be blamed for seeking to minimize the disadvantages of the agreement once they had been forced to accept its more onerous terms as a condition of doing business.... We therefore hold that the doctrine of *in pari delicto,* with its complex scope, contents, and effect, is not to be recognized as a defense to an antitrust action.[26]

"Unclean hands" is a second defense which the Supreme Court has found inapplicable to antitrust violations, particularly when damages are sought, as distinguished from injunctive or other equitable relief. The unclean hands defense would normally apply when the plaintiff has engaged in conduct that is in itself illegal and a violation of the antitrust laws apart from defendants' illegal conduct. Thus, *in pari delicto,* if applicable, would apply where plaintiff voluntarily participated in illegal conduct along with the the defendants, whereas, "unclean hands" would apply where plaintiff engages in wrongful conduct wholly apart from the illegal activities of the defendants.

The leading case in this area is *Kiefer-Stewart Co.* v. *Joseph E. Seagram & Sons, Inc.*[27] In that case, the plaintiff was a wholesale distributor in Indiana who sued Seagram and Calvert for fixing the wholesale price of liquor in Indiana and then forcing wholesalers to adhere to those prices. Defendants argued that plaintiff came into court with unclean hands because it had conspired with other wholesalers to fix the minimum prices at which they would sell. The Court held that this was not a defense that Seagram and Calvert could invoke. The Court stated:

If [plaintiff] and others were guilty of infractions of the antitrust laws, they could be held responsible in appropriate proceedings brought against them by the Government or by injured private persons. The alleged illegal conduct of [plaintiff], however, could not legalize the

26. *Id.* at 139–40.
27. 340 U.S. 211 (1951).

unlawful combination by [defendants] nor immunize them against liability to those they injured.[28]

In cases seeking injunctive relief, as distinguished from damages, courts have applied the "unclean hands" doctrine and barred a plaintiff's recovery. In *Heldman* v. *United States Lawn Tennis Ass'n.,*[29] the plaintiff, Gladys M. Heldman, was the past owner, editor, and publisher of *World Tennis Magazine,* having sold out to Columbia Broadcasting System in 1972. Thereafter, plaintiff organized the Virginia Slims tennis circuit for women sponsored by the Philip Morris Company. A second (intervening) plaintiff, Billie Jean King, was the then number-one-ranked woman pro in the world. Plaintiffs asserted that anyone signing with plaintiff Heldman for the Virginia Slims circuit was barred, because of a conspiracy involving the United States Lawn Tennis Association (USLTA) and its officials, from playing in the USLTA sanctioned tournaments. Plaintiffs sought a preliminary injunction to enjoin the USLTA from barring tennis pros, including Billie Jean King, who signed with Heldman from competing in USLTA sanctioned events.

Defendants argued that the plaintiff Heldman in 1972 had organized a tournament tour for women under the auspices of the USLTA and, in that capacity, had not acted in good faith and fairness to the USLTA by organizing her own Virginia Slims circuit. Because of her breach of duty and good faith owed to the USLTA, she came into court with "unclean hands" in trying to enjoin the USLTA's boycott of women who signed up with her for the Virginia Slims circuit. The court therefore denied the preliminary injunction, stating:

> Injunctive relief in advance of the trial is available only to the plaintiff
> ... who comes before the Court free of any inequitable conduct ...
> with respect to the matters in dispute. While the so-called clean hands
> doctrine may provide no defense to the antitrust violation when the
> merits are being decided, at this stage this equitable doctrine may well
> be applied; as of now, no violation of law by defendants has been tried,
> established or decided.[30]

28. *Id*. at 214.
29. 354 F.Supp. 1241 (S.D.N.Y. 1973).
30. *Id*. at 1249.

70. Class action lawsuits

One of the most potent weapons in the antitrust arsenal is the "class action" brought by private litigants. The mere threat of a class action is in itself a substantial deterrent to errant defendants engaging in potential Sherman Act conduct. Class actions can turn a $2,000 lawsuit filed by a single plaintiff into a $50 million lawsuit if the action is certified for class treatment.

Rule 23 of the Federal Rules of Civil Procedure is the vehicle by which class actions are certified by federal judges.[31] The requirements of a class action are fairly technical but cover basically the following factors. First, the class must be so numerous that it would be impracticable to have all the potential class members bring their own lawsuits or join in the pending action as individual plaintiffs. As few as thirty-five members have been held sufficient to establish a class action,[32] while in other cases the courts have held that several

---

31. Federal Rule 23 provides, in relevant part:

"(a) *Prerequisites to a Class Action.* One or more members of a class may sue or be sued as representative parties on behalf of all only if (1) the class is so numerous that joinder of all members is impracticable, (2) there are questions of law or fact common to the class, (3) the claims or defenses of the representative parties are typical of the claims or defenses of the class, and (4) the representative parties will fairly and adequately protect the interests of the class.

(b) *Class Actions Maintainable.* An action may be maintained as a class action if the prerequisites of subdivision (a) are satisfied, and in addition:

• • •

(3) the court finds that the questions of law or fact common to the members of the class predominate over any questions affecting only individual members, and that a class action is superior to other available methods for the fair and efficient adjudication of the controversy. The matters pertinent to the findings include: (A) the interest of members of the class in individually controlling the prosecution or defense of separate actions; (B) the extent and nature of any litigation concerning the controversy already commenced by or against members of the class; (C) the desirability or undesirability of concentrating the litigation of the claims in the particular forum; (D) the difficulties likely to be encountered in the management of a class action."

32. In Butkus v. Chicken Unlimited Enterprises, Inc., 1971 Trade Cas. ¶ 73,780 (N.D.Ill. 1971), the court stated: "As to the first requirement, namely, that the number of plaintiffs be so numerous that joinder of all of them is impracticable, it is clear that despite defendant Scot Lad Foods, Inc.'s contention to the contrary, that requirement is satisfied. Even if the defendant's predicition that only 35 of the over 100 franchises will join in this action is accurate, that requirement would still be met. . . . This is best seen by noting the difficulties involved in having thirty-five intervenors, all with their respective attorneys, attempt to go through the formal motions required for entrance into and participation in the suit. Creating such a situation would quite plainly be impractical."

hundred potential class members were insufficient.[33] On the other hand, class action status has been denied when there have been too many potential class members, thereby making the action unmanageable if a class were declared.

In *Eisen* v. *Carlisle & Jacquelin*,[34] the class included approximately 6 million odd-lot purchasers of stock who sued a number of brokers on the ground that they were fixing prices. The Second Circuit Court of Appeals initially ruled that a class this size did not create insurmountable problems and ordered the district court to consider further class action treatment. After the district court ruled that actual notice would be permitted to less than 10,000 of the potential class members with damages being awarded for the entire class, including those members who did not file claims, the court of appeals reversed, indicating that its earlier decision on manageability of the case had been overly optimistic and that a class should not be certified. Judge Lombard, in the initial decision of the circuit court, stated in his dissent:

> What could be less of a class action than a suit where there are more than 3,750,000 potential plaintiffs living in every state of the Union and in almost every foreign country. If this is a "class," it is so large and indiscriminate that a substantial portion of its membership will have no idea whatever that they belong to it. Just how a notice can be worded which could alert so large a "class" . . . is a mystery to me.[35]

The second requirement of a class action suit involves questions of law or fact common to all class members, which predominate over individual questions. The whole utility of class actions is bound up in the concept that by deciding such common questions of law and fact in one lawsuit, greater efficiency of the court's time and energies will result to the ultimate benefit of the public as a whole. Thus, rather than litigating five hundred independent lawsuits, one lawsuit is tried, which then resolves the rights of five hundred persons as class members. However, to achieve this result there must be overriding common questions. If individual questions predominate that would have

33. *See, e.g.,* City & County of Denver v. American Oil Co., 53 F.R.D. 620 (D.Colo. 1971) (126 public bodies); William Goldman Theatres, Inc. v. Paramount Film Distrib. Corp., 1970 Trade Cas. ¶ 73,211 (E.D.Pa. 1969) (460 theaters).

34. 479 F.2d 1005 (2d Cir. 1973), *vacated and class action dismissed on other grounds,* 417 U.S. 156 (1974).

35. 391 F.2d 555,570 (2d Cir. 1968).

to be tried separately, no advantages will result in trying the case as a class action. Thus, in determining whether to allow a case to proceed as a class action, one of the primary questions to be resolved by the court is whether common questions of law and fact are present which predominate over individual questions.

Ungar v. *Dunkin' Donuts of America, Inc.*[36] illustrates the difficulties a court can have in determining whether there are sufficient common questions to allow a case to proceed as a class action. There, the defendant Dunkin' Donuts was a franchiser of Dunkin' Donuts franchised shops throughout the United States. Dunkin' Donuts began as a small chain of company-owned coffee and doughnut shops in New England. By 1976 it was the largest coffee and doughnut franchising system in the United States, having more than 700 franchised shops.

Typically, Dunkin' Donuts provided its franchises with a "turn-key" operation, that is, it selected suitable sites for the doughnut shops, which it leased to the franchisee, built the shop and totally equipped it, provided the stores with signs and other trademark items identifying the store, and provided the food items needed to operate the stores. Plaintiffs, who were franchised store owners, claimed that it was Dunkin' Donuts' policy to grant a franchise license only on the condition that the prospective store owners accept certain "tied" items—real estate, equipment, signs, and supplies. Plaintiffs contended that Dunkin' Donuts prevented its franchises from using their own premises, thus requiring them to lease or sublease the shop premises from Dunkin' Donuts on onerous terms. Franchisees were also allegedly pressured into purchasing equipment from Dunkin' Donuts and not from the manufacturers, who, in any event, would not sell directly to franchisees. Signs could be purchased only from Dunkin' Donuts or an approved vendor that paid secret rebates to Dunkin' Donuts. Supplies could be purchased, in practice, only from approved sources, which paid rebates to Dunkin' Donuts for the right to sell to store owners.

In deciding whether the case was properly certified by the district court for class action treatment, the court of appeals noted that in a tie-in case the plaintiff had to demonstrate, if not shown in the franchise agreement itself, that each potential class member was

36. 531 F.2d 1211 (3d Cir. 1976), *cert. denied,* 429 U.S. 823 (1976).

"coerced" into purchasing the "tied" products and that each did not do so voluntarily. The issue of coercion thus became an individual question that each of the 700 store owners was required to prove individually. Thus, this individual question predominated over common questions and class action treatment was deemed inappropriate.

A contrary result was reached in *Bogosian* v. *Gulf Oil Corp.*,[37] wherein two independent service station dealers sued their respective lessors, Gulf Oil and Exxon, alleging that the lease contracts imposed tie-in restrictions in violation of Section 1 of the Sherman Act. Plaintiffs also named as defendants fourteen other major oil companies whom they alleged, together with Gulf and Exxon, had engaged in concerted action unlawfully to tie the leasing and subleasing of gas station sites to the purchase of gasoline supplied by each dealer's lessor. In other words, each independent dealer was required, as a condition of obtaining a service station lease, to purchase his gasoline requirements only from his lessor and no other producer of gasoline.

Plaintiffs sought to represent a class of all present and past independent gasoline station operators leasing stations from the defendants, some 100,000 or more. Defendants argued, and the trial court agreed, that "coercion" had to be proven on an individual basis, and therefore, there was an important individual question of fact that predominated over the common questions. The trial court, therefore, denied a class status. The court of appeals reversed and held that a class was appropriate in this action since proof of coercion was not necessary. The court noted that the lease agreements themselves precluded station operators from purchasing gasoline from others. The leases provided that each operator had to sell a certain quantity of gasoline or be terminated, which, in effect, foreclosed the operator from purchasing gasoline from other sources. Thus, "coercion" did not have to be shown and common questions of fact, that is, the restrictive terms of the leases themselves predominated. The court stated:

> If plaintiffs are able to show that the lease agreements in use by all defendants have similar clauses which have the practical economic effect of precluding sale of other than the lessor's gasoline, they will have shown that the purchase of gasoline was tied in to the lease of the service station. Under these circumstances the lease agreement

37. 561 F.2d 434 (3d Cir. 1977), *cert. denied,* 434 U.S. 1086 (1978).

itself conditions the sale of one product (here a lease) upon purchase of another, and . . . proof of coercion is not a required element of plaintiffs' case.[38]

On this basis the court of appeals found that common questions and not individual questions predominated and, therefore, class action treatment was appropriate.

A third requirement of a class action suit, pursuant to Rule 23(a)(4), requires that the plaintiffs must "fairly and adequately protect the interest of the class." In making this determination, courts have examined (1) whether the plaintiffs are capable of representing the class diligently and thoroughly, and (2) whether counsel for the plaintiffs is qualified and experienced in the type of case involved. Rarely has a class been denied because counsel was unqualified to handle the matter. However, any number of class actions have been denied where the court concluded that the plaintiffs could not adequately represent the class. For example, courts have held that a terminated distributor or franchisee could not represent a class made up of existing distributors or franchisees because their interests and objectives might be antagonistic. The plaintiff, as a terminated distributor or franchisee, is interested in damages regardless of the impact this might have on the system itself, whereas existing distributors and franchisees are as much interested in protecting their ongoing investment in a strong system or franchise operation as they are in recovering damages.[39]

In the fourth determinant of a class action, the court is compelled to determine whether proceeding as a class action is superior to other methods of litigating the issues raised. Of major concern to the court are the difficulties encountered in attempting to manage a large antitrust class action. The mechanics of mailing out one million notices to potential class members and recording the responses received alone, for example, can literally tie up the clerk of the court's office for weeks. Indeed, the full impact of litigating an antitrust class action to conclusion has never been ascertained because, to date, no case has fully litigated the issue of damages. One can surmise the overwhelming problems a court would encounter in

38. 561 F.2d at 452.
39. *See, e.g.,* Free World Foreign Cars, Inc. v. Alfa Romeo, S.p.A., 55 F.R.D. 26 (S.D.N.Y. 1972); Gaines v. Budget Rent-A-Car Corp. of America, 1972 Trade Cas. ¶ 73,-860 (N.D. Ill. 1972).

trying the individual damage claims of one million class members or, for that matter, one hundred thousand or even one thousand claims. If a court could hear ten claims a day, five days a week, it would take twenty weeks to hear one thousand claims, forty years to hear one hundred thousand claims, and four hundred years to hear one million claims.[40] Of course, there are many ways a court could handle some of these problems, but the question of manageability is still an overwhelming consideration.

Some mention should be made of the notice given to potential class members and how they remain in the class or withdraw from it. At plaintiff's cost, notice must be sent to all potential class members in the typical antitrust class action. The notice will inform the class members of the nature of the action, the names of the parties, and each class member's rights should he choose to remain in the class or exercise his option to get out of the class, which is referred to as "opting out." Upon receiving notice, a person seeking to withdraw from the lawsuit must take affirmative action and send back the form that is provided, stating his desire not to be involved in the action. If he does nothing, he will *automatically* be included in the class and bound by all decisions entered, whether they are favorable *or* adverse to the class. Under some circumstances class members may be subjected to costs along with the plaintiffs if the lawsuit is lost. It is therefore essential for the potential class member, upon receiving notice, to send back the "opt out" form if he does not wish to remain part of the action.

A final word should be made concerning large consumer-type class actions. Because of the large number of potential class members, class certification can act as a cudgel in the hands of plaintiffs' counsel rather than serving its intended purpose as an instrument furthering the public good. Not infrequently, class actions were brought where the plaintiff or plaintiffs and individual class members had only minimal losses, for example, of less than $100 per person, yet because the class was made up of hundreds of thousands or millions of persons, the accumulated treble damages were staggering. Invariably, the plaintiffs involved had little interest in the lawsuit because their recovery was so minimal and they could not recover any bonus

40. These estimates are based on the rather unrealistic assumption that a federal court's docket is limited to civil cases. Congress has mandated, however, that a federal district court give priority to hearing criminal cases.

if the class action succeeded. Thus, these actions had, as a primary goal, the financial interests of the plaintiffs' attorney, who stood to recover a very large legal fee if the class action was successful.

Courts have been acutely aware of this fact and the potential abuse of lawyers seeking out plaintiffs to commence class actions for private gain. In response to the problem, the U.S. Supreme Court has imposed upon the plaintiff the cost of notifying potential class members that an action has been certified for class action treatment. At 25 cents an envelope, which includes postage, envelopes, printing, stuffing, and mailing, a plaintiff with a $34 claim would have to spend $250 to serve one thousand potential class members, $25,000 to serve one hundred thousand class members, and $250,000 to serve one million class members. Of course, such costs are recoverable if the plaintiff wins the lawsuit; if he loses, however, there is no recovery.

In *Eisen* v. *Carlisle & Jacquelin,*[41] plaintiff sued two brokerage firms that handled 99 percent of the New York Stock Exchange's odd-lot business for monopolizing odd-lot trading and for fixing the brokerage commission on such transactions, in violation of Sections 1 and 2 of the Sherman Act. More specifically, the defendants imposed a surcharge on odd-lot transactions in addition to the standard brokerage commission applicable to round-lot transactions. For the period in question, the late 1960s, the differential was ⅛ of a point, or 12½ cents, per share on stocks trading below $40 per share and ¼ of a point, or 25 cents, per share on stocks trading at or above $40 per share.

Plaintiff only sought $70 in damages, and therefore it was essential for him to proceed as a class action or not at all because he could not, quite clearly, finance a large antitrust lawsuit for such a minimal recovery. After eight years in the courts trying to determine if a class action should be certified, the district court granted certification and ordered notice to go out. The prospective class included some six million individuals, with some 2.25 million identifiable by name and address. The cost of notice at that time for stuffing and mailing was 10 cents per notice, which a short time later became 14 cents because of an increase in postage. The total cost of a single notice would therefore have been $225,000, and subsequently $315,000.

41. 417 U.S. 156 (1974).

Plaintiff made it very clear that he could not and would not bear these costs and therefore proposed that defendants cover the costs. The trial court ultimately decided that notice would be sent to some seven thousand identifiable class members and the rest notified by publication in the *Wall Street Journal* and other local prominent papers, at a cost of $21,720. However, the plaintiff was not willing to bear even these costs, and the trial court concluded that defendants would pay 90 percent of the cost and plaintiff 10 percent or, $2,172.

The United States Supreme Court ruled that individual notice had to go to *all* identifiable class members, some 2.25 million in all. It rejected plaintiff's argument that the prohibitively high cost of providing individual notice to so many class members would end the suit as a class action and "effectively frustrate [plaintiff's] attempt to vindicate the policies underlying the antitrust and securities laws."[42] Plaintiff also argued that individual notice was unnecessary in this case because no prospective class member had a large enough stake in the matter to justify separate litigation of his individual claim; thus, there was no incentive to opt out of the class action even if notified. The Supreme Court stated:

> The short answer to these arguments is that individual notice to identifiable class members is not a discretionary consideration to be waived in a particualr case. It is, rather, an unambiguous requirement of Rule 23. As the Advisory Committee's Note explained, the Rule was intended to insure that the judgment, whether favorable or not, would bind all class members who did not request exclusion from the suit. . . . Accordingly, each class member who can be identified through reasonable effort must be notified that he may request exclusion from the action and thereby preserve his opportunity to press his claim separately or that he may remain in the class and perhaps participate in the management of the action. There is nothing in Rule 23 to suggest that the notice requirements can be tailored to fit the pocketbooks of particular plaintiffs.[43]

The Court further held that plaintiff had to bear the entire cost of notice "as part of the ordinary burden of financing his own suit."[44] Unquestionably, this holding of the Supreme Court has done more

42. *Id.* at 175–76.
43. *Id.* at 176.
44. *Id.* at 179.

than any other to halt the flood of "consumer" antitrust class action litigation by private persons. In essence, the Court's decision effectively foreclosed Eisen from proceeding any further after eight years of litigation.

In September 1976, Congress attempted to fill this void of consumer antitrust litigation by enacting legislation that permits the attorney general of any state to bring a treble damage action on behalf of natural persons who are residents of the state for any injuries sustained due to violations of the antitrust laws.[45] Significantly, damages caused by price fixing do not have to be proven on an individual basis under this statute, but rather may be "proved and assessed in the aggregate by statistical or sampling methods, by the computation of illegal overcharges, or by such other reasonable system of estimating aggregate damages as the court in its discretion may permit."[46] How effective this statute will be in vindicating consumer interests when injured by violations of the antitrust laws is yet to be seen.

71. Intracorporate conspiracies

One area of the antitrust laws that should be given special consideration by the business executive is the area of intracorporate conspiracies, that is, conspiracies between a parent and subsidiary corporations or between subsidiary corporations that might be in violation of Section 1 of the Sherman Act.[47] It will be recalled, as discussed in Chapter 3, that the plaintiff, under Section 1 of the Sherman Act, must prove that *two or more* persons or business entities conspired or agreed or combined to violate the act. A corporation operating through divisions, such as General Motors Corporation, cannot be charged with conspiring within the corporate structure because divisions are not separate legal entities capable of conspiring. The same corporation, however, changing from divisions to subsidiary corporations could be guilty of conspiratorial conduct as hereinafter discussed.

The Supreme Court has made it clear that a parent corporation

45. 15 U.S.C. §15c.
46. 15 U.S.C. §15d.
47. Intracorporate conspiracies are not necessarily limited to private treble damage actions, but could be a source of both criminal and civil governmental action.

and subsidiary or two or more subsidiaries can conspire to fix prices in violation of Section 1 of the Sherman Act. The defendants in *Kiefer-Stewart Co.* v. *Joseph E. Seagram & Sons, Inc.*[48] were a parent and two subsidiaries—Joseph E. Seagram & Sons, Inc. and its subsidiaries, Seagram Distilleries Corporation and Calvert Distilling Company. The defendants were charged with fixing the price at which wholesale distributors could sell their beverages in Indiana. Plaintiff, a wholesale distributor in Indiana, had been terminated because of its refusal to adhere to the prices so fixed by the defendants. Defendants argued that they could not be guilty of price fixing because they were related companies, "mere instrumentalities of a single manufacturing-merchandising unit." The Supreme Court rejected the argument, stating that the defendants' argument

> runs counter to our past decisions that common ownership and control does not liberate corporations from the impact of the antitrust laws. . . . The rule is especially applicable where, as here [Seagram-Distilleries and Calvert], hold themselves out as competitors.[49]

Timken Roller Bearing Co. v. *United States*[50] involved three corporations that territorially divided the world market between themselves for the manufacture and sale of antifriction bearings. The defendant was an Ohio corporation that licensed two other corporations to manufacture Timken bearings, one being British Timken, Ltd., in which the defendant owned 30 percent of the stock, and Societe Anonyme Francaise Timken, in which the defendant and a private person owned 100 percent of the stock. Defendant argued that because it owned part of the stock of the two corporations with which it allegedly conspired, the arrangement had to be treated as a joint-venture arrangement, which was legal under the Sherman Act. Even though there was joint ownership among the conspiring corporations, the Supreme Court still found that a violation existed: "The fact that there is common ownership or control of the contracting corporations does not liberate them from the impact of the antitrust laws."[51]

In *Perma Life Mufflers, Inc.* v. *International Parts Corp.,*[52] a dif-

---

48. 340 U.S. 211 (1951).
49. *Id.* at 215.
50. 341 U.S. 593 (1951).
51. *Id.* at 598.
52. 392 U.S. 134 (1968).

ferent problem existed. Midas, Inc. was charged with conspiring with its parent corporation, International Parts Corp., two other subsidiaries, and six individual defendants, who were officers or agents of the corporation. The complaint alleged that plaintiffs, who operated Midas Muffler Shops, were foreclosed from purchasing from other sources of supply and from selling outside a designated territory and that they were required to purchase other products in the Midas line and were required to sell at fixed retail prices. Midas, which was not in competition with its parent corporation or the two other subsidiaries, argued that the entire corporate organization operated as "a single business entity" and therefore was entitled to cooperate without creating an illegal conspiracy. The Supreme Court rejected the argument and held that a conspiracy had been demonstrated:

> But since respondents Midas and International [the parent corporation] availed themselves of the privilege of doing business through separate corporations, the fact of common ownership could not save them from any of the obligations that the law imposed on separate entities.[53]

The plaintiff in *Minnesota Bearing Co.* v. *White Motor Corp.*[54] sued White Motor and a wholly owned subsidiary for unlawfully terminating its distributorship agreement with the latter in the sale of White Motor "Mobilift" products and for fixing resale prices of distributors. Plaintiff alleged that White Motor and its subsidiary had agreed to give the territory to a major stockholder of White Motor who was the grandson of its founder. The defendants argued that activity between a parent and subsidiary concerning the termination of a distributor was internal in nature and could not be the basis of a Sherman Act violation. The court disagreed, stating that "common ownership does not serve to exonerate corporate entities, operating as parent and subsidiary, of the legal obligations imposed upon individual corporations."[55]

Battle v. *Liberty National Life Ins. Co.*[56] also illustrates the problems a parent-subsidiary relationship can create. There, the defendant Liberty National was in the business of issuing burial insurance in the southern part of the United States. Its wholly owned subsidiary, the defendant Brown-Service Funeral Homes Company, Inc.,

53. *Id.* at 141–42.
54. 470 F.2d 1323 (8th Cir. 1973).
55. *Id.* at 1328–29.
56. 493 F.2d 39 (5th Cir. 1974).

entered a contract with Liberty National to furnish the merchandise and services required by the burial insurance policies issued by the latter. Additionally, Brown-Service contracted with independent funeral homes in Alabama to perform its obligation under its contract with Liberty National. All funeral homes entering contracts with Brown-Service were designated "authorized" homes, and any insured of Liberty National using an "authorized" home received a casket, burial clothing, embalming, use of the funeral parlor, assistance in the performance of any services, transportation to the cemetary or church, and rail transportation to any place within the continental United States. But if a policyholder went to an unauthorized funeral home, the benefits conferred under the policy were limited only to a casket or a cash settlement. Some of the plaintiffs were unauthorized funeral homes which pleaded that they were effectively foreclosed from a large number of potential clients, those insured by Liberty National, who were being "subtly coerced" into dealing only with authorized homes due to the additional benefits and services derived.

Defendants argued that they were not competitors, but rather one organization or business unit and therefore were unable to form a combination or conspiracy within the meaning of Section 1 of the Sherman Act. The court of appeals disagreed, stating:

> Even though Liberty National and Brown-Service are not competitors, because Liberty National is in the insurance business while Brown-Service provides funeral services and merchandise, the alleged facts tend to establish that they are operationally two separate organizations entirely capable of combining or conspiring to restrain trade. That the defendants do not compete with each other in no way precludes them from combining or conspiring to suppress competition, the ultimate result of which would inure to their mutual benefit. While the existence of competition between two organizations would tend to establish their separateness and thus fulfill the requirement that it takes more than one party to create a combination or conspiracy, the absence of such competition does not preclude the existence of two separate organizations.[57]

From the above cases, it can be concluded that consideration must be given to intracorporate dealings, particularly when they affect

57. *Id.* at 44.

competitors and competition. The test of whether a conspiracy exists is not whether the corporations are in apparent competition, but whether they are treated and operated as separate entities. Separate officers, employees, offices, and products, for example, are *indicia* of the separateness required to establish a conspiracy. Of course, not all cases have found this requisite separateness and therefore no conspiracy was proven. However, the direction the law appears to be heading in the last ten years suggests that intracorporate action must be scrutinized closely.

One last observation should be made concerning potential conspiratorial activity between a corporation and its directors, officers, and/or employees. The predominant view is that a corporation cannot conspire with its own directors, officers, or employees by whom its purposes must be formed and through whom it must act if it is to take any action at all. In *Nelson Radio & Supply Co.* v. *Motorola, Inc.,*[58] the defendant Motorola was alleged to have conspired with its president-director, its sales manager, and its officers, employees, representatives, and agents, who were actively engaged in the management, direction, and control of the business and affairs of Motorola, to foreclose the plaintiff, a Motorola distributor, from selling and distributing Motorola communication equipment. Although in prior years plaintiff had sold Motorola communication equipment as well as heaters, radio receivers, radio phonograph combinations, and television receivers, under the provisions of a new distributor agreement, plaintiff was not given authority to sell communication equipment. The new distributor agreement also foreclosed plaintiff from selling the communication equipment of other manufacturers in competition with Motorola.

The court of appeals held that there was no conspiracy between Motorola and its officers and employees because said persons were acting only on behalf of Motorola and not on their own behalf. The court specifically noted that there was no allegation that "these officers, agents and employees were actuated by any motives personal to themselves. Obviously, they were acting only for the defendant corporation."[59]

The above analysis concerning intracorporate conspiracies is at

58. 200 F.2d 911 (5th Cir. 1952), *cert. denied,* 345 U.S. 925 (1953).
59. *Id.* at 914.

best cursory, but sufficient to alert any executive officer to the problems that may cloud intracorporate transactions affecting prices, territorial allocations, refusals to deal, and tie-in restrictions. There are definite limitations that limit the freedom with which intracorporate matters are conducted. The single-business entity concept cannot be relied upon as a defense to otherwise illegal conduct.

Chapter Eight

Exemptions from
the Antitrust Laws

Statutory exemptions have been written into the antitrust laws that protect certain areas of the American economy from the strictures of the antitrust laws. This chapter will, in summary fashion, consider the nature of those exemptions that are applicable to agricultural and fishing cooperatives, insurance, organized labor, government contracts, and small businesses. Also considered will be certain judicially created exemptions applicable in very limited areas.

72. Agricultural cooperatives

Section 6 of the Clayton Act has granted limited immunity to agricultural and fishing cooperatives. That section provides that

> nothing contained in the antitrust laws shall be construed to forbid the existence and operation of . . . agricultural, or horticultural organizations instituted for the purposes of mutual help and not having capital stock or conducted for profit, or to forbid or restrain individual members of such organizations from lawfully carrying out the legitimate objects thereof; nor shall such organizations . . . be held or construed to be illegal combinations or conspiracies in restraint of trade, under the antitrust laws.[1]

1. 15 U.S.C. §17.

In 1922 this exemption was expanded by the Capper-Volstead Act. Section 1 provides:

> Persons engaged in the production of agricultural products ... may act together in associations, corporate or otherwise, with or without capital stock, in collectively possessing, preparing for market, handling, and marketing ... such products ... [and] may have marketing agencies in common ... [and] make the necessary contracts and agreements to effect such purposes.[2]

Section 2 of the act authorizes the Secretary of Agriculture to proceed against any cooperative association that has monopolized or restrained commerce "to such an extent that the price of any agricultural product is unduly enhanced."[3]

Finally, the Cooperative Marketing Act of 1926 authorizes agricultural producers and associations to acquire and exchange "past, present and prospective" pricing, production, and marketing data.[4] Internal payments by cooperatives to their members are also exempted from the Robinson-Patman Act.[5]

The immunity granted by these acts extends no further than to allow producers to join together in the formation of agricultural cooperatives, which will then act as agents for the producers in the processing, handling, and marketing of their products. This then places farmers on a parity with shareholders of private corporations in pooling their resources to the mutual advantage of each. However, when cooperatives exceed the bounds of the exemption created by Congress, they run afoul of the antitrust laws.

In *United States* v. *Borden Co.,*[6] the U.S. Supreme Court upheld an indictment charging a cooperative agricultural association with conspiring with several major milk distributors, labor officials, municipal officials, and others to maintain artificial and noncompetitive prices to be paid to milk producers for fluid milk produced in Illinois and neighboring states for sale in the Chicago area. The defendant agricultural association argued that it was exempt from

---

2. 7 U.S.C. §291.

3. *Id.* §292. In 1934, fishermen were likewise granted the right to form cooperatives by the Fisherman's Collective Marketing Act, which was patterned after the Capper-Volstead Act. 15 U.S.C. §§521–22.

4. 7 U.S.C. §455.

5. 15 U.S.C. §13b.

6. 308 U.S. 188 (1939).

the Sherman Act because it was organized according to the terms of the Capper-Volstead Act. The Supreme Court rejected this argument, noting that the exemption covered only joint action of farmers to prepare and market their produce and to enter joint contracts necessary to that end. This did not, however, give agricultural associations the right to conspire with others, such as milk producers and municipal officials, to fix prices. The Supreme Court stated:

> The right of these agricultural producers thus to unite in preparing for market and in marketing their products, and to make the contracts which are necessary for that collaboration, cannot be deemed to authorize any combination or conspiracy with other persons in restraint of trade that these producers may see fit to devise. In this instance, the conspiracy charged is not that of merely forming a collective association of producers to market their product but a conspiracy, or conspiracies, with major distributors and their allied groups, with labor officials, municipal officials, and others, in order to maintain artificial and non-competitive prices to be paid to all producers for all fluid milk produced in Illinois and neighboring states and marketed in the Chicago area, and thus in effect, as the indictment is construed by the court, "to compel independent distributors to exact a like price from their customers" and also to control "the supply of fluid milk permitted to be brought to Chicago." ... Such a combined attempt of all defendants, producers, distributors and their allies, to control the market finds no justification in §1 of the Capper-Volstead Act.[7]

The Supreme Court reached a similar result in *Maryland and Virginia Milk Producers Ass'n, Inc.* v. *United States*,[8] in which a milk producers' association, supplying 86 percent of the milk purchased by local milk dealers in the Washington, D.C. metropolitan area, was charged with a number of violations, including violations of Sections 2 and 3[9] of the Sherman Act and Section 7 of the Clayton Act. The monopolization charge, Section 2 of the Sherman Act, was that the defendant association had threatened and induced milk dealers in the Washington area to purchase milk from it and it also purchased those

---

7. *Id.* at 204–05.

8. 362 U.S. 458 (1960).

9. Section 3 of the Sherman Act is substantially the same as Section 1 of the Sherman Act except that it applies to commerce in or with the District of Columbia and/or the territories.

dealers' outlets which had refused to purchase from the defendant. In one instance, the association engaged in a boycott of a feed and farm supply store to compel the owner, who also owned a dairy, to purchase milk from the association.

The Section 7 charge was that the defendant purchased the assets of Embassy Dairy, thereby eliminating the largest purchaser of non-association milk in the area, forced former Embassy Dairy milk producers either to join the association or to ship to Baltimore, eliminated the association's prime competitive dealer from government contract milk bidding, and increased the association's control of the Washington market. The Section 3 charge included all of the above charges as well as an agreement that the prior Embassy Dairy owners would not compete in the Washington area for ten years. It was established that Embassy Dairy was eliminated as a competitor because the association had been "unhappy" with Embassy Dairy's price cutting and its generally "disruptive" competitive practices that had made Embassy Dairy a "thorn in the side of the Association for many years."

The primary defense raised was that because the defendant was a cooperative composed exclusively of dairy farmers, it was exempted and immunized from the antitrust laws by Section 6 of the Clayton Act and Sections 1 and 2 of the Capper-Volstead Act. The Supreme Court held that the defendants' association conduct was not immunized from the antitrust laws:

> We hold that the privilege the Capper-Volstead Act grants producers to conduct their affairs collectively does not include a privilege to combine with competitors so as to use a monopoly position as a lever further to suppress competition by and among independent producers and processors.[10]

From the case law it is clear that farmers may combine among themselves without fearing the strictures of the antitrust laws. However, their immunity ends when they go outside the association and combine or conspire with others to violate the antitrust laws. As demonstrated by both the *Borden* and *Maryland and Virginia Milk Producer* cases, the Supreme Court has come down hard on associations when their conduct has exceeded that protected by the Clayton Act and the Capper-Volstead Act.

10. 362 U.S. at 472.

73. Insurance

Under the McCarran-Ferguson Act,[11] Congress has delegated to the states the power to regulate and tax the business of insurance. Under the act, the Sherman, Clayton, and Federal Trade Commission acts apply to the business of insurance only to the extent that such business is not regulated by state law or the activity questioned does not constitute a boycott or acts of coercion or intimidation. The act does not define what the business of insurance is nor the kind of state regulation required to trigger the exemption.

The Supreme Court in *Group Life & Health Insurance Co.* v. *Royal Drug Co.,*[12] held that the business of insurance does not encompass agreements between insurers and third-party providers of goods and services. In that case Blue Shield of Texas offered to enter into agreements with pharmacies in order to hold down the cost of prescription drugs to its policyholders. The Supreme Court held that the agreements were not the business of insurance even though they might have had an indirect effect on insurance rates paid by insureds, for the real purpose of the agreements was to minimize costs and maximize profits. This decision means that any arrangements between insurance companies and service and supply industries, such as doctors and hospitals (health insurance), body shops, auto glass shops, and trim shops (auto insurance), will not be immunized by the McCarran-Ferguson Act.

In those areas where the business of insurance is involved, the next question raised is whether the state has undertaken to regulate the activity. In order to invoke this exemption, the state statute must be specifically directed at the insurance company and its policyholders rather than some other aspect of the company's business. In *Federal Trade Commission* v. *National Casualty Co.,*[13] the Supreme Court held that state legislation prohibiting deceptive advertising by insurance companies within the state's borders was sufficient to exempt those advertising practices from the jurisdiction of the Federal Trade Commission.

In *Ohio AFL-CIO* v. *Insurance Rating Board,*[14] it was argued that

11. 15 U.S.C. §§1011–15.
12. 440 U.S. 205 (1979).
13. 357 U.S. 560 (1958).
14. 451 F.2d 1178 (6th Cir. 1971), *cert. denied,* 409 U.S. 917 (1972).

the Ohio insurance laws were ineffective in regulating new premium rates because such laws permitted a private rating bureau to place new premium rates into effect simply by filing the rate increases with the state insurance department. Because the state agency had never challenged or disapproved a rate increase and lacked the trained personnel to do so, it was alleged that there was a total absence of state regulation. The Sixth Circuit Court of Appeals disagreed and held that the state had sufficiently regulated the business of insurance to invoke the McCarran-Ferguson Act exemption when it enacted a statute proscribing, permitting, or authorizing the challenged conduct.[15]

It is clear from the recent case law that the rather unique exempt status of insurance companies is slowly being eroded and that the antitrust laws are being more aggressively enforced against insurance companies. Thus, insurance executives must consider anew the antitrust laws and their impact on insurance activities.

74. Organized labor

Although the organization of a union was not generally considered to be an unlawful restraint of trade at common law, the Sherman Act, at its inception, was used against union activities. In *Loewe* v. *Lawlor (the Danbury Hatters case),*[16] the Supreme Court held that a union had violated the Sherman Act when it organized a nationwide secondary boycott of nonunion-made hats as part of an organized strike against the manufacturer. Congress reacted to this case by adopting Section 6 of the Clayton Act, which provides:

> The labor of a human being is not a commodity or article of commerce. Nothing contained in the antitrust laws shall be construed to forbid the existence and operation of labor . . . organizations, . . . or to forbid or restrain individual members of such organizations from lawfully carrying out the legitimate objectives thereof; nor shall such organizations, or members thereof, be held or construed to be illegal combinations or conspiracies in restraint of trade, under the antitrust laws.[17]

15. 451 F.2d at 1181.
16. 208 U.S. 274 (1908).
17. 15 U.S.C. §17.

Section 20 of the Clayton Act prohibits the issuance of federal injunctions against strikes, boycotts, or picketing "in any case between an employer and employees, or between employers and employees, or between employees, or between persons employed and persons seeking employment, involving, or growing out of, a dispute concerning terms or conditions of employment," and concludes with the broad prohibition that, "nor shall any of the acts specified in this paragraph be considered or held to be violations of any laws of the United States."[18]

In 1932, Congress enacted the Norris-LaGuardia Act,[19] which was intended to plug certain loopholes that had arisen in the application of the Clayton Act labor exemptions. In broad terms the Norris-LaGuardia Act deprived the federal courts of all jurisdiction to issue injunctions "in a case involving or growing out of a labor dispute," except under very limited conditions or when the dispute was "contrary to the public policy declared by this chapter." Specific conduct on the part of persons "participating or interested in" a labor dispute was also expressly exempted from restraint by injunction.[20]

As in the case of agricultural cooperatives and insurance companies, whenever a union combines with third parties concerning matters outside the immediate concern of labor, the Supreme Court has found that the union had lost its insulation from the antitrust laws. The first case addressing this question was *Allen Bradley Co.* v. *Local No. 3, IBEW,*[21] which held that the labor exemption did not apply because the union had conspired with a group of companies to restrain competition. In that case, the defendant was a labor union, Local No. 3 of the International Brotherhood of Electrical Workers, which had jurisdiction only over the metropolitan area of New York City. In an attempt to expand its membership, obtain shorter hours, and increase wages, the union waged an aggressive campaign to obtain closed-shop agreements with all local electrical equipment manufacturers and contractors.

Through the use of strikes and boycotts, closed-shop agreements were entered into that provided that contractors were obligated to

18. 29 U.S.C. §52.
19. *Id.* at §§101–115.
20. *Id.* at §106.
21. 325 U.S. 797 (1945).

purchase equipment only from local manufacturers who also had closed-shop agreements with the union, and manufacturers were obligated to confine their New York City sales to contractors employing the union's members. To enforce these agreements, agencies—composed of representatives from the union, manufacturers, and contractors—were set up to boycott recalcitrant local contractors and manufacturers and to bar the introduction of equipment manufactured from outside the area. As a result of those efforts all prospered—the manufacturers had phenomenal growth, with prices of electrical equipment soaring, the union obtained more jobs for its members along with higher wages and shorter hours, and contractors as well as manufacturers financially benefitted. Some New York manufacturers sold their products in the protected New York market at one price and a substantially lower price outside the market.

Plaintiffs were electrical manufacturers outside the New York City market that were foreclosed from selling in that market because of the agreements and conduct in question. The Supreme Court held that by combining with business groups, the union had lost its immunity under the antitrust laws. The Court stated that "Congress never intended that unions could, consistently with the Sherman Act, aid non-labor groups to create business monopolies and to control the marketing of goods and services."[22] The Court also stated:

> Since union members can without violating the Sherman Act strike to enforce a union boycott of goods, it is said they may settle the strike by getting their employers to agree to refuse to buy the goods. Employers and the union did here make bargaining agreements in which the employers agreed not to buy goods manufactured by companies which did not employ the members of Local No. 3. We may assume that such an agreement standing alone would not have violated the Sherman Act. But it did not stand alone. It was but one element in a far larger program in which contractors and manufacturers united with one another to monopolize all the business in New York City, to bar all other businessmen from that area, and to charge the public prices above a competitive level.... So far as the union might have achieved this result acting alone, it would have been the natural consequences of labor union activities exempted by the Clayton Act from the coverage of the Sherman Act.... But when the unions participated with a combination of businessmen who had com-

22. *Id.* at 808.

plete power to eliminate all competition among themselves and to prevent all competition from others, a situation was created not included within the exemptions of the Clayton and Norris-LaGuardia Act.[23]

A similar question was presented in *United Mine Workers of America* v. *Pennington.*[24] There, the plaintiff Phillips Brothers Coal Company, a small coal producer, filed a cross claim against the UMW for conspiring with certain large coal operators to restrain and monopolize interstate commerce, in violation of Sections 1 and 2 of the Sherman Act. Because of overproduction in the coal industry in the late 1940s, an agreement had been entered into between the UMW and certain large coal operators to eliminate the smaller coal producers. This was done in order to reduce coal production, permit mechanization, increase wages, and generally better control the coal market. The large coal producers further agreed not to lease coal land to nonunion operators and, in 1958, not to sell or buy coal from such companies. The companies and the union jointly induced the Secretary of Labor to establish, under the Walsh-Healy Act, higher minimum wages for employees of contractors selling coal to the TVA. These minimum wages were much higher than in other industries and made it difficult for small companies to compete in the TVA contract market. Thereafter, four of the largest companies, including two in which the defendant union had large investments and over which it was in a position to exercise control, waged a destructive and collusive price-cutting campaign in the TVA "spot market" for coal.

The Supreme Court concluded that the UMW's collusive activities with the large coal producers destroyed any exemption it had from the antitrust laws:

> We have said that a union may make wage agreements with a multi-employer bargaining unit and may in pursuance of its own union interests seek to obtain the same terms from other employers. No case under the antitrust laws could be made out on evidence limited to such union behavior. But we think a union forfeits its exemption from the antitrust laws when it is clearly shown that it has agreed with one set of employers to impose a certain wage scale on other bargaining units. One group of employers may not conspire to eliminate competitors from the industry and the union is liable with the employers if it

23. *Id.* at 809.
24. 381 U.S. 657 (1965).

becomes a party to the conspiracy. This is true even though the union's part in the scheme is an undertaking to secure the same wages, hours or other conditions of employment from the remaining employers in the industry.[25]

A different result was achieved in *Local Union No. 189, Amalgamated Meat Cutters & Butcher Workmen of North America, AFL-CIO* v. *Jewel Tea Co.*[26] There, the defendant unions, which represented virtually all butchers in the Chicago area, attempted to impose upon all retail stores the following restriction on the operating hours of food store meat departments:

> Market operating hours shall be 9:00 a.m. to 6:00 p.m. Monday through Saturday, inclusive. No customer shall be served who comes into the market before or after the hours set forth above.[27]

All retail stores agreed upon this restriction in their collective bargaining agreements except National Tea Co. and the plaintiff Jewel Tea, although both subsequently agreed to it to avert a threatened strike. Jewel Tea sued the union and an association of retail stores that supported the restriction. The latter, in fact, insisted that included in all collective bargaining agreements entered into by the union be the hours restriction and the restrictions that no union employee could work after 6 p.m. or before 9 a.m., and that no retail store could sell meat with or without a union employee during those hours. The intent of the defendant retail stores was to foreclose the large chain stores from selling prepackaged meat at self-service counters because of their inability to compete with the chains.

The Supreme Court held that the union conduct in question was exempted because it predominantly concerned matters of wages, hours, and working conditions. The Court stated:

> Thus, the issue in this case is whether the marketing-hours restrictions, like wages, and unlike prices, is so intimately related to wages, hours and working conditions that the union's successful attempt to obtain that provision through bona fide, arm's length bargaining in pursuit of their own labor relations policies, and not at the behest of or in combination with non-labor groups, falls within the protection of

25. *Id.* at 665–66.
26. 381 U.S. 676 (1965).
27. *Id.* at 679–80.

the national labor policy and is therefore exempt from the Sherman Act. We think that it is.[28]

The case law seems to suggest that when a union negotiates with employers concerning wages, hours, and working conditions, which are mandatory subjects of collective bargaining, no antitrust violation can occur even though a combination of a labor group and several competing employers is achieved through industry-wide bargaining. But should a union and employers agree on matters outside these mandatory subjects, such as prices or foreclosing competition by eliminating certain employers, the labor exemption will be lost.

75. Government contracts and small business

Additional statutory exemptions from the antitrust laws should be noted in passing. The Defense Production Act of 1950[29] grants an exemption for voluntary agreements and programs entered into at the request of the president or his delegate in the interest of national defense. Section 708(a) of the act provides for "the approval by the President (or his delegate) of voluntary agreements and programs to further the objectives of this Act," and Section 708(b) provides: "No act or omission . . . pursuant to this Act . . . if requested by the President pursuant to a voluntary agreement or program approved under subsection (a) and found by the President to be in the public interest as contributing to the national defense shall be construed to be within the prohibitions of the antitrust laws or the Federal Trade Commission Act. . . ."[30]

If the president delegates the power to approve such agreements to another person, said person must consult with the attorney general and the chairman of the Federal Trade Commission and have the approval of the attorney general.[31] The attorney general is also authorized to terminate the exemption by withdrawing his approval,[32] and is required to investigate the anticompetitive effects of any such

28. *Id.* at 689–90.
29. 50 U.S.C. App. §§2061–2166.
30. *Id.* §2158(a) and (b).
31. *Id.* §2158(c).
32. *Id.* §2158(d).

agreements or programs and to report periodically his findings to Congress and the president.[33]

The Small Business Act[34] also provides limited exemptions from the antitrust laws as to certain activities approved by the Small Business administrator or by the president. The Small Business administrator may make loans to corporations formed by groups of small businesses to enable them to purchase raw materials, equipment inventories, or supplies or to benefit from joint research and development or for establishing facilities for such purposes.[35] Such combined efforts are exempt from antitrust scrutiny under Section 7(a)(6)[36] of the act, which provides: "No act or omission to act, if requested by the Administrator . . . and if found and approved by the Administrator as contributing to the needs of small business, shall be construed to be within the prohibitions of antitrust laws or the Federal Trade Commision Act. . . ."

Section 9(d)[37] of the act authorizes the administrator to encourage and approve joint programs of research and development by small business concerns, which are granted exemption from the antitrust laws and the Federal Trade Commission Act pursuant to Section 9(d)(3).[38] Similar to the Defense Production Act, the administrator must consult with the attorney general and the chairman of the Federal Trade Commission and have the written approval of the former prior to approving such a small business loan or a joint research and development program.[39]

76. Noerr-Pennington exemption

In addition to the above described statutory exemptions, there are also judicially created exemptions to the antitrust laws that should be considered in passing. The most important of these exemptions is the so-called *Noerr-Pennington* doctrine, which permits business con-

33. *Id.* §2158(e).
34. 15 U.S.C. §§631–47.
35. *Id.* §636(a)(5).
36. *Id.* §636(a)(6).
37. *Id.* §638(d).
38. *Id.* §638(d)(3).
39. *Id.* §638(a) and (d)(2).

cerns to join together in lobbying or attempting to influence governmental action, even if done with an anticompetitive purpose.⌐

In *Eastern Railroad Presidents Conference* v. *Noerr Motor Freight, Inc.,*[40] twenty-four eastern railroads, an association of the presidents of those railroads, and a public relations firm were charged with conducting a publicity campaign, through the public relations firm, against truckers designed to foster the adoption and retention of laws and law enforcement practices destructive of the trucking business, to create an atmosphere of distaste for the truckers among the general public, and to impair the relationship existing between truckers and their customers. The campaign was described as "vicious, corrupt, and fraudulent" and motivated solely by the desire to injure and destroy truckers in the long-distance freight business. The defendants directly influenced legislation against the truckers by seeking the passage of state laws relating to truck weight limits and tax rates on heavy trucks, and they persuaded the governor of Pennsylvania to veto a measure known as the "Fair Truck Bill," which would have permitted truckers to carry heavier loads over Pennsylvania roads.

The Supreme Court, in holding such conduct exempt from the antitrust laws, stated that the "Sherman Act does not prohibit two or more persons from associating together in an attempt to persuade the legislature or the executive to take particular action with respect to a law that would produce a restraint or a monopoly."[41] The Court reasoned that a contrary rule would impede the power of the government to operate, based on the people's direct access to their representatives:

> To hold that the government retains the power to act in this representative capacity and yet hold, at the same time, that the people cannot freely inform the government of their wishes would impute to the Sherman Act a purpose to regulate, not business activity, but political activity, a purpose which would have no basis whatever in the legislative history of that Act.[42]

The Supreme Court also noted that denial of the citizenry's free access to their governmental representatives would amount to the

40. 365 U.S. 127 (1961).
41. *Id.* at 136.
42. *Id.* at 137.

denial of the right to petition, "one of the freedoms protected by the Bill of Rights."[43]

The second case developing this doctrine is the labor of *United Mine Workers of America* v. *Pennington,*[44] already discussed in this chapter. One of the allegations of conspiracy in that case was that the UMW and certain large coal producers had jointly approached the Secretary of Labor and persuaded him to establish minimum wages under the Walsh-Healey Act for employees of contractors selling coal to the TVA. The minimum wages established were much higher than those in other industries, thereby making it difficult for the small coal producers to compete in the TVA term contract market.

The Supreme Court ruled that the joint effort of the union and the large coal producers to influence the Secretary of Labor, even when done with the intent and purpose to injure the small producers, could not violate the Sherman Act under the *Noerr* ruling:

> Joint efforts to influence public officials do not violate the antitrust laws even though intended to eliminate competition. Such conduct is not illegal, either standing alone or as part of a broader scheme itself violative of the Sherman Act. . . .[45]

The *Noerr-Pennington* exemption does have its limitations, as noted by the Supreme Court in *California Motor Transport Co.* v. *Trucking Unlimited.*[46] There, the defendants, who were licensed highway carriers, sought to bar the plaintiffs from obtaining highway carrier licenses in California. To effectuate this goal the defendants were alleged to have instituted state and federal proceedings to resist and defeat plaintiffs' applications to acquire operating rights or to transfer or register those rights. It was further contended that the power, strategy, and resources of the defendants were used "to harass and deter respondents [plaintiffs] in their use of administrative and judicial proceedings so as to deny them 'free and unlimited access' to those tribunals."[47] Further, "the machinery of the agencies and the courts was effectively closed to respondents [plaintiffs], and petition-

---

43. *Id.* at 138.
44. 381 U.S. 657 (1965).
45. *Id.* at 670.
46. 404 U.S. 508 (1972).
47. *Id.* at 511.

ers [defendants] indeed became 'the regulators of the grants of rights, transfers, and registrations' to respondents—thereby depleting and diminishing the value of the businesses of respondents and aggrandizing petitioners' economic and monopoly power."[48]

The Supreme Court concluded that defendants' use of the legislative, executive, or judicial branches of the government for the "sham" purpose of exercising First Amendment rights will not bar the courts from applying the antitrust laws to test the legality of their conduct:

> First Amendment rights may not be used as the means or the pretext for achieving "substantive evils" ... which the legislature has the power to control. Certainly the constitutionality of the antitrust laws is not open to debate. A combination of entrepreneurs to harass and deter their competitors from having "free and unlimited access" to the agencies and courts, to defeat that right by massive, concerted, and purposeful activities of the group are ways of building up one empire and destroying another. ... If these facts are proved, a violation of antitrust laws has been established. If the end result is unlawful, it matters not that the means used in violation may be lawful.[49]

The so-called "sham" exception to the *Noerr-Pennington* rule has found increasing usage in more recent cases, thereby demonstrating an increasing reluctance of the courts to exempt conduct that is otherwise illegal under the antitrust laws.

77. The Parker v. Brown rule

Action of a state that results in price fixing or other conduct otherwise illegal if effectuated by private parties is exempted from the antitrust laws under the so-called *Parker* v. *Brown* doctrine. In *Parker* v. *Brown*,[50] a producer and packer of raisins brought a lawsuit to enjoin certain state officials administering a state marketing program under the California Agricultural Prorate Act. The challenged act authorized the establishment of marketing programs that restricted competition among growers and fixed the prices of certain agricultural products. The purpose of the act was to prevent economic waste

48. *Ibid.*
49. *Id.* at 515.
50. 317 U.S. 341 (1943).

and destruction of competition in the marketing of agricultural products.

The program for raisins provided for three classifications of raisins—standard, substandard, and inferior. Substandard and 20 percent of the standard raisins were placed in a "surplus pool" and sold at $25 to $27.50 per ton. Fifty percent of the remaining standard raisins were placed in a "stabilization pool" and disposed of by a committee "in such a manner as to obtain stability in the market," with producers receiving $50 to $55 per ton. The balance of the standard raisins were denominated "free tonnage" and sold through ordinary commercial channels if the producer paid a fee of $2.50 per ton.

Plaintiff challenged the entire raisin program as violating the Sherman Act. However, the U.S. Supreme Court validated the program because it involved state action, which was exempt from antitrust scrutiny. The Court noted that the program would unquestionably have violated the Sherman Act if it had been organized and effectuated through a contract, combination, or conspiracy of private persons, individual or corporate:

> But it is plain that the prorate program here was never intended to operate by force of individual agreement or combination. It derived its authority and its efficacy from the legislative command of the state and was not intended to operate or become effective without that command. We find nothing in the language of the Sherman Act or in its history which suggests that its purpose was to restrain a state or its officers or agents from activities directed by its legislature. In a dual system of government in which, under the Constitution, the states are sovereign, save only as Congress may constitutionally subtract from their authority, an unexpressed purpose to nullify a state's control over its officers and agents is not lightly to be attributed to Congress.[51]

The *Parker* v. *Brown* rule is limited to action taken by the state to effectuate what would otherwise be illegal conduct. If private parties act in an illegal manner in violation of the Sherman Act, their conduct does not become immune simply because it was approved by the state or even required by state law. The Detroit Edison Co., in *Cantor* v. *Detroit Edison Co.,*[52] furnished residential customers, free of

51. *Id.* at 350–51.
52. 428 U.S. 579 (1976).

charge, with 50 percent of the most frequently used standard-sized light bulbs, this cost being included in the rate structure established by Detroit Edison and approved by the state. This practice was long-standing and even antedated state regulation of electric utilities. After the Michigan Public Service Commission was established, it specifically approved the practice as part of Detroit Edison's rate structure, and, pursuant to the regulations of the commission, the practice could not be changed unless a new tariff was submitted to and approved by the commission.

Plaintiff, a retail druggist selling light bulbs, brought this action, claiming that Detroit Edison was using its monopoly power in the distribution of electricity to restrain competition in the sale of light bulbs, in violation of the Sherman Act. The district court, relying on the *Parker* v. *Brown rule,* granted summary judgment to Detroit Edison on the ground that the Michigan Public Service Commission's approval of Detroit Edison's light bulb marketing practices exempted such conduct from the scrutiny of the Sherman Act. The Supreme Court disagreed and held that the rule of *Parker* v. *Brown* can apply only when the state action is the modus operandi by which the restraint is effectuated, not when it merely approves or compels private action. The Court stated:

> In this case, unlike *Parker,* the only defendant is a private utility. No public officials or agencies are named as parties and there is no claim that any state action violated the antitrust laws. Conversely, in *Parker* there was no claim that any private citizen or company had violated the law. . . . Since the case now before us does not call into question the legality of any act of the State of Michigan or any of its officials or agents, it is not controlled by the *Parker* decision.[53]

78. Regulated industries

In addition to the above judicial and statutory exemptions to the antitrust laws, additional exemptions have been carried out in certain regulated industries. Although narrowly applied, exemptions have been found in five industries—banking, securities, communications, fuel and energy, and transportation. Because federal agencies have been set up to regulate these industries, including matters that would

53. *Id.* at 591–92.

otherwise have antitrust implications, the Supreme Court has said that they have primary and, in some instances, exclusive jurisdiction over the industries in question, including antitrust questions. Such preemption may be statutory, as discussed earlier concerning agricultural cooperatives and labor unions, or it may be implicit in the pervasive nature of the congressionally mandated regulatory scheme. Exclusive agency jurisdiction is evident when the statutory scheme contains a provision explicitly immunizing agency action from antitrust coverage.

Hughes Tool Co. v. *Trans World Airlines, Inc.*[54] is an example of an agency, the Civil Aeronautics Board, having exclusive jurisdiction to approve acquisitions that were exempt from the antitrust laws. Howard Hughes became interested in TWA at the invitation of his friend, Jack Frye, the president of TWA. Hughes began acquiring TWA stock through Toolco, which he solely owned. By 1942, Toolco had acquired 42.1 percent of TWA's outstanding stock and, for all practical purposes, was in a position to control the day-to-day affairs of the carrier. In 1944, because Toolco engaged in certain phases of the aeronautics industry, it sought CAB approval of its control over TWA. Such approval was required by law and, when granted, made conduct of the person receiving such authorization immune from the antitrust laws. The CAB entered an order approving the acquisition as being in the public interest. In 1950, after extensive hearings, the CAB entered an order permitting Toolco to take effective control of TWA subject to certain conditions.

In 1960, when TWA sought financing from financial institutions for its proposed jet airliner fleet, the relationship between Toolco and TWA was substantially altered. At the insistence of the financial institutions providing the funds in question, Toolco's TWA stock was placed in a voting trust, thus ending Toolco's control of TWA. In 1961 TWA, now no longer under the control of Toolco, commenced a lawsuit against Toolco, claiming violations of the antitrust laws to the injury of TWA's business. Toolco pleaded that its conduct was immune from the antitrust laws because every acquisition from 1944 through 1960 of aircraft by TWA from Toolco and each financing of TWA by Toolco was approved by the CAB.

During the course of the litigation Howard Hughes was ordered

---

54. 409 U.S. 363 (1973).

to appear for a deposition, but he refused to do so, choosing rather to rely on the affirmative defense that the conduct in question was immune from the antitrust laws. A default judgment was entered against Toolco on May 3, 1963. The case was then reviewed by the court of appeals and the default judgment affirmed. A special master then awarded damages totaling $137,611,435.95, and the district court added $7,500,000 as a reasonable attorney's fee.

On review in the United States Supreme Court the judgment was reversed and the complaint ordered dismissed on the ground that the conduct in question was exempt from the antitrust laws. Justice Douglas wrote the opinion of the Court in which he stated that

> where, as here, the CAB authorizes control of an air carrier to be acquired by another person or corporation, and where it specifically authorizes as in the public interest specific transactions between the parent and the subsidiary, the way in which that control is exercised in those precise situations is under the surveillance of the CAB, not in the hands of those who can invoke the sanctions of the antitrust laws. As noted, the parent company which controls an air carrier is subject to pervasive control by the CAB. The control which the CAB is authorized to grant or to deny under §408 involves an appraisal of the impact of that control in terms of monopoly and competition; and the ongoing supervision entrusted to the CAB by §415 is broad enough to put all transactions between parent and subsidiary—as originally conceived or subsequently exercised—under CAB supervision.[55]

The complaint in *Pan American World Airways, Inc.* v. *United States,*[56] brought by the United States, alleged that Pan American and W. R. Grace & Co., each of whom owned 50 percent of the stock of defendant Panagra, formed Panagra in 1928 under an agreement that Panagra would have the exclusive right to traffic along the west coast of South America, free from Pan American competition, and that the latter was to be free from competition of Panagra in other areas of South America and between the Canal Zone and the United States. The complaint also charged that Pan American and Grace were monopolizing and conspiring to monopolize air commerce between the eastern coastal areas of the United States and the western coastal areas of South America.

55. *Id.* at 387–88.
56. 371 U.S. 296 (1963).

The district court rejected Pan American's argument that the conduct in question was subject to the primary jurisdiction and control of the CAB and therefore exempt from the antitrust laws. The Supreme Court, however, reversed; examining the legislative history of the Civil Aeronautics Act, the Court concluded that the CAB was to have broad jurisdiction over air carriers. Although the regulatory scheme did not completely displace the antitrust laws, still

> [t]hat does not, however, end our inquiry. Limitations of routes and divisions of territories and the relation of common carriers to air carriers are basic in the regulatory scheme. Those acts charged in this civil suit as antitrust violations are precise ingredients of the Board's authority in granting, qualifying, or denying certificates to air carriers, in modifying, suspending, or revoking them, and in allowing affiliations between common carriers. . . .
>
> It would be strange, indeed, if a division of territories or an allocation of routes which met the requirements of the "public interest" as defined in §102 were held to be antitrust violations. It would also be odd to conclude that an affiliation between a common carrier and an air carrier that passed muster under §408 should run afoul of the antitrust laws. Whether or not transactions of that character meet the standards of competition and monopoly provided by the Act is peculiarly a question for the Board, subject of course to judicial review.[57]

The Supreme Court in *Silver* v. *New York Stock Exchange*[58] reached a different conclusion. In that case, two broker-dealers who were not members of the New York Stock Exchange sued for treble damages and injunctive relief, alleging a conspiracy of the exchange with member firms to deprive the broker-dealers of their private wire connections and stock ticket service. Plaintiffs had arranged for several firms, who were members of the exchange, to provide wire connections for them on the floor of the exchange. The firms in question, pursuant to exchange rules, applied for approval of the connections but were refused; thus they terminated the connections and services. The district court ruled for plaintiffs, but the court of appeals reversed, holding that the Securities Exchange Act of 1934 gave the exchange disciplinary powers over members, that the actions of the

57. *Id.* at 305, 309.
58. 373 U.S. 341 (1963).

exchange were within the authority of the exchange, and that "(t)he exchange is exempt from the restrictions of the Sherman Act because it is exercising a power which it is required to exercise by the Securities Exchange Act."[59]

The Supreme Court reversed, holding that the conduct in question was not exempt from antitrust laws. The Court noted that there was nothing in the Securities Exchange Act that exempted regulated conduct from the purview of the antitrust laws. "This means that any repealer of the antitrust laws must be discerned as a matter of implication and '[i]t is a cardinal principle of construction that repeals by implication are not favored.'"[60] The Court then added, "repeal is to be regarded as implied only if necessary to make the Securities Exchange Act work, and even then only to the minimum extent necessary."[61] Finally, the Court held that although the act in question gives the Securities and Exchange Commission the power to request the New York Stock Exchange and other exchanges to make changes in their rules, and therefore, the power to disapprove rule changes, it did not give the commission jurisdiction to review particular instances of enforcement of exchange rules. This absence of commission jurisdiction meant that there was nothing built into the regulatory scheme "which performs the antitrust function of insuring that an exchange will not in some cases apply its rules so as to do injury to competition which cannot be justified as furthering legitimate self-regulative ends."[62]

This case should be compared to *Pan American* and *Hughes Tool Co.* cases where an antitrust exemption was written into the act in question and the CAB acted pursuant to powers given it to approve or disapprove the conduct in question.

A different question from that in the *Silver* case was presented in *Ricci* v. *Chicago Mercantile Exchange.*[63] In that case, the plaintiff Ricci filed a complaint against the Chicago Mercantile Exchange, its president, vice president, and chairman of the Board, and against the Siegel Trading Company, a member of the exchange, and its president, charging a conspiracy in violation of Section 1 of the Sherman

59. *Id.* at 346–47.
60. *Id.* at 357.
61. *Ibid.*
62. *Id.* at 358.
63. 409 U.S. 289 (1973).

Act. Ricci had purchased a membership in the exchange in 1967, using funds borrowed from the Siegel Trading Company, and in February 1969 the exchange, at the insistence of Siegel Trading Company, transferred the membership to another, without notice and hearing, utilizing a blank transfer authorization that had been previously revoked. This conduct allegedly violated the rules of both the exchange and the Commodity Exchange Act and was done intentionally to restrain Ricci's business.

The district court dismissed the complaint; the court of appeals, however, reversed and ordered the district court to stay further proceedings until the Commodity Exchange Commission had the opportunity to pass on the question first. The Supreme Court agreed with the court of appeals that the action should be stayed in order that the Commodity Exchange Commission could pass on the validity of defendants' conduct under the Commodity Exchange Act. Unlike the SEC in *Silver,* the Commodity Exchange Commission had statutory authority to consider a challenge to a specific application of the exchange's rules. If the challenged conduct was found by the commission to have been improper, as alleged, there would be no immunity and the antitrust case could then proceed ahead. If the conduct in question was found by the commission to have been proper by a valid membership rule, then the court, and not the commission, would determine whether this particular regulatory scheme provided antitrust immunity or whether, in fact, any rule of the exchange should take precedence over the antitrust laws.

The relationship of the antitrust laws to the rules, regulations, and decisions of the various administrative agencies raises difficult questions concerning "exemptions." As seen from the cases discussed the Supreme Court's approach has varied, depending upon the context in which the issue has been presented. For purposes here it is sufficient simply to allude to the question as an additional area of consideration for the businessman.

The following appendix sets forth the basic antitrust laws, with some deletions, and their amendments through 1979.

Sherman Act[1]

SEC. 1. Every contract, combination in the form of trust or otherwise, or conspiracy, in restraint of trade or commerce among the several States, or with foreign nations, is hereby declared to be illegal. Every person who shall make any contract or engage in any combination or conspiracy hereby declared to be illegal shall be deemed guilty of a felony and, on conviction thereof, shall be punished by fine not exceeding one million dollars if a corporation, or, if any other person, one hundred thousand dollars, or by imprisonment not exceeding three years, or by both said punishments, in the discretion of the court.

SEC. 2. Every person who shall monopolize, or attempt to monopolize, or combine or conspire with any other person or persons, to monopolize any part of the trade or commerce among the several States, or with foreign nations, shall be deemed guilty of a felony, and, on conviction thereof, shall be punished by fine not exceeding one million dollars if a corporation, or, if any other person, one hundred thousand dollars, or by imprisonment not exceeding three years, or by both said punishments, in the discretion of the court.

SEC. 3. Every contract, combination in form of trust or otherwise, or conspiracy, in restraint of trade or commerce in any Territory of the United States or of the District of Columbia, or in restraint of trade or commerce between any such Territory and another, or between any such Territory or Territories and any State or States or the District of Columbia, or with foreign nations, or between the District of Columbia and any State or States or foreign nations, is hereby declared illegal. Every person who shall make any such contract or engage in any such combination or conspiracy, shall

[1]The Sherman Act is the act of July 2, 1890, c. 617, 26 Stat. 209, 15 U.S.C.A. §§ 1–7. By an act of July 7, 1955, c. 281, 69 Stat. 282, the fine was increased from $5,000 to $50,000, and by the Antitrust Procedures and Penalties Act, Public Law 93–528, 88 Stat. 1706 (1974), the fine was increased to $1,000,000 for corporations and $100,000 for other persons and the maximum term was increased to three years.

be deemed guilty of a felony, and, on conviction thereof, shall be punished by fine not exceeding one million dollars if a corporation, or, if any other person, one hundred thousand dollars, or by imprisonment not exceeding three years, or by both said punishments, in the discretion of the court.

SEC. 4.   The several district courts of the United States are invested with jurisdiction to prevent and restrain violations of this act; and it shall be the duty of the several United States attorneys, in their respective districts, under the direction of the Attorney General, to institute proceedings in equity to prevent and restrain such violations. Such proceedings may be by way of petition setting forth the case and praying that such violation shall be enjoined or otherwise prohibited. When the parties complained of shall have been duly notified of such petition the court shall proceed, as soon as may be, to the hearing and determination of the case; and pending such petition and before final decree, the court may at any time make such temporary restraining order or prohibition as shall be deemed just in the premises.

SEC. 5.   Whenever it shall appear to the court before which any proceeding under section four of this act may be pending, that the ends of justice require that other parties should be brought before the court, the court may cause them to be summoned, whether they reside in the district in which the court is held or not; and subpoenas to that end may be served in any district by the marshal thereof.

SEC. 6.   Any property owned under any contract or by any combination, or pursuant to any conspiracy (and being the subject thereof) mentioned in section one of this act, and being in the course of transportation from one State to another, or to a foreign country, shall be forfeited to the United States, and may be seized and condemned by like proceedings as those provided by law for the forfeiture, seizure, and condemnation of property imported into the United States contrary to law.

SEC. 8.   The word "person," or "persons," wherever used in this act shall be deemed to include corporations and associations existing under or authorized by the laws of either the United States, the laws of any of the Territories, the laws of any State, or the laws of any foreign country.

Clayton Act[2]

AN ACT To supplement existing laws against unlawful restraints and monopolies, and for other purposes.

SEC. 1. *Be it enacted by the Senate and House of Representatives of the United States of America in Congress assembled,* That "antitrust laws," as used herein, includes the Act entitled "An Act to protect trade and commerce against unlawful restraints and monopolies," approved July second, eighteen hundred and ninety; sections seventy-three to seventy-seven, inclusive, of an Act entitled "An Act to reduce taxation, to provide revenue for the Government, and for other purposes," of August twenty-seventh, eighteen hundred and ninety-four; an Act entitled "An Act to amend sections seventy-three and seventy-six of the Act of August twenty-seventh, eighteen hundred and ninety-four, entitled 'An Act to reduce taxation, to provide revenue for the Government, and for other purposes,'" approved February twelfth, nineteen hundred and thirteen; and also this Act.

"Commerce," as used herein, means trade or commerce among the several States and with foreign nations, or between the District of Columbia or any Territory of the United States and any State, Territory or foreign nation, or between any insular possessions or other places under the jurisdiction of the United States, or between any such possession or place and any State or Territory of the United States or the District of Columbia or any foreign nation, or within the District of Columbia or any Territory or any insular possession or other place under the jurisdiction of the United States: *Provided,* That nothing in this Act contained shall apply to the Philippine Islands.

[2]The Clayton Act is the act of October 15, 1914, c. 223, 38 Stat. 730, 15 U.S.C.A. §§12–27. Section 2 of the Clayton Act was amended by the Robinson-Patman Act, Act of June 19, 1936, c 592, 49 Stat. 1526. Section 3 of the Robinson-Patman Act made price discrimination criminal in certain instances. Sections 4A and 4B were added by the Act of July 7, 1955, c. 283, 69 Stat. 282–283. Sections 4c–4h were added by amendment on September 30, 1976, pub. L. 94–435, 90 Stat. 1394–1396. Section 5 was amended by the act of December 21, 1974, Pub. L. 93-528 Section 2, 88 Stat. 1706 and by the act of September 30, 1976, Pub. L. 94–435, 90 Stat. 1396. Section 7 of the Clayton Act was amended by the Celler-Kefauver Act of December 29, 1950. c. 1184, 64 Stat. 1125. Section 9 was repealed by the act of June 25, 1948. c. 645, 62 Stat. 862. Sections 17 through 19 and 21 through 25 were repealed by the act of June 25, 1948, c. 646, 62 Stat. 992.

The word "person" or "persons" wherever used in this Act shall be deemed to include corporations and associations existing under or authorized by the laws of either the United States, the laws of any of the Territories, the laws of any State, or the laws of any foreign country.

SEC. 2.   (a) That it shall be unlawful for any person engaged in commerce, in the course of such commerce, either directly or indirectly, to discriminate in price between different purchasers of commodities of like grade and quality, where either or any of the purchases involved in such discrimination are in commerce, where such commodities are sold for use, consumption, or resale within the United States or any Territory thereof or the District of Columbia or any insular possession or other place under the jurisdiction of the United States, and where the effect of such discrimination may be substantially to lessen competition or tend to create a monopoly in any line of commerce, or to injure, destroy, or prevent competition with any person who either grants or knowingly receives the benefit of such discrimination, or with customers of either of them: *Provided,* That nothing herein contained shall prevent differentials which make only due allowance for differences in the cost of manufacture, sale, or delivery resulting from the differing methods or quantities in which such commodities are to such purchasers sold or delivered: *Provided, however,* That the Federal Trade Commission may, after due investigation and hearing to all interested parties, fix and establish quantity limits, and revise the same as it finds necessary, as to particular commodities or classes of commodities, where it finds that available purchasers in greater quantities are so few as to render differentials on account thereof unjustly discriminatory or promotive of monopoly in any line of commerce; and the foregoing shall then not be construed to permit differentials based on differences in quantities greater than those so fixed and established: *And provided further,* That nothing herein contained shall prevent persons engaged in selling goods, wares, or merchandise in commerce from selecting their own customers in bona fide transactions and not in restraint of trade: *And provided further,* That nothing herein contained shall prevent price changes from time to time where in response to changing conditions affecting the market for or the marketability of the goods concerned, such as but not limited to actual or imminent deterioration of perishable goods, obsolescence of seasonal goods, distress sales under court process, or sales in good faith in discontinuance of business in the goods concerned.

(b) Upon proof being made, at any hearing on a complaint under this section, that there has been discrimination in price or services or facilities furnished, the burden of rebutting the prima facie case thus made by showing justification shall be upon the person charged with a violation of this section, and unless justification shall be affirmatively shown, the Commission is authorized to issue an order terminating the discrimination: *Provided, however,* That nothing herein contained shall prevent a seller rebutting the prima facie case thus made by showing that his lower price or the furnishing of services or facilities to any purchaser or purchasers was made in good faith to meet an equally low price of a competitor, or the services or facilities furnished by a competitor.

(c) That it shall be unlawful for any person engaged in commerce in the course of such commerce, to pay or grant, or to receive or accept, anything of value as a commission, brokerage, or other compensation, or any allowance or discount in lieu thereof, except for services rendered in connection with the sale or purchase of goods, wares, or merchandise, either to the other party to such transaction or to an agent, representative, or other intermediary therein where such intermediary is acting in fact for or in behalf, or is subject to the direct or indirect control, of any party to such transaction other than the person by whom such compensation is so granted or paid.

(d) That it shall be unlawful for any person engaged in commerce to pay or contract for the payment of anything of value to or for the benefit of a customer of such person in the course of such commerce as compensation or in consideration for any services or facilities furnished by or through such customer in connection with the processing, handling, sale, or offering for sale of any products or commodities manufactured, sold, or offered for sale by such person, unless such payment or consideration is available on proportionally equal terms to all other customers competing in the distribution of such products or commodities.

(e) That it shall be unlawful for any person to discriminate in favor of one purchaser against another purchaser or purchasers of a commodity bought for resale, with or without processing, by contracting to furnish or furnishing, or by contributing to the furnishing of, any services or facilities connected with the processing, handling, sale, or offering for sale of such commodity so purchased upon terms not accorded to all purchasers on proportionally equal terms.

(f) That it shall be unlawful for any person engaged in commerce, in the course of such commerce, knowingly to induce or receive a discrimination in price which is prohibited by this section.

SEC. 3.   That it shall be unlawful for any person engaged in commerce, in the course of such commerce, to lease or make a sale or contract for sale of goods, wares, merchandise, machinery, supplies or other commodities, whether patented or unpatented, for use, consumption or resale within the United States or any Territory thereof or the District of Columbia or any insular possession or other place under the jurisdiction of the United States, or fix a price charged therefor, or discount from or rebate upon, such price, on the condition, agreement or understanding that the lessee or purchaser thereof shall not use or deal in the goods, wares, merchandise, machinery, supplies, or other commodities of a competitor or competitors of the lessor or seller, where the effect of such lease, sale, or contract for sale or such condition, agreement or understanding may be to substantially lessen competition or tend to create a monopoly in any line of commerce.

SEC. 4.   That any person who shall be injured in his business or property by reason of anything forbidden in the antitrust laws may sue therefor in any district court of the United States in the district in which the defendant resides or is found or has an agent, without respect to the amount in controversy, and shall recover threefold the damages by him sustained, and the cost of suit, including a reasonable attorney's fee.

SEC. 4A.   Whenever the United States is hereafter injured in its business or property by reason of anything forbidden in the antitrust laws it may sue therefor in the United States district court for the district in which the defendant resides or is found or has an agent, without respect to the amount in controversy, and shall recover actual damages by it sustained and the cost of suit.

SEC. 4B.   Any action to enforce any cause of action under sections 4, 4A or 4C shall be forever barred unless commenced within four years after the cause of action accrued. No cause of action barred under existing law on the effective date of this section and sections 4A and 5 of this Act shall be revived by said sections.

SEC. 4C.   (a)(1) Any attorney general of a State may bring a civil action in the name of such State, as parens patriae on behalf of natural persons residing in State, in any district court of the United States having jurisdiction of the defendant, to secure monetary relief as provided in this section for injury sustained by natural persons to their property by reason of any violation of the Sherman Act. The court shall exclude from the amount of monetary relief awarded in such action any amount of monetary relief (A) which duplicates amounts which have been awarded for the same injury, or (B) which is property allocable to (i) natural persons who have excluded their claims pursuant to subsection (b)(2) of this section, and (ii) any business entity. (2) The court shall award the State as monetary relief threefold the total damage sustained as described in paragraph (1) of this subsection, and the cost of suit, including a reasonable attorney's fee.

(b)(1) In any action brought under subsection (a)(1) of this section, the State attorney general shall, at such times, in such manner, and with such content as the court may direct, cause notice thereof to be given by publication. If the court finds that notice given solely by publication would deny due process of law to any person or persons, the court may direct further notice to such person or persons according to the circumstances of the case. (2) Any person on whose behalf an action is brought under subsection (a)(1) may elect to exclude from adjudication the portion of the State claim for monetary relief attributable to him by filing notice of such election with the court within such time as specified in the notice given pursuant to paragraph (1) of this subsection. (3) The final judgment in an action under subsection (a)(1) shall be res judicata as to any claim under section 4 of this Act by any person on behalf of whom such action was brought and who fails to give such notice within the period specified in the notice given pursuant to paragraph (1) of this subsection.

(c) An action under subsection (a)(1) shall not be dismissed or compromised without the approval of the court, and notice of any proposed dismissal or compromise shall be given in such manner as the court directs.

(d) In any action under subsection (a)—(1) the amount of the plaintiffs' attorney's fee, if any, shall be determined by the court; and (2) the court may, in its discretion, award a reasonable attorney's fee to a prevailing defendant upon a finding that the State attorney general has acted in bad faith, vexatiously, wantonly, or for oppressive reasons.

SEC. 4D. In any action under section 4c(a)(1), in which there has been a determination that a defendant agreed to fix prices in violation of the Sherman Act, damages may be proved and assessed in the aggregate by statistical or sampling methods, by the computation of illegal overcharges, or by such other reasonable system of estimating aggregate damages as the court in its discretion may permit without the necessity of separately proving the individual claim of, or amount of damage to, persons on whose behalf the suit was brought.

SEC. 4E. Monetary relief recovered in an action under section 4c(a)(1) shall—(1) be distributed in such manner as the district court in its discretion may authorize; or (2) be deemed a civil penalty by the court and deposited with the State as general revenues; subject in either case to the requirement that any distribution procedure adopted afford each person a reasonable opportunity to secure his appropriate portion of the net monetary relief.

SEC. 4F. (a) Whenever the Attorney General of the United States has brought an action under the antitrust laws, and he has reason to believe that any State attorney general would be entitled to bring an action under this Act based substantially on the same alleged violation of the antitrust laws, he shall promptly give written notification thereof to such State attorney general.

(b) To assist a State attorney general in evaluating the notice or in bringing any action under this Act, the Attorney General of the United States shall, upon request by such State attorney general, make available to him, to the extent permitted by law, any investigative files or other materials which are or may be relevant or material to the actual or potential cause of action under this Act.

SEC. 4G. [Definitions]

SEC. 4H. Sections 4C, 4D, 4E, 4F, and 4G shall apply in any State, unless such State provides by law for its nonapplicability in such State.

SEC. 5. (a) A final judgment or decree heretofore or hereafter rendered in any civil or criminal proceeding brought by or on behalf of the United States under the antitrust laws to the effect that a defendant has violated said laws shall be prima facie evidence against such defendant in any action or proceeding brought by any other party against such defendant under said laws or by the United States under section 4A, as to all matters respecting which said judgment or decree would be an estoppel as between the parties thereto: *Provided,* That this section shall not apply to consent judgments or decrees entered before any testimony has been taken or to judgments or decrees entered in actions under section 4A.

(b) Any proposal for a consent judgment submitted by the United States for entry in any civil proceeding brought by or on behalf of the United States under the antitrust laws shall be filed with the district court before which such proceeding is pending and published by the United States in the Federal Register at least 60 days prior to the effective date of such judgment. Any written comments relating to such proposal and any responses by the United States thereto, shall also be filed with such district court and published by the United States in the Federal Register within such sixty-day period. Copies of such proposal and any other materials and documents which the United States considered determinative in formulating such proposal, shall also be made available to the public at the district court and in such other districts as the court may subsequently direct. Simultaneously with the filing of such proposal, unless otherwise instructed by the court, the United States shall file with the district court, publish in the Federal Register, and thereafter furnish to any person upon request, a competitive impact statement which shall recite—

(1) the nature and purpose of the proceeding;

(2) a description of the practices or events giving rise to the alleged violation of the antitrust laws;

(3) an explanation of the proposal for a consent judgment, including an explanation of any unusual circumstances giving rise to such proposal or any provision contained therein, relief to be obtained thereby, and the anticipated effects on competition of such relief;

(4) the remedies available to potential private plaintiffs damaged by the alleged violation in the event that such proposal for the consent judgment is entered in such proceeding;

(5) a description of the procedures available for modification of such proposal; and

(6) a description and evaluation of alternatives to such proposal actually considered by the United States.

(c) The United States shall also cause to be published, commencing at least 60 days prior to the effective date of the judgment described in subsection (b) of this section, for 7 days over a period of 2 weeks in newspapers of general circulation of the district in which the case has been filed, in the District of Columbia, and in such other districts as the court may direct—

(i) a summary of the terms of the proposal for the consent judgment,

(ii) a summary of the competitive impact statement filed under subsection (b) of this section,

(iii) and a list of the materials and documents under subsection (b) of this section which the United States shall make available for purposes of meaningful public comment, and the place where such materials and documents are available for public inspection.

(d) During the 60-day period as specified in subsection (b) of this section, and such additional time as the United States may request and the court may grant, the United States shall receive and consider any written comments relating to the proposal for the consent judgment submitted under subsection (b) of this section. The Attorney General or his designee shall establish procedures to carry out the provisions of this subsection, but such 60-day time period shall not be shortened except by order of the district court upon a showing that (1) extraordinary circumstances require such shortening and (2) such shortening is not adverse to the public interest. At the close of the period during which such comments may be received, the United States shall file with the district court and cause to be published in the Federal Register a response to such comments.

(e) Before entering any consent judgment proposed by the United States under this section, the court shall determine that the entry of such judgment is in the public interest. For the purpose of such determination, the court may consider—

(1) the competitive impact of such judgment, including termination of alleged violations, provisions for enforcement and modi-

fication, duration or relief sought, anticipated effects of alternative remedies actually considered, and any other considerations bearing upon the adequacy of such judgment;

(2) the impact of entry of such judgment upon the public generally and individuals alleging specific injury from the violations set forth in the complaint including consideration of the public benefit, if any, to be derived from a determination of the issues at trial.

(f) In making its determination under subsection (e) of this section, the court may—

(1) take testimony of Government officials or experts or such other expert witnesses, upon motion of any party or participant or upon its own motion, as the court may deem appropriate;

(2) appoint a special master and such outside consultants or expert witnesses as the court may deem appropriate; and request and obtain the views, evaluations, or advice of any individual, group or agency of government with respect to any aspects of the proposed judgment or the effect of such judgment, in such manner as the court deems appropriate;

(3) authorize full or limited participation in proceedings before the court by interested persons or agencies, including appearance amicus curiae, intervention as a party pursuant to the Federal Rules of Civil Procedure, examination of witnesses or documentary materials, or participation in any other manner and extent which serves the public interest as the court may deem appropriate;

(4) review any comments including any objections filed with the United States under subsection (d) of this section concerning the proposed judgment and the responses of the United States to such comments and objections; and

(5) take such other action in the public interest as the court may deem appropriate.

(g) Not later than 10 days following the date of the filing of any proposal for a consent judgment under subsection (b) of this section, each defendant shall file with the district court a description of any and all written or oral communications by or on behalf of such defendant, including any and all written or oral communications on behalf of such defendant, or other person, with any officer or employee of the United States concerning or relevant to such proposal, except that any such communications made by counsel of record alone with the Attorney General or the employees of the Department of Justice alone shall be excluded from the requirements of this subsection. Prior to the entry of any consent judgment pursuant to the antitrust laws, each defendant shall certify to the district court that the requirements of this subsection have been complied with and that such filing is a true and complete description of such communications known to the defendant or which the defendant reasonably should have known.

(h) Proceedings before the district court under subsections (e) and (f) of this section, and the competitive impact statement filed under subsection (b) of this section, shall not be admissible against any defendant in any action or proceeding brought by any other party against such defendant under the antitrust laws or by the United States under section 4A nor constitute a basis for the introduction of the consent judgment as prima facie evidence against such defendant in any such action or proceeding.

(i) Whenever any civil or criminal proceeding is instituted by the United States to prevent, restrain, or punish violations of any of the antitrust laws, but not including an action under section 4A, the running of the statute of limitations in respect of every private right of action arising under said laws and based in whole or in part on any matter complained of in said proceeding shall be suspended during the pendency thereof and for one year thereafter: *Provided, however,* That whenever the running of the statute of limitations in respect of a cause of action arising under section 4 and 4C is suspended hereunder, any action to enforce such cause of action shall be forever barred unless commenced either within the period of suspension or within four years after the cause of action accrued.

SEC. 6.   That the labor of a human being is not a commodity or article of commerce. Nothing contained in the antitrust laws shall be construed to forbid the existence and operation of labor, agricultural, or horticultural organizations, instituted for the purposes of mutual help, and not having capital stock or conducted for profit, or to forbid or restrain individual members of such organizations from lawfully carrying out the legitimate objects thereof; nor shall such organizations, or the members thereof, be held or construed to be illegal combinations or conspiracies in restraint of trade, under the antitrust laws.

Sec. 7.   That no corporation engaged in commerce shall acquire directly or indirectly, the whole or any part of the stock or other share capital and no corporation subject to the jurisdiction of the Federal Trade Commission shall acquire the whole or any part of the assets of another corporation engaged also in commerce, where in any line of commerce in any section of the country, the effect of such acquisition may be substantially to lessen competition, or to tend to create a monopoly.

No corporation shall acquire, directly or indirectly, the whole or any part of the stock or other share capital and no corporation subject to the jurisdiction of the Federal Trade Commission shall acquire the whole or any part of the assets of one or more corporations engaged in commerce, where in any line of commerce in any section of the country, the effect of such acquisition, of such stocks or assets, or of the use of such stock by the voting or granting of proxies or otherwise, may be substantially to lessen competition, or to tend to create a monopoly.

This section shall not apply to corporations purchasing such stock solely for investment and not using the same by voting or otherwise to bring about, or in attempting to bring about, the substantial lessening of competition. Nor shall anything contained in this section prevent a corporation engaged in commerce from causing the formation of subsidiary corporations for the actual carrying on of their immediate lawful business, or the natural and legitimate branches or extensions thereof, or from owning and holding all or a part of the stock of such subsidiary corporations, when the effect of such formation is not to substantially lessen competition.

Nor shall anything herein contained be construed to prohibit any common carrier subject to the laws to regulate commerce from aiding in the construction of branches or short lines so located as to become feeders to the main line of the company so aiding in such construction or from acquiring or owning all or any part of the stock of such branch lines, nor to prevent any such common carrier from acquiring and owning all or any part of the stock of a branch or short line constructed by an independent company where there is no substantial competition between the company owning the branch line so constructed and the company owning the main line acquiring the property or an interest therein, nor to prevent such common carrier from extending any of its lines through the medium of the acquisition of stock or otherwise of any other common carrier where there is no substantial competition between the company extending its lines and the company whose stock, property, or an interest therein is so acquired.

Nothing contained in this section shall be held to affect or impair any right heretofore legally acquired: *Provided,* That nothing in this section shall be held or construed to authorize or make lawful anything heretofore prohibited or made illegal by the antitrust laws, nor to exempt any person from the penal provisions thereof or the civil remedies therein provided.

Nothing contained in this section shall apply to transactions duly consummated pursuant to authority given by the Civil Aeronautics Board, Federal Communications Commission, Federal Power Commission, Interstate Commerce Commission, the Securities and Exchange Commission in the exercise of its jurisdiction under section 10 of the Public Utility Holding Company Act of 1935, the United States Maritime Commission, or the Secretary of Agriculture under any statutory provision vesting such power in such Commission, Secretary, or Board.

SEC. 8.   No private banker or director, officer, or employee of any member bank of the Federal Reserve System or any branch thereof shall be at the same time a director, officer, or employee of any other bank, banking association, savings bank, or trust company organized under the National Bank Act or organized under the laws of any State or of the District of Columbia, or any branch thereof, except that the Board of Governors of the Federal Reserve System may by regulation permit such service as a director, officer, or employee of not more than one other such institution or branch thereof; but the foregoing prohibition shall not apply in the case of any one or more of the following or any branch thereof:

(1) A bank, banking association, savings bank, or trust company, more than 90 per centum of the stock of which is owned directly or indirectly by the United States or by any corporation of which the United States directly or indirectly owns more than 90 per centum of the stock.

(2) A bank, banking association, savings bank, or trust company which has been placed formally in liquidation or which is in the hands of a receiver, conservator, or other official exercising similar functions.

(3) A corporation, principally engaged in international or foreign banking or banking in a dependency or insular possession of the United States which has entered into an agreement with the Board of Governors of the Federal Reserve System pursuant to sections 601 to 604a of Title 12.

(4) A bank, banking association, savings bank, or trust company, more than 50 per centum of the common stock of which is owned directly or indirectly by persons who own directly or indirectly more than 50 per centum of the common stock of such member bank.

(5) A bank, banking association, savings bank, or trust company not located and having no branch in the same city, town, or village as that in which such member bank or any branch thereof is located, or in any city, town, or village contiguous or adjacent thereto.

(6) A bank, banking association, savings bank, or trust company not engaged in a class or classes of business in which such member bank is engaged.

(7) A mutual savings bank having no capital stock.

Until February 1, 1939, nothing in this section shall prohibit any director, officer, or employee of any member bank of the Federal Reserve System, or any branch thereof, who is lawfully serving at the same time as a private banker or as a director, officer, or employee of any other bank, banking association, savings bank, or trust company, or any branch thereof, on August 23, 1935, from continuing such service.

The Board of Governors of the Federal Reserve System is authorized and directed to enforce compliance with this section, and to prescribe such rules and regulations as it deems necessary for that purpose.

No person at the same time shall be a director in any two or more corporations, any one of which has capital, surplus, and undivided profits aggregating more than $1,000,000, engaged in whole or in part in commerce, other than banks, banking associations, trust companies, and common carriers subject to the Act to regulate commerce, approved February fourth, eighteen hundred and eighty-seven, if such corporations are or shall have been theretofore, by virtue of their business and location of operation, competitors, so that the elimination of competition by agreement between them would constitute a violation of any of the provisions of any of the antitrust laws. The eligibility of a director under the foregoing provision shall be determined by the aggregate amount of the capital, surplus, and undivided profits, exclusive of dividends declared but not paid to stockholders, at the end of the fiscal year of said corporation next preceding the election of directors, and when a director has been elected in accordance with the provisions of this Act it shall be lawful for him to continue as such for one year thereafter.

When any person elected or chosen as a director or officer or selected as an employee of any bank or other corporation subject to the provisions of this Act is eligible at the time of his election or selection to act for such bank or other corporation in such capacity his eligibility to act in such capacity shall not be affected and he shall not become or be deemed amenable to any of the provisions hereof by reason of any change in the affairs of such bank or other corporation from whatsoever cause, whether specifically excepted by any of the provisions hereof or not, until the expiration of one year from the date of his election or employment.

SEC. 10. No common carrier engaged in commerce shall have any dealings in securities, supplies, or other articles of commerce, or shall make or have any contracts for construction or maintenance of any kind, to the amount of more than $50,000, in the aggregate, in any one year, with another corporation, firm, partnership, or association when the said common carrier shall have upon its board of directors or as its president, manager, or as its purchasing or selling officer, or agent in the particular transaction, any person who is at the same time a director, manager, or purchasing or selling officer of, or who has any substantial interest in, such other corporation, firm, partnership, or association, unless and except such purchases shall be made from, or such dealings shall be with, the bidder whose bid is the most favorable to such common carrier, to be ascertained by competitive bidding under regulations to be prescribed by rule or otherwise by the Interstate Commerce Commission. No bid shall be received unless the name and address of the bidder or the names and addresses of the officers, directors, and general managers thereof, if the bidder be a corporation, or of the members, if it be a partnership or firm, be given with the bid.

Any person who shall, directly or indirectly, do or attempt to do anything to prevent anyone from bidding, or shall do any act to prevent free and fair competition among the bidders or those desiring to bid, shall be punished as prescribed in this section in the case of an officer or director.

Every such common carrier having any such transactions or making any such purchases shall, within thirty days after making the same, file with the Interstate Commerce Commission a full and detailed statement of the transaction showing the manner of the competitive bidding, who were the bidders, and the names and addresses of the directors and officers of the corporations and the members of the firm or partnership bidding; and whenever the said commission shall, after investigation or hearing, have reason to believe that the law has been violated in and about the said purchases or transactions, it shall transmit all papers and documents and its own views or findings regarding the transaction to the Attorney General.

If any common carrier shall violate this section, it shall be fined not exceeding $25,000; and every such director, agent, manager, or officer thereof who shall have knowingly voted for or directed the act constituting such violation, or who shall have aided or abetted in such violation, shall be deemed guilty of a misdemeanor and shall be fined not exceeding $5,000 or confined in jail not exceeding one year, or both, in the discretion of the court.

SEC. 11.   (a) That authority to enforce compliance with sections 2, 3, 7, and 8 of this Act by the persons respectively subject thereto is hereby vested in the Interstate Commerce Commission where applicable to common carriers subject to the Interstate Commerce Act, as amended; in the Federal Communications Commission where applicable to common carriers engaged in wire or radio communication or radio transmission of energy; in the Civil Aeronautics Board where applicable to air carriers and foreign air carriers subject to the Civil Aeronautics Act of 1938; in the Federal Reserve Board where applicable to banks, banking associations, and trust companies; and in the Federal Trade Commission where applicable to all other character of commerce to be exercised as follows:

(b) Whenever the Commission or Board vested with jurisdiction thereof shall have reason to believe that any person is violating or has violated any of the provisions of sections 2, 3, 7, and 8 of this Act, it shall issue and serve upon such person and the Attorney General a complaint stating its charges in that respect, and containing a notice of hearing upon a day and at a place therein fixed at least thirty days after the service of said complaint. The person so complained of shall have the right to appear at the place and time so fixed and show cause why an order should not be entered by the Commission or Board requiring such person to cease and desist from the violation of the law so charged in said complaint. The Attorney General shall have the right to intervene and appear in said proceeding and any person may make application, and upon good cause shown may be allowed by the Commission or Board, to intervene and appear in said proceeding by counsel or in person. The testimony in any such proceeding shall be reduced to writing and filed in the office of the Commission or Board. If upon such hearing the Commission or Board, as the case may be, shall be of the opinion that any of the provisions of said sections have been or are being violated, it shall make a report in writing, in which it shall state its findings as to the facts, and shall issue and cause to be served on such person an order requiring such person to cease and desist from such violations, and divest itself of the stock, or other share capital, or assets, held or rid itself of the directors chosen contrary to the provisions of sections 7 and 8 of this Act, if any there be, in the manner and within the time fixed by said order. Until the expiration of the time allowed for filing a petition for review, if no such petition has been duly filed within such time, or, if a petition for review has been filed within such time then until the record in the proceeding has been filed in a court of appeals of the United States, as hereinafter provided, the Commission or Board may at any time, upon such notice and in such manner as it shall deem proper, modify or set aside, in whole or in part, any report or any order made or issued by it under this section. After the expiration of the time allowed for filing a petition for review, if no such petition has been duly filed within such time, the Commission or Board may at any time, after notice and opportunity for hearing, reopen and alter, modify, or set aside, in whole or in part, any report or order made or issued by it under this section, whenever in the opinion of the Commission or Board conditions of fact or of law have so changed as to require such action or if the public interest shall so require: *Provided, however,* That the said person may, within sixty days after service upon him or it of said report or order entered after such a reopening, obtain a review thereof in the appropriate court of appeals of the United States, in the manner provided in subsection (c) of this section.

(c) Any person required by such order of the commission or board to cease and desist from any such violation may obtain a review of such order in the court of appeals of the United States for any circuit within which such violation occurred or within which such person resides or carries on business, by filing in the court, within sixty days after the date of the service of such order, a written petition praying that the order of the commission or board be set aside. A copy of such petition shall be forthwith transmitted by the clerk of the court to the commission or board, and thereupon the commission or board shall file in the court the record in the proceeding, as provided in section 2112 of title 28, United States Code. Upon such filing of the petition the court shall have jurisdiction of the proceeding and of the question determined therein concurrently with the commission or board until the filing of the record, and shall have power to make and enter a decree affirming, modifying, or setting aside the order of the commission or board, and enforcing the same to the extent that such order is affirmed, and to issue such writs as are ancillary to its jurisdiction or are necessary in its judgment to prevent injury to the public or to competitors pendente lite. The findings of the commission or board as to the facts, if supported by substantial evidence, shall be conclusive. To the extent that the order of the commission or board is affirmed, the court shall issue its own order commanding obedience to the terms of such order of the commission or board. If either party shall apply to the court for leave to adduce additional evidence, and shall show to the satisfaction of the court that such additional evidence is material and that there were reasonable grounds for the failure to adduce such evidence in the proceeding before the commission or board, the court may order such additional evidence to be taken before the commission or board, and to be adduced upon the hearing in such manner and upon such terms and conditions as to the court may seem proper. The commission or board may modify its findings as to the facts, or make new findings, by reason of the additional evidence so taken, and shall file such modified or new findings, which, if supported by substantial evidence, shall be conclusive, and its recommendation, if any, for the modification or setting aside of its original order, with the return of such additional evidence. The judgment and decree of the court shall be final, except that the same shall be subject to review by the Supreme Court upon certiorari, as provided in section 1254 of title 28 of the United States Code.

(d) Upon the filing of the record with it the jurisdiction of the court of appeals to affirm, enforce, modify, or set aside orders of the commission or board shall be exclusive.

(e) Such proceedings in the court of appeals shall be given precedence over other cases pending therein, and shall be in every way expedited. No order of the commission or board or judgment of the court to enforce the same shall in anywise relieve or absolve any person from any liability under the antitrust laws.

(f) Complaints, orders, and other processes of the commission or board under this section may be served by anyone duly authorized by the commission or board, either (1) by delivering a copy thereof to the person to be served, or to a member of the partnership to be served, or to the president, secretary, or other executive officer or a director of the corporation to be served; or (2) by leaving a copy thereof at the residence or the principal office or place of business of such person; or (3) by mailing by registered or certified mail a copy thereof addressed to such person at his or its residence or principal office or place of business. The verified return by the person so serving said complaint, order, or other process setting forth the manner of said service shall be proof of the same, and the return post office receipt for said complaint, order, or other process mailed by registered or certified mail as aforesaid shall be proof of the service of the same.

(g) Any order issued under subsection (b) shall become final—

(1) upon the expiration of the time allowed for filing a petition for review, if no such petition has been duly filed within such time; but the commission or board may thereafter modify or set aside its order to the extent provided in the last sentence of subsection (b); or

(2) upon the expiration of the time allowed for filing a petition for certiorari, if the order of the commission or board has been affirmed, or the petition for review has been dismissed by the court of appeals, and no petition for certiorari has been duly filed; or

(3) upon the denial of a petition for certiorari, if the order of

the commission or board has been affirmed or the petition for review has been dismissed by the court of appeals; or

(4) upon the expiration of thirty days from the date of issuance of the mandate of the Supreme Court, if such Court directs that the order of the commission or board be affirmed or the petition for review be dismissed.

(h) If the Supreme Court directs that the order of the commission or board be modified or set aside, the order of the commission or board rendered in accordance with the mandate of the Supreme Court shall become final upon the expiration of thirty days from the time it was rendered, unless within such thirty days either party has instituted proceedings to have such order corrected to accord with the mandate, in which event the order of the commission or board shall become final when so corrected.

(i) If the order of the commission or board is modified or set aside by the court of appeals, and if (1) the time allowed for filing a petition for certiorari has expired and no such petition has been duly filed, or (2) the petition for certiorari has been denied, or (3) the decision of the court has been affirmed by the Supreme Court, then the order of the commission or board rendered in accordance with the mandate of the court of appeals shall become final on the expiration of thirty days from the time such order of the commission or board was rendered, unless within such thirty days either party has instituted proceedings to have such order corrected so that it will accord with the mandate, in which event the order of the commission or board shall become final when so corrected.

(j) If the Supreme Court orders a rehearing; or if the case is remanded by the court of appeals to the commission or board for a rehearing, and if (1) the time allowed for filing a petition for certiorari has expired, and no such petition has been duly filed, or (2) the petition for certiorari has been denied, or (3) the decision of the court has been affirmed by the Supreme Court, then the order of the commission or board rendered upon such rehearing shall become final in the same manner as though no prior order of the commission or board had been rendered.

(k) As used in this section the term 'mandate,' in case a mandate has been recalled prior to the expiration of thirty days from the date of issuance thereof, means the final mandate.

(l) Any person who violates any order issued by the commission or board under subsection (b) after such order has become final, and while such order is in effect, shall forfeit and pay to the United States a civil penalty of not more than $5,000 for each violation, which shall accrue to the United States and may be recovered in a civil action brought by the United States. Each separate violation of any such order shall be a separate offense, except that in the case of a violation through continuing failure or neglect to obey a final order of the commission or board each day of continuance of such failure or neglect shall be deemed a separate offense.

SEC. 12.   That any suit, action, or proceeding under the antitrust laws against a corporation may be brought not only in the judicial district whereof it is an inhabitant, but also in any district wherein it may be found or transacts business; and all process in such cases may be served in the district of which it is an inhabitant, or wherever it may be found.

SEC. 13.   That in any suit, action, or proceeding brought by or on behalf of the United States subpoenas for witnesses who are required to attend a court of the United States in any judicial district in any case, civil or criminal, arising under the antitrust laws may run into any other district: *Provided,* That in civil cases no writ of subpoena shall issue for witnesses living out of the district in which the court is held at a greater distance than one hundred miles from the place of holding the same without the permission of the trial court being first had upon proper application and cause shown.

SEC. 14.   That whenever a corporation shall violate any of the penal provisions of the antitrust laws, such violation shall be deemed to be also that of the individual directors, officers, or agents of such corporation who shall have authorized, ordered, or done any of the acts constituting in whole or in part such violation, and such violation shall be deemed a misdemeanor, and upon conviction therefor of any such director, officer, or agent he shall be punished by a fine of not exceeding $5,000 or by imprisonment for not exceeding one year, or by both, in the discretion of the court.

SEC. 15.   That the several district courts of the United States are hereby invested with jurisdiction to prevent and restrain violations of this Act, and it shall be the duty of the several district attorneys of the United States, in their respective districts, under the direction of the Attorney General, to institute proceedings in equity to prevent and restrain such violations. Such proceedings may be by way of petition setting forth the case and praying that such violation shall be enjoined or otherwise prohibited. When the parties complained of shall have been duly notified of such petition, the court shall proceed, as soon as may be, to the hearing and determination of the case; and pending such petition, and before final decree, the court may at any time make such temporary restraining order or prohibition as shall be deemed just in the premises. Whenever it shall appear to the court before which any such proceeding may be pending that the ends of justice require that other parties should be brought before the court, the court may cause them to be summoned whether they reside in the district in which the court is held or not, and subpoenas to that end may be served in any district by the marshal thereof.

SEC. 16.   Any person, firm, corporation, or association shall be entitled to sue for and have injunctive relief, in any court of the United States having jurisdiction over the parties, as against threatened loss or damage by a violation of the antitrust laws, including sections two, three, seven, and eight of this Act, when and under the same conditions and principles as injunctive relief against threatened conduct that will cause loss or damage is granted by courts of equity, under the rules governing such proceedings, and upon the execution of proper bond against damages for an injunction improvidently granted and a showing that the danger of irreparable loss or damage is immediate, a preliminary injunction may issue: *Provided,* That nothing herein contained shall be construed to entitle any person, firm, corporation, or association, except the United States, to bring suit in equity for injunctive relief against any common carrier subject to the provisions of the Act to regulate commerce, approved February fourth, eighteen hundred and eighty-seven, in respect of any matter subject to the regulation, supervision, or other jurisdiction of the Interstate Commerce Commission.

SEC. 20.   That no restraining order or injunction shall be granted by any court of the United States, or a judge or the judges thereof, in any case between an employer and employees, or between employers and employees, or between employees, or between persons employed and persons seeking employment, involving, or growing out of, a dispute concerning terms or conditions of employment, unless necessary to prevent irreparable injury to property, or to a property right, of the party making the application, for which injury there is no adequate remedy at law, and such property or property right must be described with particularity in the application, which must be in writing and sworn to by the applicant or by his agent or attorney.

And no such restraining order or injunction shall prohibit any person or persons, whether singly or in concert, from terminating any relation of employment, or from ceasing to perform any work or labor, or from recommending, advising, or persuading others by peaceful means so to do; or from attending at any place where any such person or persons may lawfully be, for the purpose of peacefully obtaining or communicating information, or from peacefully persuading any person to work or to abstain from working; or from ceasing to patronize or to employ any party to such dispute, or from recommending, advising, or persuading others by peaceful and lawful means so to do; or from paying or giving to, or withholding from, any persons engaged in such dispute, any strike benefits or other moneys or things of value; or from peaceably assembling in a lawful manner, and for lawful purposes; or from doing any act or thing which might lawfully be done in the absence of such dispute by any party thereto; nor shall any of the acts specified in this paragraph be considered or held to be violations of any law of the United States.

SEC. 26.   If any clause, sentence, paragraph, or part of this Act shall, for any reason, be adjudged "* * * invalid, such judgment shall not affect, impair, or invalidate the remainder thereof * * *."

Federal Trade Commission Act[3]

AN ACT To create a Federal Trade Commission, to define its powers and duties and for other purposes.

[3]The Federal Trade Commission Act is the act of September 26, 1914, c. 311, 38 Stat. 717, 15 U.S.C.A. §§41–51. Sections 12 through 18 were added by the Wheeler-Lea Act. 52 Stat. 114 (1938). Section 5 was amended by the McQuire Fair Trade Act, act of July 14, 1952, c. 745, 66 Stat. 632, which made certain so-called fair trade agreements legal. Those amendments were repealed by the act of December 2, 1975, Public Law 94–145. Substantial amendments were also made in Sections 5 and 10 by the Act of January 4, 1975, Public Law 93–637, Title II, Section 203(c), 88 Stat. 2193. Section 13(b) was amended and 13(c) was added by the act of November 16, 1973, Public L. 93–153, Title IV, Section 408(f), 87 Stat. 592. Section 16 was amended by the act of January 4, 1975, Public Law 93–637, Title II, Section 204(a), 88 Stat. 2199. The act of January 4, 1975, Public Law 93–637 Title II, Sections 202(a), 88 Stat. 2193, 206(a), 88 Stat. 2201, and 207, 88 Stat. 2203, added Sections 19 through 21. Portions of the act not deemed relevant to antitrust issues have been omitted from this Appendix.

SEC. 1. *Be it created by the Senate and House of Representatives of the United States of America in Congress assembled,* That a commission is hereby created and established, to be known as the Federal Trade Commission (hereinafter referred to as the commission), which shall be composed of five commissioners, who shall be appointed by the President, by and with the advice and consent of the Senate. Not more than three of the commissioners shall be members of the same political party. The first commissioners appointed shall continue in office for terms of three, four, five, six, and seven years, respectively, from the date of the taking affect of this Act, the term of each to be designated by the President, but their successors shall be appointed for terms of seven years, except that any person chosen to fill a vacancy shall be appointed only for the unexpired term of the commissioner whom he shall succeed: *Provided, however,* That upon the expiration of his term of office a Commissioner shall continue to serve until his successor shall have been appointed and shall have qualified. The President shall choose a chairman from the commission's membership. No commissioner shall engage in any other business, vocation, or employment. Any commissioner may be removed by the President for inefficiency, neglect of duty or malfeasance in office. A vacancy in the commission shall not impair the right of the remaining commissioners to exercise all the powers of the commission.

The commission shall have an official seal, which shall be judicially noticed.

SEC. 2. That each commissioner shall receive a salary * * *

SEC. 3. * * *

SEC. 4. The words defined in this section shall have the following meaning when found in this Act, to wit:

"Commerce" means commerce among the several States or with foreign nations, or in any Territory of the United States or in the District of Columbia, or between any such Territory and another, or between any such Territory and any State or foreign nation, or between the District of Columbia and any State or Territory or foreign nation.

"Corporation" shall be deemed to include any company, trust, so-called Massachusetts trust, or association, incorporated or unincorporated, which is organized to carry on business for its own profit or that of its members, and has shares of capital or capital stock or certificates of interest, and any company, trust, so-called Massachusetts trust, or association, incorporated or unincorporated, without shares of capital or capital stock or certificates of interest, except partnerships, which is organized to carry on business for its own profit or that of its members.

"Documentary evidence" includes all documents, papers, correspondence, books of account, and financial and corporate records.

"Acts to regulate commerce" means the Act entitled "An Act to regulate commerce," approved February 14, 1887, and all Acts amendatory thereof and supplementary thereto and the Communications Act of 1934 and all Acts amendatory thereof and supplementary thereto.

"Antitrust Acts," means the Act entitled "An Act to protect trade and commerce against unlawful restraints and monopolies," approved July 2, 1890; also sections 73 to 77, inclusive, of an Act entitled "An Act to reduce taxation, to provide revenue for the Government, and for other purposes," approved August 27, 1894; also the Act entitled "An Act to amend sections 73 and 76 of the Act of August 27, 1894, entitled 'An Act to reduce taxation, to provide revenue for the Government, and for other purposes,'" approved February 12, 1913; and also the Act entitled "An Act to supplement existing laws against unlawful restraints and monopolies, and for other purposes," approved October 15, 1914.

Sec. 5.   (a)(1) Unfair methods of competition in or affecting commerce, and unfair or deceptive acts or practices in or affecting commerce, are hereby declared unlawful.

(2) The Commission is hereby empowered and directed to prevent persons, partnerships, or corporations, except banks, savings and loan institutions described in section 57a (FX3) of this title, common carriers subject to the Acts to regulate commerce, air carriers and foreign air carriers subject to the Federal Aviation Act of 1958, and persons, partnerships, or corporations insofar as they are subject to the Packers and Stockyards Act, 1921, as amended, except as provided in section 406(b) of said Act, from using unfair methods of competition in or affecting commerce and unfair or deceptive acts or practices in or affecting commerce.

(b) Whenever the Commission shall have reason to believe that any such person, partnership, or corporation has been or is using any unfair method of competition or unfair or deceptive act or practice in or affecting commerce, and if it shall appear to the Commission that a proceeding by it in respect thereof would be to the interest of the public, it shall issue and serve upon such person, partnership, or corporation a complaint stating its charges in that respect and containing a notice of a hearing upon a day and at a place therein fixed at least thirty days after the service of said complaint. The person, partnership, or corporation so complained of shall have the right to appear at the place and time so fixed and show cause why an order should not be entered by the Commission requiring such person, partnership, or corporation to cease and desist from the violation of the law so charged in said complaint. Any person, partnership, or corporation may make application, and upon good cause shown may be allowed by the Commission to intervene and appear in said proceeding by counsel or in person. The testimony in any such proceeding shall be reduced to writing and filed in the office of the Commission. If upon such hearing the Commission shall be of the opinion that the method of competition or the act or practice in question is prohibited by this Act, it shall make a report in writing in which it shall state its findings as to the facts and shall issue and cause to be served on such person, partnership, or corporation an order requiring such person, partnership, or corporation to cease and desist from using such method of competition or such act or practice. Until the expiration of the time allowed for filing a petition for review, if no such petition has been duly filed within such time, or, if a petition for review has been filed within such time then until the record in the proceeding has been filed in a court of appeals of the United States, as hereinafter provided, the Commission may at any time, upon such notice and in such manner as it shall deem proper, modify or set aside, in whole or in part, any report or any order made or issued by it under this section. After the expiration of the time allowed for filing a petition for review, if no such petition has been duly filed within such time, the Commission may at any time, after notice and opportunity for hearing, reopen and alter, modify, or set aside, in whole or in part, any report or order made or issued by it under this section, whenever in the opinion of the Commission conditions of fact or of law have so changed as to require such action or if the public interest shall so require: *Provided, however,* That the said person, partnership, or corporation may, within sixty days after service upon him or it of said report or order entered after such a reopening, obtain a review thereof in the appropriate court of appeals of the United States, in the manner provided in subsection (c) of this section.

(c) Any person, partnership, or corporation required by an order of the Commission to cease and desist from using any method of competition or act or practice may obtain a review of such order in the court of appeals of the United States, within any circuit where the method of competition or the act or practice in question was used or where such person, partnership, or corporation resides or carries on business, by filing in the court, within sixty days from the date of the service of such order, a written petition praying that the order of the Commission be set aside. A copy of such petition shall be forthwith transmitted by the clerk of the court to the Commission, and thereupon the Commission shall file in the court the record in the proceeding, as provided in section 2112 of title 28, United States Code. Upon such filing of the petition the court shall have jurisdiction of the proceeding and of the question determined therein concurrently with the Commission until the filing of the record and shall have power to make and enter a decree affirming, modifying, or setting aside the order of the Commission, and enforcing the same to the extent that such order is affirmed and to issue such writs as are ancillary to its jurisdiction or are necessary in its judgment to prevent injury to the public or to competitors pendente lite. The findings of the Commission as to the facts, if supported by evidence, shall be conclusive. To the extent that the order of the Commission is affirmed, the court shall thereupon issue its own order commanding obedience to the terms of such order of the Commission. If either party shall apply to the court for leave to adduce additional evidence, and shall show to the satisfaction of the court that such additional evidence is material and that there were reasonable grounds for the failure to adduce such evidence in the proceeding before the Commission, the court may order such additional evidence to be taken before the Commission and to be adduced upon the hearing in such manner and upon such terms and conditions as to the court may seem proper. The Commission may modify its findings as to the facts, or make new findings, by reason of the additional evidence so taken, and it shall file such modified or new findings, which, if supported by evidence, shall be conclusive, and its recommendation, if any, for the modification or setting aside of its original order, with the return of such additional evidence. The judgment and decree of the court shall be final, except that the same shall be subject to review by the Supreme Court upon certiorari, as provided in section 1254 of Title 28.

(d) Upon the filing of the record with it the jurisdiction of the court of appeals of the United States to affirm, enforce, modify, or set aside orders of the Commission shall be exclusive.

(e) Such proceedings in the court of appeals shall be given precedence over other cases pending therein, and shall be in every way expedited. No order of the Commission or judgment of court to enforce the same shall in anywise relieve or absolve any person, partnership, or corporation from any liability under the Antitrust Acts.

(f) Complaints, orders, and other processes of the Commission under this section may be served by anyone duly authorized by the Commission, either (a) by delivering a copy thereof to the person to be served, or to a member of the partnership to be served, or the president, secretary, or other executive officer or a director of the corporation to be served; or (b) by leaving a copy thereof at the residence or the principal office or place of business of such person, partnership, or corporation; or (c) by registering and mailing a copy thereof addressed to such person, partnership, or corporation at his or its residence or principal office or place of business. The verified return by the person so servicing said complaint, order, or other process setting forth the manner of said service shall be proof of the same, and the return post office receipt for said complaint, order, or other process registered and mailed as aforesaid shall be proof of the service of the same.

(g) An order of the Commission to cease and desist shall become final—

(1) Upon the expiration of the time allowed for filing a petition for review, if no such petition has been duly filed within such time; but the Commission may thereafter modify or set aside its order to the extent provided in the last sentence of subsection (b); or

(2) Upon the expiration of the time allowed for filing a petition for certiorari, if the order of the Commission has been affirmed, or

the petition for review dismissed by the court of appeals, and no petition for certiorari has been duly filed; or

(3) Upon the denial of a petition for certiorari, if the order of the Commission has been affirmed or the petition for review dismissed by the court of appeals; or

(4) Upon the expiration of thirty days from the date of issuance of the mandate of the Supreme Court, if such Court directs that the order of the Commission be affirmed or the petition for review dismissed.

(h) If the Supreme Court directs that the order of the Commission be modified or set aside, the order of the Commission rendered in accordance with the mandate of the Supreme Court shall become final upon the expiration of thirty days from the time it was rendered, unless within such thirty days either party has instituted proceedings to have such order corrected to accord with the mandate, in which event the order of the Commission shall become final when so corrected.

(i) If the order of the Commission is modified or set aside by the court of appeals, and if (1) the time allowed for filing a petition for certiorari has expired and no such petition has been duly filed, or (2) the petition for certiorari has been denied, or (3) the decision of the court has been affirmed by the Supreme Court, then the order of the Commission rendered in accordance with the mandate of the court of appeals shall become final on the expiration of thirty days from the time such order of the Commission was rendered, unless within such thirty days either party has instituted proceedings to have such order corrected so that it will accord with the mandate, in which event the order of the Commission shall become final when so corrected.

(j) If the Supreme Court orders a rehearing; or if the case is remanded by the court of appeals to the Commission for a rehearing, and if (1) the time allowed for filing a petition for certiorari has expired, and no such petition has been duly filed, or (2) the petition for certiorari has been denied, or (3) the decision of the court has been affirmed by the Supreme Court, then the order of the Commission rendered upon such rehearing shall become final in the same manner as though no prior order of the Commission had been rendered.

(k) As used in this section the term "mandate," in case a mandate has been recalled prior to the expiration of thirty days from the date of issuance thereof, means the final mandate.

(l) Any person, partnership, or corporation who violates an order of the Commission after it has become final, and while such order is in effect, shall forfeit and pay to the United States a civil penalty of not more than $10,000 for each violation, which shall accrue to the United States and may be recovered in a civil action brought by the Attorney General of the United States. Each separate violation of such an order shall be a separate offense, except that in the case of a violation through continuing failure to obey or neglect to obey a final order of the Commission, each day of continuance of such failure or neglect shall be deemed a separate offense. In such actions, the United States district courts are empowered to grant mandatory injunctions and such other and further equitable relief as they deem appropriate in the enforcement of such final orders of the Commission.

(m)(1)(A) The Commission may commence a civil action to recover a civil penalty in a district court of the United States against any person, partnership, or corporation which violates any rule under this chapter respecting unfair or deceptive acts or practices (other than an interpretive rule or a rule violation of which the Commission has provided is not an unfair or deceptive act or practice in violation of subsection (a)(1) of this section) with actual knowledge or knowledge fairly implied on the basis of objective circumstances that such act is unfair or deceptive and is prohibited by such rule. In such action, such person, partnership, or corporation shall be liable for a civil penalty of not more than $10,000 for each violation.

(B) If the Commission determines in a proceeding under subsection (b) of this section that any act or practice is unfair or deceptive, and issues a final cease and desist order with respect to such act or practice, then the Commission may commence a civil action to obtain a civil penalty in a district court of the United States against any person, partnership, or corporation which engages in such act or practice—

(1) after such cease and desist order becomes final (whether or not such person, partnership, or corporation was subject to such cease and desist order), and

(2) with actual knowledge that such act or practice is unfair or deceptive and is unlawful under subsection (a)(1) of this section.

In such action, such person, partnership, or corporation shall be liable for a civil penalty of not more than $10,000 for each violation.

(C) In the case of a violation through continuing failure to comply with a rule or with subsection (a)(1) of this section, each day of continuance of such failure shall be treated as a separate violation, for purposes of subparagraphs (A) and (B). In determining the amount of such a civil penalty, the court shall take into account the degree of culpability, any history of prior such conduct, ability to pay, effect on ability to continue to do business, and such other matters as justice may require.

(2) If the cease and desist order establishing that the act or practice is unfair or deceptive was not issued against the defendant in a civil penalty action under paragraph (1)(B) the issues of fact in such action against such defendant shall be tried de novo.

(3) The Commission may compromise or settle any action for a civil penalty if such compromise or settlement is accompanied by a public statement of its reasons and is approved by the court.

SEC. 6.   That the commission shall also have power—

(a) To gather and compile information concerning, and to investigate from time to time the organization, business, conduct, practices, and management of any person, partnership, or corporation engaged in or whose business affects commerce, excepting banks and common carriers subject to the Act to regulate commerce, and its relation to other corporations and to individuals, associations, and partnerships.

(b) To require, by general or special orders, persons, partnerships, and corporations engaged in or whose business affects commerce, excepting banks, and common carriers subject to the Act to regulate commerce, or any class of them, or any of them, respectively, to file with the commission in such form as the commission may prescribe annual or special, or both annual and special, reports or answers in writing to specific questions, furnishing to the commission such information as it may require as to the organization, business, conduct, practices, management, and relation to other corporations, partnerships, and individuals of the respective persons, partnerships, and corporations filing such reports or answers in writing. Such reports and answers shall be made under oath, or otherwise, as the commission may prescribe, and shall be filed with the commission within such reasonable period as the commission may prescribe, unless additional time be granted in any case by the commission.

(c) Whenever a final decree has been entered against any defendant corporation in any suit brought by the United States to prevent and restrain any violation of the antitrust Acts, to make investigation, upon its own initiative, of the manner in which the decree has been or is being carried out, and upon the application of the Attorney General it shall be its duty to make such investigation. It shall transmit to the Attorney General a report embodying its findings and recommendations as a result of any such investigation, and the report shall be made public in the discretion of the commission.

(d) Upon the direction of the President or either House of Congress to investigate and report the facts relating to any alleged violations of the antitrust Acts by any corporation.

(e) Upon the application of the Attorney General to investigate and make recommendations for the readjustment of the business of any corporation alleged to be violating the antitrust Acts in order that the corporation may thereafter maintain its organization, management, and conduct of business in accordance with law.

(f) To make public from time to time such portions of the information obtained by it hereunder, except trade secrets and names of customers, as it shall deem expedient in the public interest; and to make annual and special reports to the Congress and to submit therewith recommendations for additional legislation; and to provide for the publication of its reports and decisions in such form and manner as may be best adapted for public information and use.

(g) From time to time to classify corporations and (except as provided in section 18(a)(2) of this Act) to make rules and regulations for the purpose of carrying out the provisions of this Act.

(h) To investigate, from time to time, trade conditions in and with foreign countries where associations, combinations, or practices of manufacturers, merchants, or traders, or other conditions, may affect the foreign trade of the United States, and to report to Congress thereon, with such recommendations as it deems advisable.

Provided, That the exception of "banks and common carriers subject to the Act to regulate commerce" from the Commission's powers defined in clauses (a) and (b) of this section, shall not be construed to limit the Commission's authority to gather and compile information, to investigate, or to require reports or answers from, any person, partnership, or corporation to the extent that such action is necessary to the investigation of any person, partnership, or corporation, group of persons, partnerships, or corporations, or industry which is not engaged or is engaged only incidentally in banking or in business as a common carrier subject to the Act to regulate commerce.

Sec. 7.   That in any suit in equity brought by or under the direction of the Attorney General as provided in the antitrust Acts, the court may, upon the conclusion of the testimony therein, if it shall be then of opinion that the complainant is entitled to relief, refer said suit to the commission, as a master in chancery, to ascertain and report an appropriate form of decree therein. The commission shall proceed upon such notice to the parties and under such rules of procedure as the court may prescribe, and upon the coming in of such report such exceptions may be filed and such proceedings had in relation thereto as upon the report of a master in other equity causes, but the court may adopt or reject such report, in whole or in part, and enter such decree as the nature of the case may in its judgment require.

Sec. 8.   That the several departments and bureaus of the Government when directed by the President shall furnish the commission, upon its request, all records, papers, and information in their possession relating to any corporation subject to any of the provisions of this Act, and shall detail from time to time such officials and employees to the commission as he may direct.

Sec. 9.   That for the purposes of this Act the commission, or its duly authorized agent or agents, shall at all reasonable times have access to, for the purpose of examination, and the right to copy any documentary evidence of any person, partnership, or corporation being investigated or proceeded against; and the commission shall have power to require by subpoena the attendance and testimony of witnesses and the production of all such documentary evidence relating to any matter under investigation. Any member of the commission may sign subpoenas, and members and examiners of the commission may administer oaths and affirmations, examine witnesses, and receive evidence.

Such attendance of witnesses, and the production of such documentary evidence, may be required from any place in the United States, at any designated place of hearing. And in case of disobedience to a subpoena the commission may invoke the aid of any court of the United States in requiring the attendance and testimony of witnesses and the production of documentary evidence.

Any of the district courts of the United States within the jurisdiction of which such inquiry is carried on may, in case of contumacy or refusal to obey a subpoena issued to any person, partnership, or corporation issue an order requiring such person, partnership or corporation to appear before the commission, or to produce documentary evidence if so ordered, or to give evidence touching the matter in question; and any failure to obey such order of the court may be punished by such court as a contempt thereof.

Upon the application of the Attorney General of the United States, at the request of the commission, the district courts of the United States shall have jurisdiction to issue writs of mandamus commanding any person, partnership, or corporation to comply with the provisions of this Act or any order of the commission made in pursuance thereof.

The Commission may order testimony to be taken by deposition in any proceeding or investigation pending under this Act at any stage of such proceeding or investigation. Such depositions may be taken before any person designated by the commission and having power to administer oaths. Such testimony shall be reduced to writing by the person taking the deposition, or under his direction, and shall then be subscribed by the deponent. Any person may be compelled to appear and depose and to produce documentary evidence in the same manner as witnesses may be compelled to appear and testify and produce documentary evidence before the commission as hereinbefore provided.

Witnesses summoned before the Commission shall be paid the same fees and mileage that are paid witnesses in the courts of the United States, and witnesses whose depositions are taken, and the persons taking the same shall severally be entitled to the same fees as are paid for like services in the courts of the United States.

SEC. 10.   That any person who shall neglect or refuse to attend and testify, or to answer any lawful inquiry, or to produce documentary evidence, if in his power to do so, in obedience to the subpoena or lawful requirement of the commission, shall be guilty of an offense and upon conviction thereof by a court of competent jurisdiction shall be punished by a fine of not less than $1,000 nor more than $5,000, or by imprisonment for not more than one year, or by both such fine and imprisonment.

Any person who shall willfully make, or cause to be made, any false entry or statement of fact in any report required to be made under this Act, or who shall willfully make, or cause to be made, any false entry in any account, record, or memorandum kept by any person, partnership, or corporation subject to said Act, or who shall willfully neglect or fail to make, or to cause to be made, full, true, and correct entries in such accounts, records, or memoranda of all facts and transactions appertaining to the business of such person, partnership, or corporation or who shall willfully remove out of the jurisdiction of the United States, or willfully mutilate, alter, or by any other means falsify any documentary evidence of such person, partnership, or corporation or who shall willfully refuse to submit to the Commission or to any of its authorized agents, for the purpose of inspection and taking copies, any documentary evidence of such person, partnership, or corporation in his possession or within his control, shall be deemed guilty of an offense against the United States, and shall be subject, upon conviction in any court of the United States of competent jurisdiction, to a fine of not less than $1,000 nor more than $5,000, or to imprisonment for a term of not more than three years, or to both such fine and imprisonment.

If any persons, partnership, or corporation required by this Act to file any annual or special report shall fail so to do within the time fixed by the Commission for filing the same, and such failure shall continue for thirty days after notice of such default, the corporation shall forfeit to the United States the sum of $100 for each and every day of the continuance of such failure, which forfeiture shall be payable into the Treasury of the United States, and shall be recoverable in a civil suit in the name of the United States brought in the case of a corporation or partnership in the district where the corporation or partnership has its principal office or in any district in which it shall do business, and in the case of any person in the district where such person resides or has his principal place of business. It shall be the duty of the various United States attorneys, under the direction of the Attorney General of the United States, to prosecute for the recovery of forfeitures. The costs and expenses of such prosecution shall be paid out of the appropriation for the expenses of the courts of the United States.

Any officer or employee of the commission who shall make public any information obtained by the commission without its authority, unless directed by a court, shall be deemed guilty of a misdemeanor, and, upon conviction thereof, shall be punished by a fine not exceeding $5,000, or by imprisonment not exceeding one year, or by fine and imprisonment, in the discretion of the court.

SEC. 11. Nothing contained in this Act shall be construed to prevent or interfere with the enforcement of the provisions of the antitrust Acts or the Acts to regulate commerce, nor shall anything contained in the Act be construed to alter, modify, or repeal the said antitrust Acts or the Acts to regulate commerce or any part or parts thereof.

SEC. 12. * * *

SEC. 13 (a). * * *

(b) Whenever the Commission has reason to believe—

(1) that any person, partnership, or corporation is violating, or is about to violate, any provision of law enforced by the Federal Trade Commission, and

(2) that the enjoining thereof pending the issuance of a complaint by the Commission and until such complaint is dismissed by the Commission or set aside by the court on review, or until the order of the Commission made thereon has become final, would be in the interest of the public—

the Commission by any of its attorneys designated by it for such purpose may bring suit in a district court of the United States to enjoin any such act or practice. Upon a proper showing that, weighing the equities and considering the Commission's likelihood of ultimate success, such action would be in the public interest, and after notice to the defendant, a temporary restraining order or a preliminary injunction may be granted without bond: *Provided, however,* That if a complaint is not filed within such period (not exceeding 20 days) as may be specified by the court after issuance of the temporary restraining order or preliminary injunction, the order or injunction shall be dissolved by the court and be of no further force and effect: *Provided further,* That in proper cases the Commission may seek, and after proper proof, the court may issue, a permanent injunction. Any such suit shall be brought in the district in which such person, partnership, or corporation resides or transacts business.

(c) Whenever it appears to the satisfaction of the court in the case of a newspaper, magazine, periodical, or other publication, published at regular intervals—

(1) that restraining the dissemination of a false advertisement in any particular issue of such publication would delay the delivery of such issue after the regular time therefor, and

(2) that such delay would be due to the method by which the manufacture and distribution of such publication is customarily conducted by the publisher in accordance with sound business practice, and not to any method or device adopted for the evasion of this section or to prevent or delay the isssuance of an injunction or restraining order with respect to such false advertisement or any other advertisement,

the court shall exclude such issue from the operation of the restraining order or injunction.

SEC. 14.   * * *

SEC. 15.   * * *

SEC. 16.   (a)(1) Except as otherwise provided in paragraph (2) or (3), if—

(A) before commencing, defending, or intervening in, any civil action involving this chapter (including an action to collect a civil penalty) which the Commission, or the Attorney General on behalf of the Commission, is authorized to commence, defend, or intervene in, the Commission gives written notification and undertakes to consult with the Attorney General with respect to such action; and

(B) the Attorney General fails within 45 days after receipt of such notification to commence, defend, or intervene in, such action;

the Commission may commence, defend, or intervene in, and supervise the litigation of, such action and any appeal of such action in its own name by any of its attorneys designated by it for such purpose.

(2) Except as otherwise provided in paragraph (3), in any civil action—

(A) under section 13 of this Act (relating to injunctive relief);

(B) * * *

(C) to obtain judicial review of a rule prescribed by the Commission, or a cease and desist order issued under section 5 of this Act; or

(D) under the second paragraph of section 9 of this Act (relating to enforcement of a subpoena) and under the fourth paragraph of such section * * *;

the Commission shall have exclusive authority to commence or defend, and supervise the litigation of, such action and any appeal of such action in its own name by any of its attorneys designated by it for such purpose, unless the Commission authorizes the Attorney General to do so. The Commission shall inform the Attorney General of the exercise of such authority and such exercise shall not preclude the Attorney General from intervening on behalf of the United States in such action and any appeal of such action as may be otherwise provided by law.

(3)(A) If the Commission makes a written request to the Attorney General, within the 10-day period which begins on the date of the entry of the judgment in any civil action in which the Commission represented itself pursuant to paragraph (1) or (2), to represent itself through any of its attorneys designated by it for such purpose before the Supreme Court in such action, it may do so, if—

(i) the Attorney General concurs with such request; or

(ii) the Attorney General, within the 60-day period which begins on the date of the entry of such judgment—

(a) refuses to appeal or file a petition for writ of certiorari with respect to such civil action, in which case he shall give written notification to the Commission of the reasons for such refusal within such 60-day period; or

(b) the Attorney General fails to take any action with respect to the Commission's request.

(B) In any case where the Attorney General represents the Commission before the Supreme Court in any civil action in which the Commission represented itself pursuant to paragraph (1) or (2), the Attorney General may not agree to any settlement, compromise, or dismissal of such action, or confess error in the Supreme Court with respect to such action, unless the Commission concurs.

(C) For purposes of this paragraph (with respect to representation before the Supreme Court), the term "Attorney General" includes the Solicitor General.

(4) If, prior to the expiration of the 45-day period specified in paragraph (1) of this section or a 60-day period specified in paragraph (3), any right of the Commission to commence, defend, or intervene in, any such action or appeal may be extinguished due to any procedural requirement of any court with respect to the time in which any pleadings, notice of appeal, or other acts pertaining to such action or appeal may be taken, the Attorney General shall have one-half of the time required to comply with any such procedural requirement of the court (including any extension of such time granted by the court) for the purpose of commencing, defending, or intervening in the civil action pursuant to paragraph (1) or for the purpose of refusing to appeal or file a petition for writ of certiorari and the written notification or failing to take any action pursuant to paragraph 3(A)(ii).

(5) The provisions of this subsection shall apply notwithstanding chapter 31 of Title 28, or any other provision of law.

(b) Whenever the Commission has reason to believe that any person, partnership, or corporation is liable for a criminal penalty under this chapter, the Commission shall certify the facts to the Attorney General, whose duty it shall be to cause appropriate criminal proceedings to be brought.

SEC. 17.   If any provision of this Act, or the application thereof to any person, partnership, corporation, or circumstance, is held invalid, the remainder of the Act and the application of such provision to any other person, partnership, corporation, or circumstance, shall not be affected thereby.

SEC. 18.   (a)(1) The Commission may prescribe—

(A) interpretative rules and general statements of policy with respect to unfair or deceptive acts or practices in or affecting commerce (within the meaning of section 5(a)(1) of this Act), and

(B) rules which define with specificity acts or practices which are unfair or deceptive acts or practices in or affecting commerce (within the meaning of section 5(a)(1) of this Act). Rules under this subparagraph may include requirements prescribed for the purpose of preventing such acts or practices.

(2) The Commission shall have no authority under this chapter, other than its authority under this section, to prescribe any rule with respect to unfair or deceptive acts or practices in or affecting commerce (within the meaning of section 5(a)(1) of this Act). The preceding sentence shall not affect any authority of the Commission to prescribe rules (including interpretative rules), and general statements of policy, with respect to unfair methods of competition in or affecting commerce.

(b) When prescribing a rule under subsection (a)(1)(B) of this section, the Commission shall proceed in accordance with section 553 of Title 5 (without regard to any reference in such section to sections 556 and 557 of such title), and shall also (1) publish a notice of proposed rulemaking stating with particularity the reason for the proposed rule; (2) allow interested persons to submit written data, views, and arguments, and make all such submissions publicly available; (3) provide an opportunity for an informal hearing in accordance with subsection (c) of this section; and (4) promulgate, if appropriate, a final rule based on the matter in the rulemaking record (as defined in subsection (e)(1)(B) of this section), together with a statement of basis and purpose.

(c) The Commission shall conduct any informal hearings required by subsection (b)(3) of this section in accordance with the following procedure:

(1) Subject to paragraph (2) of this subsection, an interested person is entitled—

(A) to present his position orally or by documentary submissions (or both), and

(B) if the Commission determines that there are disputed issues of material fact it is necessary to resolve, to present such rebuttal submissions and to conduct (or have conducted under paragraph (2)(B)) such cross-examination of persons as the Commission determines (i) to be appropriate, and (ii) to be required for a full and true disclosure with respect to such issues.

(2) The Commission may prescribe such rules and make such rulings concerning proceedings in such hearings as may tend to avoid unnecessary costs or delay. Such rules or rulings may include (A) imposition of reasonable time limits on each interested person's oral presentations, and (B) requirements that any cross-examination to which a person may be entitled under paragraph (1) be conducted by the Commission on behalf of that person in such manner as the Commission determines (i) to be appropriate, and (ii) to be required for a full and true disclosure with respect to disputed issues of material fact.

(3)(A) Except as provided in subparagraph (B), if a group of persons each of whom under paragraphs (1) and (2) would be entitled to conduct (or have conducted) cross-examination and who are determined by the Commission to have the same or similar interests in the proceeding cannot agree upon a single representative of such interests for purposes of cross-examination, the Commission may make rules and rulings (i) limiting the representation of such interest, for such purposes, and (ii) governing the manner in which such cross-examination shall be limited.

(B) When any person who is a member of a group with respect to which the Commission has made a determination under subparagraph (A) is unable to agree upon group representation with the other members of the group, then such person shall not be denied under the authority of subparagraph (A) the opportunity to conduct (or have conducted) cross-examination as to issues affecting his particular interests if (i) he satisfies the Commission that he has made a reasonable and good faith effort to reach agreement upon group representation with the other members of the group and (ii) the Commission determines that there are substantial and relevant issues which are not adequately presented by the group representative.

(4) A verbatim transcript shall be taken of any oral presentation, and cross-examination, in an informal hearing to which this subsection applies. Such transcript shall be available to the public.

(d)(1) The Commission's statement of basis and purpose to accompany a rule promulgated under subsection (a)(1)(B) of this section shall include (A) a statement as to the prevalence of the acts or practices treated by the rule; (B) a statement as to the manner and context in which such acts or practices are unfair or deceptive; and (C) a statement as to the economic effect of the rule, taking into account the effect on small business and consumers.

(2)(A) The term "Commission" as used in this subsection and subsections (b) and (c) of this section includes any person authorized to act in behalf of the Commission in any part of the rulemaking proceeding.

(B) A substantive amendment to, or repeal of, a rule promulgated under subsection (a)(1)(B) of this section shall be prescribed, and subject to judicial review, in the same manner as a rule prescribed under such subsection. An exemption under subsection (g) of this section shall not be treated as an amendment or repeal of a rule.

(3) When any rule under subsection (a)(1)(B) of this section takes effect a subsequent violation thereof shall constitute an unfair or deceptive act or practice in violation of section 5(a)(1) of this Act, unless the Commission otherwise expressly provides in such rule.

(e)(1)(A) Not later than 60 days after a rule is promulgated under subsection (a)(1)(B) of this section by the Commission, any interested person (including a consumer or consumer organization) may file a petition, in the United States Court of Appeals for the District of Columbia circuit or for the circuit in which such person resides or has his principal place of business, for judicial review of such rule. Copies of the petition shall be forthwith transmitted by the clerk of the court to the Commission or other officer designated by it for that purpose. The provisions of section 2112 of Title 28 shall apply to the filing of the rulemaking record of proceedings on which the Commission based its rule and to the transfer of proceedings in the courts of appeals.

(B) For purposes of this section, the term "rulemaking record" means the rule, its statement of basis and purpose, the transcript required by subsection (c)(4) of this section, any written submissions, and any other information which the Commission considers relevant to such rule.

(2) If the petitioner or the Commission applies to the court for leave to make additional oral submissions or written presentations and shows to the satisfaction of the court that such submissions and presentations would be material and that there were reasonable grounds for the submissions and failure to make such submissions and presentations in the proceeding before the Commission, the court may order the Commission to provide additional opportunity to make such submissions and presentations. The Commission may modify or set aside its rule or make a new rule by reason of the additional submissions and presentations and shall file such modified or new rule, and the rule's statement of basis of purpose, with the return of such submissions and presentations. The court shall thereafter review such new or modified rule.

(3) Upon the filing of the petition under paragraph (1) of this subsection, the court shall have jurisdiction to review the rule in accordance with chapter 7 of Title 5 and to grant appropriate relief, including interim relief, as provided in such chapter. The court shall hold unlawful and set aside the rule on any ground specified in subparagraphs (A), (B), (C), or (D) of section 706(2) of Title 5 (taking due account of the rule of prejudicial error), or if—

(A) the court finds that the Commission's action is not supported by substantial evidence in the rulemaking record (as defined in paragraph (1)(B) of this subsection) taken as a whole, or

(B) the court finds that—

(i) a Commission determination under subsection (c) of this section that the petitioner is not entitled to conduct cross-examination or make rebuttal submissions, or

(ii) a Commission rule or ruling under subsection (c) of this section limiting the petitioner's cross-examination or rebuttal submissions,

has precluded disclosure of disputed material facts which was necessary for fair determination by the Commission of the rulemaking proceeding taken as a whole.

The term "evidence," as used in this paragraph, means any matter in the rulemaking record.

(4) The judgment of the court affirming or setting aside, in whole or in part, any such rule shall be final, subject to review by the Supreme Court of the United States upon certiorari or certification, as provided in section 1254 of Title 28.

(5)(A) Remedies under the preceding paragraphs of this subsection are in addition to and not in lieu of any other remedies provided by law.

(B) The United States Courts of Appeal shall have exclusive jurisdiction of any action to obtain judicial review (other than in an enforcement proceeding) of a rule prescribed under subsection (a)(1)(B) of this section, if any district court of the United States would have had jurisdiction of such action but for this subparagraph. Any such action shall be brought in the United States Court of Appeals for the District of Columbia circuit, or for any circuit which includes a judicial district in which the action could have been brought but for this subparagraph.

(C) A determination, rule, or ruling of the Commission described in paragraph (3)(B)(i) or (ii) may be reviewed only in a proceeding under this subsection and only in accordance with paragraph (3)(B). Section 706(2)(E) of Title 5 shall not apply to any rule promulgated under subsection (a)(1)(B) of this section. The contents and adequacy of any statement required by subsection (b)(4) of this section shall not be subject to judicial review in any respect.

(f) * * *

(g)(1) Any person to whom a rule under subsection (a)(1)(B) of this section applies may petition the Commission for an exemption from such rule.

(2) If, on its own motion or on the basis of a petition under paragraph (1), the Commission finds that the application of a rule prescribed under subsection (a)(1)(B) of this section to any person or class or persons is not necessary to prevent the unfair or deceptive act or practice to which the rule relates, the Commission may exempt

such person or class from all or part of such rule. Section 553 of Title 5 shall apply to action under this paragraph.

(3) Neither the pendency of a proceeding under this subsection respecting an exemption from a rule, nor the pendency of judicial proceedings to review the Commission's action or failure to act under this subsection, shall stay the applicability of such rule under subsection (a)(1)(B) of this section.

(h)(1) The Commission may, pursuant to rules prescribed by it, provide compensation for reasonable attorneys fees, expert witness fees, and other costs of participating in a rulemaking proceeding under this section to any person (A) who has, or represents, an interest (i) which would not otherwise be adequately represented in such proceeding, and (ii) representation of which is necessary for a fair determination of the rulemaking proceeding taken as a whole, and (B) who is unable effectively to participate in such proceeding because such person cannot afford to pay costs of making oral presentations, conducting cross-examination, and making rebuttal submissions in such proceeding.

(2) The aggregate amount of compensation paid under this subsection in any fiscal year to all persons who, in rulemaking proceedings in which they receive compensation, are persons who either (A) would be regulated by the proposed rule, or (B) represent persons who would be so regulated, may not exceed 25 percent of the aggregate amount paid as compensation under this subsection to all persons in such fiscal year.

(3) The aggregate amount of compensation paid to all persons in any fiscal year under this subsection may not exceed $1,000,000.

Sec. 19. (a)(1) If any person, partnership, or corporation violates any rule under this chapter respecting unfair or deceptive acts or practices (other than an interpretive rule, or a rule violation of which the Commission has provided is not an unfair or deceptive act or practice in violation of section 5(a) of this Act), then the Commission may commence a civil action against such person, partnership, or corporation for relief under subsection (b) of this section in a United States district court or in any court of competent jurisdiction of a State.

(2) If any person, partnership, or corporation engages in any unfair or deceptive act or practice (within the meaning of section 5(a) of this Act) with respect to which the Commission has issued a final cease and desist order which is applicable to such person, partnership, or corporation, then the Commission may commence a civil action against such person, partnership, or corporation in a United States district court or in any court of competent jurisdiction of a State. If the Commission satisfies the court that the act or practice to which the cease and desist order relates is one which a reasonable man would have known under the circumstances was dishonest or fraudulent, the court may grant relief under subsection (b) of this section.

(b) The court in an action under subsection (a) of this section shall have jurisdiction to grant such relief as the court finds necessary to redress injury to consumers or other persons, partnerships, and corporations resulting from the rule violation or the unfair or deceptive act or practice, as the case may be. Such relief may include, but shall not be limited to, rescission or reformation of contracts, the refund of money or return of property, the payment of damages, and public notification respecting the rule violation or the unfair or deceptive act or practice, as the case may be; except that nothing in this subsection is intended to authorize the imposition of any exemplary or punitive damages.

(c)(1) If (A) a cease and desist order issued under section 5(b) of this Act has become final under section 5(g) of this Act with respect to any person's, partnership's, or corporation's rule violation or unfair or deceptive act or practice, and (B) an action under this section is brought with respect to such person's, partnership's, or corporation's rule violation or act or practice, then the findings of the Commission as to the material facts in the proceeding under section 5(b) of this Act with respect to such person's, partnership's, or corporation's rule violation or act or practice, shall be conclusive unless (i) the terms of such cease and desist order expressly provide that the Commission's findings shall not be conclusive, or (ii) the order became final by reason of section 5(g)(1) of this Act, in which case such finding shall be conclusive if supported by evidence.

(2) The court shall cause notice of an action under this section to

be given in a manner which is reasonably calculated, under all of the circumstances, to apprise the persons, partnerships, and corporations allegedly injured by the defendant's rule violation or act or practice of the pendency of such action. Such notice may, in the discretion of the court, be given by publication.

(d) No action may be brought by the Commission under this section more than 3 years after the rule violation to which an action under subsection (a)(1) of this section relates, or the unfair or deceptive act or practice to which an action under subsection (a)(2) of this section relates; except that if a cease and desist order with respect to any person's, partnership's, or corporation's rule violation or unfair or deceptive act or practice has become final and such order was issued in a proceeding under section 5(b) of this Act which was commenced not later than 3 years after the rule violation or act or practice occurred, a civil action may be commenced under this section against such person, partnership, or corporation at any time before the expiration of one year after such order becomes final.

(e) Remedies provided in this section are in addition to, and not in lieu of, any other remedy or right of action provided by State or Federal law. Nothing in this section shall be construed to affect any authority of the Commission under any other provision of law.

SEC. 20.   There are authorized to be appropriated to carry out the functions, powers, and duties of the Federal Trade Commission * * *.

SEC. 21.   This Act may be cited as the "Federal Trade Commission Act."

Antitrust Civil Process Act[4]

SEC. 2.   For the purposes of this chapter—

(a) The term "antitrust law" includes:

(1) Each provision of law defined as one of the antitrust laws by section 12 of this title; and

(2) Any statute enacted on and after September 19, 1962, by the Congress which prohibits, or makes available to the United

[4]The Antitrust Civil Process Act was enacted as 76 Stat. 548 (1962). It appears as 15 U.S.C.A. §§1311–14.

States in any court of the United States any civil remedy with respect to any restraint upon or monopolization of interstate or foreign trade or commerce;

(b) The term "antitrust order" means any final order, decree, or judgment of any court of the United States, duly entered in any case or proceeding arising under any antitrust law;

(c) The term "antitrust investigation" means any inquiry conducted by any antitrust investigator for the purpose of ascertaining whether any person is or has been engaged in any antitrust violation or in any activities in preparation for a merger, acquisition, joint venture, or similar transaction, which, if consummated, may result in an antitrust violation;

(d) The term "antitrust violation" means any act or omission in violation of any antitrust law or any antitrust order;

(e) The term "antitrust investigator" means any attorney or investigator employed by the Department of Justice who is charged with the duty of enforcing or carrying into effect any antitrust law;

(f) The term "person" means any natural person, partnership, corporation, association, or other legal entity, including any person acting under color or authority of State law;

(g) The term "documentary material" includes the original or any copy of any book, record, report, memorandum, paper, communication, tabulation, chart, or other document; and

(h) The term "custodian" means the custodian or any deputy custodian designated under section 1313(a) of this title.

SEC. 3. (a) Whenever the Attorney General, or the Assistant Attorney General in charge of the Antitrust Division of the Department of Justice, has reason to believe that any person may be in possession, custody, or control of any documentary material, or may have any information, relevant to a civil antitrust investigation, he may, prior to the institution of a civil or criminal proceeding thereon, issue in writing, and cause to be served upon such person, a civil investigative demand requiring such person to produce such documentary material for inspection and copying or reproduction, to answer in writing written interrogatories, to give oral testimony concerning documentary material or information, or to furnish any combination of such material, answers, or testimony.

(b) Each such demand shall—

(1) state the nature of—

(A) the conduct constituting the alleged antitrust violation, or

(B) the activities in preparation for a merger, acquisition, joint venture, or similar transaction, which, if consummated, may result in an antitrust violation.

which are under investigation and the provision of law applicable thereto;

(2) if it is a demand for production of documentary material—

(A) describe the class or classes of documentary material to be produced thereunder with such definiteness and certainty as to permit such material to be fairly identified;

(B) prescribe a return date or dates which will provide a reasonable period of time within which the material so demanded may be assembled and made available for inspection and copying or reproduction; and

(C) identify the custodian to whom such material shall be made available; or

(3) if it is a demand for answers to written interrogatories—

(A) propound with definiteness and certainty the written interrogatories to be answered;

(B) prescribe a date or dates at which time answers to written interrogatories shall be submitted; and

(C) identify the custodian to whom such answers shall be submitted; or

(4) if it is a demand for the giving of oral testimony—

(A) prescribe a date, time, and place at which oral testimony shall be commenced; and

(B) identify an antitrust investigator who shall conduct the examination and the custodian to whom the transcript of such examination shall be submitted.

(c) No such demand shall require the production of any documentary material, the submission of any answers to written interrogatories, or the giving of any oral testimony, if such material, answers, or testimony would be protected from disclosure under—

(1) the standards applicable to subpoenas or subpoenas duces tecum issued by a court of the United States in aid of a grand jury investigation, or

(2) the standards applicable to discovery requests under the Federal Rules of Civil Procedure, to the extent that the application of such standards to any such demand is appropriate and consistent with the provisions and purposes of this chapter.

(d)(1) Any such demand may be served by any antitrust investigator, or by any United States marshal or deputy marshal, at any place within the territorial jurisdiction of any court of the United States.

(2) any such demand or any petition filed under section 1314 of this title may be served upon any person who is not to be found within the territorial jurisdiction of any court of the United States, in such manner as the Federal Rules of Civil Procedure prescribe for service in a foreign country. To the extent that the courts of the United States can assert jurisdiction over such person consistent with due process, the United States District Court for the District of Columbia shall have the same jurisdiction to take any action respecting compliance with this chapter by such person that such court would have if such person were personally within the jurisdiction of such court.

(e)(1) Service of any such demand or of any petition filed under section 1314 of this title may be made upon a partnership, corporation, association, or other legal entity by—

(A) delivering a duly executed copy thereof to any partner, executive officer, managing agent, or general agent thereof, or to any agent thereof authorized by appointment or by law to receive service of process on behalf of such partnership, corporation, association, or entity;

(B) delivering a duly executed copy thereof to the principal office or place of business of the partnership, corporation, association, or entity to be served; or

(C) depositing such copy in the United States mails, by registered or certified mail, return receipt requested, duly addressed to such partnership, corporation, association, or entity at its principal office or place of business.

(2) Service of any such demand or of any petition filed under section 1314 of this title may be made upon any natural person by—

(A) delivering a duly executed copy thereof to the person to be served; or

(B) depositing such copy in the United States mails by registered or certified mail, return receipt requested, duly addressed to such person at his residence or principal office or place of business.

(f) A verified return by the individual serving any such demand or petition setting forth the manner of such service shall be proof of such service. In the case of service by registered or certified mail, such return shall be accompanied by the return post office receipt of delivery of such demand.

(g) The production of documentary material in response to a demand served pursuant to this section shall be made under a sworn certificate, in such form as the demand designates, by the person, if a natural person, to whom the demand is directed or, if not a natural person, by a person or persons having knowledge of the facts and circumstances relating to such production, to the effect that all of the documentary material required by the demand and in the possession, custody, or control of the person to whom the demand is directed has been produced and made available to the custodian.

(h) Each interrogatory in a demand served pursuant to this section shall be answered separately and fully in writing under oath, unless it is objected to, in which event the reasons for the objection shall be stated in lieu of an answer, and it shall be submitted under a sworn certificate, in such form as the demand designates, by the person, if a natural person, to whom the demand is directed or, if not a natural person, by a person or persons responsible for answering each interrogatory, to the effect that all information required by the demand and in the possession, custody, control, or knowledge of the person to whom the demand is directed has been submitted.

(i)(1) The examination of any person pursuant to a demand for oral testimony served under this section shall be taken before an officer authorized to administer oaths and affirmations by the laws of the United States or of the place where the examination is held.

The officer before whom the testimony is to be taken shall put the witness on oath or affirmation and shall personally, or by someone acting under his direction and in his presence, record the testimony of the witness. The testimony shall be taken stenographically and transcribed. When the testimony is fully transcribed, the officer before whom the testimony is taken shall promptly transmit a copy of the transcript of the testimony to the custodian.

(2) The antitrust investigator or investigators conducting the examination shall exclude from the place where the examination is held all other persons except the person being examined, his counsel, the officer before whom the testimony is to be taken, and any stenographer taking such testimony. The provisions of section 30 of this title shall not apply to such examinations.

(3) The oral testimony of any person taken pursuant to a demand served under this section shall be taken in the judicial district of the United States within which such person resides, is found, or transacts business, or in such other place as may be agreed upon by the antitrust investigator conducting the examination and such person.

(4) When the testimony is fully transcribed, the antitrust investigator or the officer shall afford the witness (who may be accompanied by counsel) a reasonable opportunity to examine the transcript; and the transcript shall be read to or by the witness, unless such examination and reading are waived by the witness. Any changes in form or substance which the witness desires to make shall be entered and identified upon the transcript by the officer or the antitrust investigator with a statement of the reasons given by the witness for making such changes. The transcript shall then be signed by the witness, unless the witness in writing waives the signing, is ill, cannot be found, or refuses to sign. If the transcript is not signed by the witness within thirty days of his being afforded a reasonable opportunity to examine it, the officer or the antitrust investigator shall sign it and state on the record the fact of the waiver, illness, absence of the witness, or the refusal to sign, together with the reason, if any, given therefor.

(5) The officer shall certify on the transcript that the witness was duly sworn by him and that the transcript is a true record of the testimony given by the witness, and the officer or antitrust

investigator shall promptly deliver it or send it by registered or certified mail to the custodian.

(6) Upon payment of reasonable charges therefor, the antitrust investigator shall furnish a copy of the transcript to the witness only, except that the Assistant Attorney General in charge of the Antitrust Division may for good cause limit such witness to inspection of the official transcript of his testimony.

(7)(A) Any person compelled to appear under a demand for oral testimony pursuant to this section may be accompanied, represented, and advised by counsel. Counsel may advise such person, in confidence, either upon the request of such person or upon counsel's own initiative, with respect to any question asked of such person. Such person or counsel may object on the record to any question, in whole or in part, and shall briefly state for the record the reason for the objection. An objection may properly be made, received, and entered upon the record when it is claimed that such person is entitled to refuse to answer the question on grounds of any constitutional or other legal right or privilege, including the privilege against self-incrimination. Such person shall not otherwise object to or refuse to answer any question, and shall not by himself or through counsel otherwise interrupt the oral examination. If such person refuses to answer any question, the antitrust investigator conducting the examination may petition the district court of the United States pursuant to section 1314 of this title for an order compelling such person to answer such question.

(B) If such person refuses to answer any question on grounds of the privilege against self-incrimination, the testimony of such person may be compelled in accordance with the provisions of Part V of title 18.

(8) Any person appearing for oral examination pursuant to a demand served under this section shall be entitled to the same fees and mileage which are paid to witnesses in the district courts of the United States.

SEC. 4.   (a) The Assistant Attorney General in charge of the Antitrust Division of the Department of Justice shall designate an antitrust investigator to serve as custodian of documentary material, answers to interrogatories, and transcripts of oral testimony received under this chapter, and such additional antitrust investigators as he shall determine from time to time to be necessary to serve as deputies to such officer.

(b) Any person, upon whom any demand under section 1312 of this title for the production of documentary material has been duly served, shall make such material available for inspection and copying or reproduction to the custodian designated therein at the principal place of business of such person (or at such other place as such custodian and such person thereafter may agree and prescribe in writing or as the court may direct, pursuant to section 1314(d) of this title) on the return date specified in such demand (or on such later date as such custodian may prescribe in writing). Such person may upon written agreement between such person and the custodian substitute copies for originals of all or any part of such material.

(c)(1) The custodian to whom any documentary material, answers to interrogatories, or transcripts of oral testimony are delivered shall take physical possession thereof, and shall be responsible for the use made thereof and for the return of documentary material, pursuant to this chapter.

(2) The custodian may cause the preparation of such copies of such documentary material, answers to interrogatories, or transcripts of oral testimony as may be required for official use by any duly authorized official or employee of the Department of Justice under regulations which shall be promulgated by the Attorney General. Notwithstanding paragraph (3) of this subsection, such material, answers, and transcripts may be used by any such official or employee in connection with the taking of oral testimony pursuant to this chapter.

(3) Except as otherwise provided in this section, while in the possession of the custodian, no documentary material, answers to interrogatories, or transcripts of oral testimony, or copies thereof, so produced shall be available for examination, without the consent of the person who produced such material, answers, or transcripts, by any individual other than a duly authorized official or employee of the Department of Justice. Nothing in this section is intended to prevent disclosure to either body of the Congress or to any authorized committee or subcommittee thereof.

(4) While in the possession of the custodian and under such reasonable terms and conditions as the Attorney General shall pre-

scribe, (A) documentary material and answers to interrogatories shall be available for examination by the person who produced such material or answers, or by any duly authorized representative of such person, and (B) transcripts of oral testimony shall be available for examination by the person who produced such testimony, or his counsel.

(d)(1) Whenever any attorney of the Department of Justice has been designated to appear before any court, grand jury, or Federal administrative or regulatory agency in any case or proceeding, the custodian of any documentary material, answers to interrogatories, or transcripts of oral testimony may deliver to such attorney such material, answers, or transcripts for official use in connection with any such case, grand jury, or proceeding as such attorney determines to be required. Upon the completion of any such case, grand jury, or proceeding, such attorney shall return to the custodian any such material, answers, or transcripts so delivered which have not passed into the control of such court, grand jury, or agency through the introduction thereof into the record of such case or proceeding.

(2) The custodian of any documentary material, answers to interrogatories, or transcripts of oral testimony may deliver to the Federal Trade Commission, in response to a written request, copies of such material, answers, or transcripts for use in connection with an investigation or proceeding under the Commission's jurisdiction. Such material, answers, or transcripts may only be used by the Commission in such manner and subject to such conditions as apply to the Department of Justice under this chapter.

(e) If any documentary material has been produced in the course of any antitrust investigation by any person pursuant to a demand under this chapter and—

(1) any case or proceeding before any court or grand jury arising out of such investigation, or any proceeding before any Federal administrative or regulatory agency involving such material, has been completed, or

(2) no case or proceeding, in which such material may be used, has been commenced within a reasonable time after completion of the examination and analysis of all documentary material and

other information assembled in the course of such investigation, the custodian shall, upon written request of the person who produced such material, return to such person any such material (other than copies thereof furnished to the custodian pursuant to subsection (b) of this section or made by the Department of Justice pursuant to subsection (c) of this section) which has not passed into the control of any court, grand jury, or agency through the introduction thereof into the record of such case or proceeding.

(f) In the event of the death, disability, or separation from service in the Department of Justice of the custodian of any documentary material, answers to interrogatories, or transcripts of oral testimony produced under any demand issued pursuant to this chapter, or the official relief of such custodian from responsibility for the custody and control of such material, answers, or transcripts, the Assistant Attorney General in charge of the Antitrust Division shall promptly (1) designate another antitrust investigator to serve as custodian of such material, answers, or transcripts, and (2) transmit in writing to the person who produced such material, answers, or testimony notice as to the identity and address of the successor so designated. Any successor designated under this subsection shall have with regard to such material, answers, or transcripts all duties and responsibilities imposed by this chapter upon his predecessor in office with regard thereto, except that he shall not be held responsible for any default or dereliction which occurred prior to his designation.

Sec. 5. (a) Whenever any person fails to comply with any civil investigative demand duly served upon him under section 1312 of this title or whenever satisfactory copying or reproduction of any such material cannot be done and such person refuses to surrender such material, the Attorney General, through such officers or attorneys as he may designate, may file, in the district court of the United States for any judicial district in which such person resides, is found, or transacts business, and serve upon such person a petition for an order of such court for the enforcement of this chapter.

(b) Within twenty days after the service of any such demand upon any person, or at any time before the return date specified in the demand, whichever period is shorter, or within such period exceeding twenty days after service or in excess of such return date as may be prescribed in writing, subsequent to service, by any antitrust investigator named in the demand, such person may file, in the district court of the United States for the judicial district within which such person resides, is found, or transacts business, and serve upon such antitrust investigator a petition for an order of such court modifying or setting aside such demand. The time allowed for compliance with the demand in whole or in part as deemed proper and ordered by the court shall not run during the pendency of such petition in the court, except that such person shall comply with any portions of the demand not sought to be modified or set aside. Such petition shall specify each ground upon which the petitioner relies in seeking such relief, and may be based upon any failure of such demand to comply with the provisions of this chapter, or upon any constitutional or other legal right or privilege of such person.

(c) At any time during which any custodian is in custody or control of any documentary material or answers to interrogatories delivered, or transcripts of oral testimony given by any person in compliance D with any such demand, such person may file, in the district court of the United States for the judicial district within which the office of such custodian is situated, and serve upon such custodian a petition for an order of such court requiring the performance by such custodian of any duty imposed upon him by this chapter.

(d) Whenever any petition is filed in any district court of the United States under this section, such court shall have jurisdiction to hear and determine the matter so presented, and to enter such order or orders as may be required to carry into effect the provisions of this chapter. Any final order so entered shall be subject to appeal pursuant to section 1291 of title 28. Any disobedience of any final order entered under this section by any court shall be punished as a comtempt thereof.

(e) To the extent that such rules may have application and are not inconsistent with the provisions of this chapter, the Federal Rules of Civil Procedure shall apply to any petition under this chapter.

(f) Any documentary material, answers to written interrogatories, or transcripts of oral testimony provided pursuant to any demand issued under this chapter shall be exempt from disclosure under section 552 of title 5.

Antitrust Procedures and Penalties Act— Expediting Act[5]

SEC. 4.   Section 1 of the Act of February 11, 1903 (32 Stat. 823), as amended (15 U.S.C. 28; 49 U.S.C. 44), commonly known as the Expediting Act, is amended to read as follows:

"Section 1. In any civil action brought in any district court of the United States under the Act entitled 'An Act to protect trade and commerce against unlawful restraints and monopolies,' approved July 2, 1890, or any other Acts having like purpose that have been or hereafter may be enacted, wherein the United States is plaintiff and equitable relief is sought, the Attorney General may file with the court, prior to the entry of final judgment, a certificate that, in his opinion, the case is of a general public importance. Upon filing of such certificate, it shall be the duty of the judge designated to hear and determine the case, or the chief judge of the district court if no judge has as yet been designated, to assign the case for hearing at the earliest practicable date and to cause the case to be in every way expedited."

SEC. 5.   Section 2 of that Act (15 U.S.C. 29; 49 U.S.C. 45) is amended to read as follows:

"(a) Except as otherwise expressly provided by this section, in every civil action brought in any district court of the United States under the Act entitled 'An Act to protect trade and commerce against unlawful restraints and monopolies,' approved July 2, 1890, or any other Acts having like purpose that have been or hereafter may be enacted, in which the United States is the complainant and equitable relief is sought, any appeal from a final judgment entered in any such action shall be taken to the court of appeals pursuant to sections 1291 and 2107 of title 28 of the United States Code. Any appeal from an interlocutory order entered in any such action shall be taken to the court of appeals pursuant to sections 1292(a)(1) and 2107 of title 28 of the United States Code but not otherwise. Any

---

[5]The Antitrust Procedures and Penalties Act was enacted as Public Law 93–528, 88 Stat. 1706. (15 U.S.C.A. §§1, 2, 3, 16, 28, 29; 47 U.S.C.A. §401; 49 U.S.C.A. §§43–45 (1976)). Sections of that act which amend the Sherman Act and the Clayton Act are reflected in those acts, as set forth in this appendix, and are deleted here. Certain other sections are also deleted.

judgment entered by the court of appeals in any such action shall be subject to review by the Supreme Court upon a writ of certiorari as provided in section 1254(1) of title 28 of the United States Code.

"(b) An appeal from a final judgment pursuant to subsection (a) shall lie directly to the Supreme Court if, upon application of a party filed within fifteen days of the filing of a notice of appeal, the district judge who adjudicated the case enters an order stating that immediate consideration of the appeal by the Supreme Court is of general public importance in the administration of justice. Such order shall be filed within thirty days after the filing of a notice of appeal. When such an order is filed, the appeal and any cross appeal shall be docketed in the time and manner prescribed by the rules of the Supreme Court. The Supreme Court shall thereupon either (1) dispose of the appeal and any cross appeal in the same manner as any other direct appeal authorized by law, or (2) in its discretion, deny the direct appeal and remand the case to the court of appeals, which shall then have jurisdiction to hear and determine the same as if the appeal and any cross appeal therein had been docketed in the court of appeals in the first instance pursuant to subsection (a)."

Index